the devil

IN EARLY MODERN ENGLAND

To Meg

the devil

IN EARLY MODERN ENGLAND

DARREN OLDRIDGE

SUTTON PUBLISHING

First published in 2000 by
Sutton Publishing Limited · Phoenix Mill
Thrupp · Stroud · Gloucestershire · GL5 2BU

British Library Cataloguing in Publication Data
A catalogue record for this book is available from the British Library

ISBN 0-7509-2092-0

Typeset in 11/13pt Photina.
Typesetting and origination by
Sutton Publishing Limited.
Printed in Great Britain by
Biddles Limited, Guildford, Surrey.

CONTENTS

PREFACE

This is a small book about an enormous subject. It is also, I hope, a book that will be accessible to general readers as well as academic historians. While I have tried to keep abreast of the latest research in each of the areas I cover, it has sometimes been impossible to include all the relevant contributions of historians working in particular fields. It has also proved impossible to address every theme connected with the title of the book. Instead, I have concentrated on two issues which seem central to early modern perceptions of Satan: the emergence of a distinctively protestant set of ideas about the devil, and the impact of these ideas on English society as a whole. I hope that my answers to these questions will stimulate further research into the subject, and that readers will excuse the omissions that have resulted from my choice of priorities.

I am grateful for the support and advice of my colleagues in the History Department at University College Worcester. In particular, I would like to thank Sue Johnson for her comments on Chapter Five, and Brian Hoggard for introducing me to the curious world of 'witch bottles'. This book would have been impossible without the encouragement, love and patience of my partner, Meg Barker, and it is dedicated to her.

LIST OF PLATES

1

INTRODUCTION:
THE SOCIAL HISTORY OF SATAN

At the beginning of the twenty-first century, it seems that the status of the devil as a popular icon is more secure than ever. From *The Blair Witch Project* to *End of Days*, the success of movies with demonic themes suggests that the prince of darkness retains his ability to attract large audiences across the western world, while the idea that a personal force lurks behind the manifest evils in human society apparently continues to exert a widespread fascination. The devil enjoys a high profile in TV talk shows, political cartoons, comic books and popular music, to name a few of the more obvious places where he can be found. Two thousand years after Christ's confrontation with Satan provided one of the central themes in the New Testament, the Christian image of the devil appears to be astonishingly endurable, even though many people no longer believe in the physical reality behind the idea.

This is a book about perceptions of Satan in sixteenth and seventeenth-century England, but it seems appropriate to begin with two more recent representations of the ancient enemy. In 1911 M.R. James published the short story *Casting the Runes*, a classic tale of the conjuration of the devil by a modern-day witch, Mr Karswell, who is eventually murdered by the creature he summons from hell. Early in the story, James offers a startlingly physical account of the killing of one of the magician's enemies by the 'frightful fiend':

> Here was this man . . . walking home along a country road late in the evening . . . and he suddenly begins to run like mad, loses his hat and stick and finally shins up a tree – quite a difficult tree – growing in the hedgerow: a dead branch gives way, and he comes down with it and breaks his neck, and there he's found next morning with the most dreadful face of fear on him that could be imagined. It was pretty evident, of course, that he had been chased by something, and people talked of savage dogs, and beasts escaped out of menageries.[1]

The concrete reality of James' devil was underlined in the 1957 film based on the story, *The Night of the Demon*. The eponymous creature was presented as a fire-snorting beast with leathery wings and dreadful, lacerating talons. The film and the story represent one of the recurrent themes in twentieth-century depictions of Satan, which can be traced back to the Middle Ages and the period considered in this book: the view that the devil is a misshapen creature walking the earth, capable of physical violence against those mortals unfortunate enough to meet him. In the figure of Karswell, it also recalls the early modern idea that men and women can harness satanic forces for their own purposes, although the story ends with the demon turning on his apparent master. Indeed, Karswell's fate echoes the grisly end of Dr Faust in some of the earliest English versions of the legend. A ballad from the 1590s described how the devil, in the shape of a terrible beast, ripped the magician's 'arms and legs in pieces' and smashed his head 'against the wall'.[2]

A rather more subtle, psychological depiction of the prince of darkness was provided in William Peter Blatty's 1972 novel, *The Exorcist*, and the film of the same name. It is ironic that Blatty's creation is often remembered for the grotesque scenes of physical violence which establish the devil's power in the movie, since the book and the film are primarily concerned with the mental and emotional impact of possession. As the ageing exorcist, Father Merrin, explains to the young priest assigned to assist him in his work, their enemy's most dangerous weapon is intellectual trickery: 'The demon is a liar. He will lie to confuse us; but he will also mix lies with the truth to attack us. The attack is psychological.' A little later, Merrin attempts to explain the motives of the unclean spirit:

> I think the demon's target is not the possessed; it is us, the observers, every person in this house. And I think the point is to make us despair; to reject our own humanity . . . to see ourselves as ultimately bestial; as ultimately vile and putrescent; without dignity; ugly; unworthy. And there lies the heart of it, perhaps: in unworthiness. For I think belief in God is not a matter of reason at all; I think it is finally a matter of love; of accepting the possibility that God could love us.[3]

In *The Exorcist*, Satan's ultimate purpose is to make people question their faith. His mission is to spread despair and doubt. But like the more physical image of the devil in *The Night of the Demon*, this interpretation belongs to a tradition which can be traced back to the sixteenth and seventeenth centuries. Although Blatty's characters are Roman Catholic priests, the view that the devil was engaged in a psychological campaign to destroy the faith of God's children was embraced with zeal by protestant reformers in the early modern period. In the hands of English theologians like William Perkins, it was used to attack the more crudely physical conceptions of Satan which had survived from the Middle Ages.

These two views of the devil – and the conflict between them – provide one of the central themes of this book. In the course of the sixteenth century, a protestant theology of Satan emerged which challenged many conventional assumptions about his power and his limitations. Like Father Merrin's description of the demon, it emphasised his role as the 'father of lies', and presented him as the source of mental temptations. As a result, the protestant reformers created an image of Satan which was more dreadful and implacable than the one favoured by many late medieval thinkers. The men and women who supported this view were not confined to any one section of the population. The protestant concept of Satan was communicated to a wide audience in picture books and ballads like the sixteenth-century *Song of Anne Askewe*, and broadsheets like *Stand Up for Your Beliefe* (1640), which presented the 'combat between Satan tempting and a Christian triumphing' as a lively dialogue between a humble protestant and the fiend.[4] The limited availability of education, however, meant that support for the Reformation tended to be concentrated geographically in towns, and socially among the more affluent members of the population. Throughout the sixteenth and seventeenth centuries, zealous protestants were always a minority, though they were well represented among the political elite. The rest of the population, characterised by the Essex pastor George Gifford as 'the common sort of Christians', retained many pre-Reformation ideas about the devil.

Protestant ideas about Satan are considered in detail in the first part of this book. Chapter Two argues that the godly minority sought to suppress the jokey, physically limited representations of the devil which had been common in the late Middle Ages, and declared war on the belief that men and women could overcome the ancient enemy by their own efforts. Their more powerful and pervasive idea of Satan imposed considerable psychological demands on those who took it seriously, and these are considered in Chapter Three. The rest of the book is concerned largely with the effect of these ideas on English society as a whole. It suggests that protestant theologians largely failed to convince ordinary people of their case, and traditional attitudes towards the devil continued to flourish. Their efforts were not, however, entirely in vain. Some reformed beliefs did achieve widespread acceptance, resulting in a partially reformed view of the devil in popular culture. This outcome is, perhaps, reflected in the diverse views of the devil which have survived into our own time, when the psychological horrors of *The Exorcist* co-exist happily with more grossly material depictions of the devil.

The second theme of this book is the social and political circumstances in which concepts of the devil developed in early modern

England. Unlike the monster in *The Night of the Demon*, these ideas did not emerge out of thin air, with no reference to the world around them. Rather, they tended to reflect the political situation of sixteenth and seventeenth-century English protestants, and cannot be understood outside this context. In 1995 the New Testament historian, Elaine Pagels, coined the phrase 'the social history of Satan' to describe the emergence of Christian teaching on the devil in the first century. She argued that the idea of a powerful, personal force for evil proved especially attractive to the early followers of Jesus, since it reflected their experience of conflict with the rest of society. In other words, it made sense for a beleaguered minority to embrace the idea that they were engaged in a cosmic struggle with Satan, whose instruments included the political leaders of the day and the mass of ordinary people.[5] This book will argue that similar considerations played a decisive role in the emergence of protestant beliefs about the devil in the sixteenth and seventeenth centuries. Beyond that, it will suggest that social and political factors were generally more important in shaping the behaviour of English protestants than purely theological concerns, and this helps to explain the apparently confused attitude of many Church of England pastors towards such subjects as witchcraft and demonic possession. Before addressing these themes in detail, however, it is necessary to review the theological background to ideas about Satan in the sixteenth century.

SATAN AND THE PROBLEM OF EVIL

If God did not exist, according to Voltaire's famous maxim, it would be necessary to invent him. The same is probably true of the devil, since his existence provides an answer to one of the most enduring problems in Christian theology. If God is loving, why does He tolerate evil? If He is all powerful, why does He do nothing to prevent it? While these questions might seem appallingly relevant at the close of the century of Auschwitz and Pol Pot, they were also a central concern of Christian theologians in the ancient and medieval world.[6] One solution, favoured by many thinkers throughout the Middle Ages, was to place an effective limit on God's power by arguing that he acted within constraints imposed by the wilful disobedience of his own creations. The first rebellion against the deity was led by the angel Lucifer, who devoted himself to the corruption of humankind once he was cast down from heaven. Through his intervention in the Garden of Eden, the first man and woman were deceived into betraying their creator. It was this act of primal disobedience, which could not have been prevented without the abolition of free will, which brought sin and death into the world.

While this formula offered an attractive solution to the problem of evil, it never achieved a position of complete dominance among Christian theologians. In particular, the works of St Augustine, the fifth-century Bishop of Hippo, challenged the view that God's power was constrained by the actions of his creatures. To Augustine, the free will exercised by Lucifer in his rebellion seemed to compromise the supreme power of his maker. Similarly, the disobedience of Adam and Eve appeared to undermine the omnipotence of God. His simple and drastic solution was to argue that mortals were incapable of doing good without the grace of the Lord, which He bestowed according to His own wishes. In effect, this position placed all earthly affairs under the ultimate control of God, and left very little room for the exercise of free will.[7] Augustine's ideas were later endorsed by Martin Luther and John Calvin, the leading protestant reformers of the sixteenth century. In Luther's view, God was the ultimate cause of everything that happened in the world, including events which appeared to be evil. The devil, accordingly, always acted according to God's will. Equally, Calvin cited biblical precedents to affirm that the Lord was ultimately responsible for the devil's actions, as when 'he turned Pharaoh over to Satan to be confirmed in the obstinacy of his breast'.[8]

By adopting this argument, protestant theologians came perilously close to asserting that God wished to cause evil events. Luther avoided this conclusion by making some subtle distinctions. First, he proposed that occurrences which seemed wicked to us were, in truth, part of God's loving plan for the world. With our flawed minds and limited sense of perspective, we were incapable of seeing the goodness which underpinned all the creator's works. Even things such as murder and natural disasters, which might at first glance appear to be evil and unjust, were designed for our ultimate benefit. Second, Luther distinguished between the will of God, which was always good, and the will of Satan, which was utterly malign. While the devil took a hideous pleasure in what he did, God allowed him to act for reasons that were loving and just. Thus 'God incites the devil to evil, but he does not do evil himself'.[9] The practical implications of this view were illustrated in an English murder case in 1603. Elizabeth Caldwell was convicted of accidentally poisoning a serving girl with ratsbane, which she had intended for her husband. A contemporary account of the crime noted that she had been inspired by the devil, but his aims were thwarted by the higher purposes of God. As a result of her experience, Elizabeth was converted to godly religion, and 'thus the deceitful devill, who hath sometime permission from God to attempt the very righteous (as Job), was now an instrument to her sorrow, but [consequently] her feeling faith the more increased'. In this instance, Satan was used by God as his tool, and the outcome of his actions was good rather than evil.[10]

The supreme power of God was further emphasised by the protestant doctrine of predestination. Originally developed by St Augustine, this concept was adopted by Martin Luther and the followers of the second-generation French reformer, John Calvin. In its Calvinist form, the doctrine asserted that God had chosen to save a portion of humankind, the 'elect', from the beginning of time, and condemned the rest to damnation. This divine edict was immutable and could not be affected by the behaviour or 'merit' of individual men and women. In 1563, this belief was enshrined in the Thirty-Nine Articles which set out the official doctrine of the Church of England. According to the seventeenth article, 'predestination to life is the everlasting purpose of God, whereby (before the foundations of the world were laid) he has constantly decreed by his council secret to us, to deliver from curse and damnation those whom he has chosen in Christ out of mankind, and to bring them by Christ to everlasting salvation'. While the precise interpretation of these words was the subject of scholarly debate, the most influential protestant theologians of the late Elizabethan period were firmly committed to the doctrine. William Perkins made it the centrepiece of his best-selling introductions to protestant theology in the 1590s, and the doctrine was publicised by other devotional writers like George Gifford and Arthur Dent.[11]

By underlining the power of God, the doctrine of predestination appeared to diminish further the role of the devil in human affairs. Not only did the Lord employ Satan as his instrument, but he retained absolute control over the salvation and damnation of individual men and women. Although the ancient enemy wished to draw people into hell for his own malicious pleasure, he had no ultimate power over their fate. To human eyes, the decision of God to damn one person and save another might appear to be arbitrary and unjust, but – just like the existence of other apparent evils in the world – it reflected the deity's eternal wisdom and ultimate purpose for humankind. The faithful were encouraged to submit themselves to the divine will, and examine their consciences for 'signs' that they had been numbered among the elect.

The theology of protestantism, therefore, provided a radical solution to the problem of evil. The author of the most complete recent history of the devil, Jeffrey Burton Russell, has argued that the leading reformers were 'unflinchingly consistent in affirming the total omnipotence of God', with the result that Satan was reduced to no more than 'God's tool, like a pruning hook or a hoe that he uses to cultivate his garden'.[12] In theory at least, this radical position had two major implications. First, it removed the need for people to fear the devil's influence in human affairs. Since God held complete power over Satan, and only allowed him to act for his own just and loving purposes, Christians could rely on the Lord to triumph over the ancient

Satan and demons, from the pamphlet *Newes from Avernus* (1642).

enemy. Second, it challenged popular beliefs about the activity of supernatural beings, such as fairies, demons and imps, which were widely assumed to exercise power in the world. By asserting the absolute authority of God, protestants effectively abolished the influence of all other entities, and condemned any attempt to exploit their knowledge or power as 'superstition'. The same logic was used to denounce all forms of magic, whatever the intentions of those who practised them. This view was spelt out bluntly by William Perkins, who asserted that 'all diviners, charmers, jugglers, [and] all wizzards commonly called wise men and wise women' were guilty of the sin of witchcraft. As such, he argued, they all deserved to be hanged.[13]

In practice, however, the protestant theology of Satan had very different consequences to those outlined above. Most notably, the advocates of the new creed actually emphasised the power of the devil, and elevated the struggle against him to the centrepiece of religious life. In this respect, the teaching of John Calvin was entirely typical:

The fact that the devil is everywhere called God's adversary and ours also ought to fire us to an unceasing struggle against him. For if we have God's glory at heart, as we should have, we ought with all our strength to contend against him who is trying to extinguish it. If we are minded to affirm Christ's kingdom as we ought, we must wage irreconcilable war with him who is plotting its ruin. Again, if we care about our salvation at all, we ought to have neither peace nor truce with him who continually lays traps to destroy it.[14]

As we will see in Chapter Three, Calvin's 'irreconcilable war' with the fiend was joined with fervour by many English protestants, who wasted few opportunitites to emphasise his terrible influence over their lives. Thus the potential of protestant doctrines to allay anxieties about Satan was not realised; in fact, English Calvinism had precisely the opposite effect.

Similarly, the idea that God's power relegated the activity of demons and imps to the world of 'superstitious folly' was never entirely accepted in early modern England. In large part, this reflected the failure of protestant doctrines to sink deep roots into popular culture. Despite the best efforts of godly preachers and propagandists, pre-Reformation ideas continued to flourish in the sixteenth and seventeenth centuries, as will be shown in Chapter Four. At the same time, however, English protestants were divided about such matters as demonic possession and witchcraft. Some thinkers, such as Reginald Scot and Samuel Harsnet, decried popular beliefs about the agency of evil spirits as remnants of catholicism. According to Scot, the supreme power of God meant that none of the feats attributed to witches or demons were achieved through their own agency. In *The Discoverie of Witchcraft* (1584), he argued that 'if all the divels in hell were dead, and all the witches in England burnt or hanged . . . we should not faile to have raine, haile and tempests as now we have, according to the appointment and will of God, and according to the constitution of the elements, and the course of the planets, wherein God hath set a perfect and perpetuall order'. Likewise, he dismissed the instruments used to perform magic as 'baubles devised by cozeners to abuse the people'.[15]

The devil walks the earth, from the title page of *Grand Plutoes Remonstrance* (1642).

Such views were challenged, however, by puritan exorcists like John Darrel, whose ministry in the 1590s tacitly endorsed many folk beliefs about witchcraft and possession. This tendency continued in the seventeenth century, when committed protestants sometimes played a leading role in the casting out of demons and the prosecution of witches.

How can these anomalies be explained? Why did a religion which explicitly reduced the devil to the status of God's tool come to emphasise his appalling power in the world, and why did many of its adherents embrace folk traditions about demonic possession and witchcraft? The answer to these questions cannot be found in theology. Indeed, the obvious contradictions between the theory and practice of protestantism in early modern England suggest that non-theological factors played a major role in the movement, even though its supporters expressed themselves in the language of the reformed faith. The development of their views is best understood in the social and political context of the English Reformation, to which we now turn.

SATAN AND RELIGIOUS DIVISION

From the 1520s onwards, the successful establishment of protestant churches in Germany and northern Europe fragmented the unity of the medieval church. It was the existence of this division, rather than the theology of protestantism itself, which profoundly affected ideas of the devil in early modern Europe. Throughout the Middle Ages, the defenders of the western church had identified heresy as the work of Satan. This tradition continued in the early years of the Reformation, with the leaders of both religious factions condemning their opponents as the devil's agents; and this rhetoric intensified as the protestant states consolidated themselves and religious warfare engulfed the continent in the second half of the sixteenth century. For Martin Luther, catholicism was 'the devil's church' and the pope was his earthly representative, or Antichrist, while the extremists within his own camp were 'bewitched of the devil'.[16] Similarly, the Roman church and its political allies denounced the satanic origins of all branches of protestantism. As a consequence, the profile of the ancient enemy increased considerably on both sides of the religious divide.

This process helps to explain the emergence of witch-hunting in both protestant and catholic territories in the sixteenth century. While the roots of the witch-hunt can be traced to the late Middle Ages, and the first wave of persecution occurred before the outbreak of religious conflict in the 1520s, the intensification of witch trials in the later sixteenth century can be attributed in part to the religious instability engendered by the Reformation. As Brian Levack has argued, both protestants and catholics viewed witches as a kind of satanic fifth column within their own communities, whose elimination was part of their wider conflict with the devil. Witches were not identified directly as members of the enemy camp, but they did represent another manifestation of Satan's activity on earth, and were therefore appropriate targets for persecution.[17] The fact of religious division also forced political leaders to identify with one of the two rival churches, with the effect that the religious beliefs of ordinary people assumed a new political importance. Since 'false' opinions now represented a threat to the state, the leaders of both camps attempted to educate and coerce their populations into religious uniformity. One consequence of this was an attack on 'unofficial' beliefs and 'secret crimes', including the practice of magic, which probably contributed to the witch hunts of the early modern period.[18]

In England, the effects of religious division were complicated by the peculiar history of the national Reformation. The protestant reforms introduced cautiously by Henry VIII, and more boldly during the brief reign of his son Edward, were swept away by the Catholic Mary Tudor in the mid-1550s. Mary's reign, which resulted in the execution of about 300 protestants and the exile of many others, encouraged later English reformers to identify their faith with persecution and conflict. Following the accession of her protestant sister, Elizabeth, this perception was expressed most forcibly in John Foxe's *Acts and Monuments* (1563), the contents of which were summed up neatly by its popular title, *The Book of Martyrs*. As Foxe declared in the preface to the 1570 edition, the history of protestantism was the story of 'what Christian blood hath been spilt, what persecutions raised, what tyranny exercised, what torments devised, what treachery used against the poor flock and church of Christ, in such sort as since Christ's time greater hath not been seen'.[19] This preoccupation with conflict was reinforced after 1588 by the war with Spain, which many protestants perceived as a struggle against the Roman Antichrist. The view that religion was a kind of warfare was further encouraged by the hostility of many ordinary people to the perceived excesses of protestant pastors and their supporters among the laity. The most zealous English protestants, who were derided by their enemies as 'puritans' and known to one another as 'godly' Christians, sought to impose their own model of religious discipline on a largely unenthusiastic population. Their efforts divided many parishes between a minority of 'godly professors' and their more easy-going neighbours. This tendency, which is considered in detail in Chapter One, predisposed the godly minority to perceive itself as an embattled vanguard of 'true Christianity'. Thus by the end of the sixteenth century, many English protestants believed that their religion was besieged by enemies at home and powerful adversaries abroad. This perception, in turn, encouraged them to develop an intense awareness of the devil's power.

Division within the Church

Another factor which influenced protestant perceptions of Satan was the incomplete nature of the English Reformation. On her accession in 1558, Elizabeth sought to introduce an inclusive religious settlement, which was capable of satisfying the wishes of her protestant supporters without alienating the catholic majority of the population. Like her father, Henry VIII, she also favoured the traditional model of church government by bishops, which reinforced the authority of the crown. Consequently, the Elizabethan church retained much of the administrative structure of its catholic predecessor, along with a liturgy and style of worship which was similar in some respects to catholicism. The survival of these 'popish trappings' was resented by a sizeable portion of the protestant community, which hoped that future concessions from the crown would complete the unfinished business of the Reformation. This group expressed their views in diverse ways: most accepted the rites of the English church but looked for their eventual reform, while the more extreme pursued a policy of 'nonconformity', refusing to participate in what they regarded as the offensive rites prescribed in the Book of Common Prayer. More generally, all puritans favoured a style of protestant worship based on preaching instead of ritual. The strength of puritan feeling was indicated in 1603 when the queen's successor, James VI of Scotland, was presented with a 1,000-name petition for reform of the church as he journeyed south to claim the English throne. Among other reforms, this requested the end to the requirement for pastors to mark infants' heads with the sign of the cross during the service of baptism, and the abolition of the catholic-style vestments they were obliged to wear. The new king considered these proposals at the Hampton Court Conference in 1604, but no significant concessions were made. Subsequently, the Elizabethan religious settlement remained in force until the 1640s, when it was violently overthrown by the puritan supporters of Parliament in the Civil War.

These tensions within the English church meant that committed protestants faced conflict on two different fronts. In their own parishes, they were surrounded by unconverted 'worldlings', as they called them, who failed to embrace the message of reformed Christianity with wholehearted zeal, and condemned their more godly neighbours as 'busy controllers'. At the same time, they were potentially at odds with the leaders of their own church. The relationship between the godly and the ecclesiastical hierarchy was often ambiguous, not least because the crown relied on zealous pastors to enforce the Reformation in the localities. Periodically, however, the differences within the church flared into open confrontation. In 1566 Archbishop Parker's attempt to impose uniformity in clerical dress led to the suspension of dozens of London clergy. During the 1580s, Archbishop Whitgift moved to suppress the 'excessive' and potentially subversive preaching of the more radical puritan pastors. Following the Hampton Court Conference, the demand that all ministers subscribe to the rites of the Book of Common Prayer provoked furious controversy and a flood of petitions from godly ministers and their supporters among the laity. Eventually, around sixty pastors were ejected for refusing to subscribe. The most bitter conflict between the godly and the hierarchy was sparked in the 1630s, when William Laud, Charles I's Archbishop of Canterbury, attempted to restrict preaching and promote a more ceremonial style of worship, centred on the reintroduction of altars in parish churches. These actions fuelled demands for a 'thorough' reform of the English church in the Parliament which met in 1640, which were later taken up by the parliamentarian party in the Civil War.

The sporadic conflict between puritans and the crown produced some curious results, which are explored at length in this book. On one hand, godly protestants were determined to educate ordinary people in the essentials of reformed Christianity, including their own interpretation of the devil. This emphasised the ubiquitous power of the ancient enemy, and his role as the source of mental temptations. Such views challenged traditional beliefs about the physical nature of Satan and the ability of mortals to overcome him through their own efforts. They also undermined the widespread belief that the world was populated by a host of supernatural entities – ghosts, fairies, demons and imps – which could intervene in human affairs for good or ill. Instead, godly protestants reduced religion to a stark dichotomy between God and the devil, whose baleful presence was felt in all aspects of life. On the other hand, many zealous protestants were dissatisfied with the established church, and occasionally found themselves in conflict with its hierarchy. Puritan ministers in particular were keen to defend their own authority and promote a style of worship at odds with the Book of Common Prayer. In order to do this, it was sometimes necessary to compromise with the beliefs of the 'ungodly multitude'. It was the remarkable consequence of this process that some of the most ardent English protestants came to accept folk traditions about the devil, even though these appeared to contradict their theological views.

The English Exorcist

This contradiction was exemplified in the career of John Darrel, the puritan exorcist.[20] Darrel achieved fame – or notoriety – through his involvement in a series of spectacular cases of demonic possession in the 1590s. In 1596 he was called to aid Thomas Darling, 'the boy of Burton', who was apparently possessed by an unclean spirit sent by a local witch. After an intense confrontation with the spirit tormenting the boy, which contorted his body and spoke in 'a big and hollow voice', the pastor succeeded in expelling the demon. A year later, he drove out the devils possessing seven young girls in Cleworth in Lancashire. Then in 1598 he confronted the demon possessing William Sommers in Nottingham, ousting the creature after a prolonged struggle in which the victim blasphemed, gnashed his teeth and bellowed like a 'horse or boare'.[21] In these cases, the behaviour of the possessed individuals, or 'demoniacs', was influenced strongly by folk beliefs which owed little to protestant teachings. The boy of Burton and William Sommers experienced the devil as a corporeal presence, rather like a parasite, which entered and departed through their mouths and moved around beneath their skin. All Darrel's subjects claimed that their condition was caused by witchcraft, and identified those responsible for sending the spirits into their bodies. Sommers' account of his encounter with the witch, which is reproduced in the appendix to this book, echoed folk tales about the devil; and Darling's description of the creature sent to torment him – 'a little partie-coloured dog' called Minnie – belonged to the world of fairies and imps rather than godly theology. Such beliefs were barely consistent with the image of Satan developed by godly thinkers in the sixteenth century, and challenged the model of witchcraft advanced by protestant demonologists like Perkins.

Why did Darrel endorse these ideas? The answer, as we shall see in Chapter Six, is that demonic possession and exorcism provided an ideal opportunity for puritan pastors to communicate their message to large audiences and demonstrate their authority. They were compelling pieces of propaganda, whether or not their participants conceived of them as such. It was for this reason that the church hierarchy decided to act against Darrel and his supporters. The published account of the case of Thomas Darling was suppressed and the printer imprisoned. In 1599 the exorcist himself was accused of fraud, and arraigned before Archbishop Whitgift's court in London. The principal witness against him was William Sommers, who alleged that his possession had been an elaborate deception concocted by the pastor. Darrel was 'condemned for a counterfeyte' and removed from the ministry. He was briefly imprisoned, but appears to have been free two years later. The case provoked a pamphlet war between Darrel's godly supporters and those responsible for his persecution. On the bishops' side, John Deacon and John Walker published lengthy treatises against the exorcist, while much pithier attacks on his alleged fabrications were penned by Samuel Harsnet, the future bishop of Norwich. In 1603 Harsnet described how easy it was for young people – especially those suffering from 'natural' diseases such as epilepsy – to feign the symptoms of possession in order to accuse their neighbours of witchcraft:

If any of you have . . . an idle girle of the wheele, or a young drab
. . . and hath not fat enough for her porredge, nor her father and
mother butter enough for their bread, and she have a little helpe of . . .
epilepsie, or cramp, to teach her to role her eyes, gnash her teeth,
startle with her body, hold her armes and hands stiffe, make anticke
faces, grine, mow and mop like an ape, tumble like a hedgehogge, and
can mutter out two or three words of gibberish, as obus bobus; and
then if old Mother Nobs hath called her by chaunce 'idle young
huswife', or bid the devil scratch her, then no doubt but Mother Nobs
is the witch, the young girl is owle-blasted, and possessed.[22]

In response to this onslaught, the beleaguered exorcist published new
accounts of the possession cases in which he had been involved,
complete with detailed descriptions of the physical symptoms of those
suffering from 'unclean spirits'. These symptoms, he maintained, were
so remarkable that they could not have been produced by fraud or
natural illness. In the case of William Sommers, for instance, swellings
had appeared in the boy's body which were so large that they snapped
off the buttons of his clothes, and these travelled up and down his limbs
during his exorcism.[23]

The controversy between Darrel and Harsnet provides a sharp
illustration of the complexity of religious politics in sixteenth-century
England. It also shows how theological consistency was sometimes
abandoned for the sake of political advantage. Darrel's ministry
endorsed a constellation of folk beliefs which bore little relation to godly
protestantism, and were condemned by the puritan clergy in other
circumstances. Darrel made this compromise because it enhanced his
authority – and that of the party he represented within the church – by
allowing him to act as an exorcist. On the other side, Harsnet employed
godly arguments to discredit his puritan opponents. He pointed out that
belief in possession appeared to limit the power of God, since it implied
that the devil was capable of miracles; and he repeatedly cited the work
of Reginald Scot, who argued that popular belief in possession and
witchcraft was no more than popish superstition. In many ways, these
views were more consistent with puritan ideology than the position
adopted by Darrel and his supporters, but they were expressed by a
churchman whose hostility to puritanism was so intense that Darrel
dubbed him a 'secret friend of Rome'.[24]

In theological terms, the bizarre career of John Darrel is very difficult
to explain. But his spectacular rise and fall make sense in the political
and social circumstances of late Elizabethan England. Puritan pastors
like Darrel embraced demonic possession and exorcism as an aid to
their ministry, and it continued to serve as a focus for preaching and

'godly exercises' throughout the seventeenth century. The conflict between the church hierarchy and protestant exorcists was essentially political: it was part of a wider dispute between the crown, which sought to maintain the institutional power of the established church, and puritan clergy who saw themselves as the leaders of the Christian community. In these circumstances, it was hardly surprising that each side used the best arguments to hand, despite the contradictions which this entailed. The case of John Darrel is a reminder that human behaviour seldom conforms neatly to philosophical or theological systems. Religious ideas have to be applied to real-life situations, and non-intellectual factors often play a crucial role in shaping human actions. This principle applies as much to the theology of Satan as to any other set of beliefs. Despite the claim in the New Testament that the devil was the 'prince of this world', it appears that perceptions of the old enemy in sixteenth and seventeenth-century England were shaped largely by the political circumstances of different social groups.

2
THE DEVIL AND THE
ENGLISH REFORMATION

MEDIEVAL PERSPECTIVES

A 'merry tale' published in 1526 provides a lively illustration of late medieval attitudes towards the devil. It tells the story of a Suffolk man named John who acted the part of Satan in a town play, then walked home at night wearing the costume he had put on for the role. His path took him through a wood, where he stumbled on the activities of a gang of poachers. As he approached in the failing light, they mistook him for 'the devyll in dede, [and] for fere ran away', abandoning their horse and a large booty of dead rabbits. When John realised what had happened, he took the horse with the rabbits hanging from its saddle and rode to the house of the gentleman who owned the estate, intending to return his property. This act of good neighbourliness inspired panic among the gentleman's servants when they caught sight of the strange visitor advancing towards them. At John's arrival, the steward informed his master that the devil 'is at the gate sytting upon a horse laden al wyth sowlles, and by likelyhoode he is com for your soule'. Marshalling the spiritual forces at his disposal, the gentleman called his chaplain and 'as many of his servaunts as durst go with hym' to the gate, armed with holy water and a blessed candle. Here the priest confronted the dreadful rider. He declared 'in the name of the father, sonne and holy ghost, I conjure thee and charge thee in the holy name of God to tell me why and wherefore thowe commest hither'. At this, John explained his intentions and announced that he was 'a good divell'. The company recognised his voice, and their 'fere and dred was turned to myrth'.

This tale offers a useful starting point from which to explore late medieval attitudes towards Satan. While it does not encompass every view that was expressed about 'the evil one' in this period, it contains many elements that were common in contemporary descriptions of him. Perhaps its most striking feature was the assumption that the devil could appear as a physical being. Without this belief, the actions of the poachers and the inhabitants of the house would have seemed unconvincing, and the story

16

would have lost much of its humour. Indeed, the author notes at the end of the tale that sightings of 'spyrytts & devyls' were widely reported and believed.[1] The idea that the devil could assume a physical form was underlined in a similar story from Germany in the fifteenth century. In this version a stranger arrived at a town during a carnival, just as a man in a devil costume was chasing an old woman outside the walls. Unaware that the carnival was taking place, the visitor attempted to rescue the woman by attacking her assailant with an axe. His defence at the ensuing murder trial was that he had genuinely believed the performer to be the devil, and that his actions were intended to save the woman's life.[2] Just as carnival players could be mistaken for the devil, Satan himself could masquerade convincingly in human form. So realistic were his disguises that English folklore identified tokens, such as the possession of one cloven hoof, by which his counterfeits could be discovered. The author of the fourteenth-century mystical tract, *The Cloud of Unknowing*, affirmed that the fiend could be detected in any guise by the fact that he 'has never more than one large and flaring nostril'.[3] Such concern for physical details emphasised the bodily reality of the devil, which appears to have been taken for granted by many people in the late Middle Ages.

Even when the devil manifested himself invisibly he was generally assumed to occupy real space. The concept of demonic possession, in which an unclean spirit was physically located inside the body of its victim, was a vivid illustration of this idea. A common treatment for the condition was to beat the possessed individual so the invader was made uncomfortable in its lodgings. Accounts of exorcisms affirmed that bystanders could themselves become possessed when the demon, expelled from the body of one host, fled into another person who happened to be nearby.[4] Such ideas reflected a tendency to view supernatural phenomena in ways which can seem shockingly materialistic to twentieth-century eyes. The arrival of the devil at the gates in the 'merry tale' indicated that he intended literally to carry away the gentleman's soul, adding it to the collection of damned spirits hanging from his saddle. Another story from the same collection described a night-time encounter between a priest

Christ performs an exorcism in an illumination from a thirteenth-century Psalter.

A medieval depiction of the jaws of hell.

and a poacher, carrying a sheep on his back. When the priest saw the poacher he thought he was 'the devyll with the spiryt of [a] dede man on hys nek'.[5] The same kind of literalism was apparent in visual depictions of the fiend. A stained-glass window in the parish church of Fairford in Gloucestershire, for instance, shows Satan carting off souls in a wheelbarrow. He is depicted in a carving in Worcester cathedral with a bundle of damned souls trussed up on his back. Similarly, it was widely assumed that hell and purgatory were physical places, and their precise location was a subject of serious debate among late medieval scholars. Most accepted the traditional view that they were placed somewhere beneath the surface of the earth. Academics attempted to calculate the precise dimensions of the infernal region, based on estimates of the number of damned souls that it had to accommodate and the arrangements in which they were housed. In the sixteenth century, protestant authors regarded such literalist views with scornful amusement, and this response is probably shared by most western people today. But the concrete reality of the devil, hell and the souls of the damned can be viewed as a logical component of medieval religion, and is perhaps more consistent than the modern tendency to retain such concepts while interpreting them in purely 'spiritual' or metaphorical terms.[6]

The Devil's Limitations

As well as illustrating the physical reality of the devil, the story of the Suffolk player indicates the availability of defences against him. These followed in part from the limitations imposed by his material form, which made it possible for mortals to run away, hide, or even attack him with an axe. When the poachers encountered the evil one in the wood, their immediate response was to run for their lives; later, the inhabitants of the house fended him off by shutting the gates. In the other 'merry tale' about the priest and the poacher, the hero tried to escape the fiend by jumping into a ditch. Greater bravery was attributed to St Dunstan who, according to legend, grabbed Satan by his nose with a pair of tongs.[7] The physical vulnerability of the ancient enemy was also depicted in church carvings. In Tewkesbury abbey, for example, the tomb of Robert Forthington, a thirteenth-century abbot famed for his skills as an exorcist, bears a spandrel depicting the abbot thrusting his sword into the devil's throat. A similar motif is found in wood carvings in Carlisle cathedral and the parish church of St Andrews in Greystoke near Penrith, which show St Michael plunging his sword into the gaping mouth of the fiend.

The torments of those guilty of the sin of anger, from the medieval *Vision of Lazarus*.

While Satan's physical limitations made him vulnerable to attack, it was much more common to deploy supernatural weapons against him, such as the candle and holy water employed by the chaplain in the 'merry tale'. Such instruments were typical of the 'sacramentals', or consecrated objects, which were recognised in folklore and theology to offer protection against wicked spirits. Similar powers were attributed to certain passages of scripture, such as the story of the annunciation in St Luke's gospel, which were recited or written on paper and placed in amulets to protect both humans and animals from the devil's assaults. Ultimately, these deterrents relied for their potency on the authority of the medieval church. The church also offered direct protection against Satan through a variety of services dedicated to this purpose, including the baptism of infants and the annual blessing of parishes on the days before the celebration of Christ's ascension. More routinely, many theologians and layfolk accepted that the ringing of church bells could offer protection against flying demons.[8]

The punishments of the proud in hell, from the *Vision of Lazarus*.

The existence of such protections meant that Satan, though fearsome, was to some extent constrained in the exercise of his power. This was also apparent from the legends surrounding saints such as Dunstan and figures from folklore like John Schorn, who was reputed to have trapped the devil in a boot. It is possible that Schorn's legend was connected to the practice of burying shoes in the chimneys of houses in late medieval and sixteenth-century England; these objects were apparently believed to trap evil spirits which attempted to enter the buildings.[9] In a different context, the resourceful heroes of folk tales also exposed the devil's limitations by their habit of outwitting or deceiving him. The belief that the devil could be tricked was illustrated in a remarkable trial from Norfolk in 1465. It was alleged that a weaver, Robert Hikkes, and his accomplice, John Cans, had used 'unlawful arts' to summon up an 'accursed spirit' and asked it to reveal the location of buried treasure. They had enticed the demon to divulge this information by promising it 'the body of a Christian', but deceived the fiend by baptising a cockerel with holy water, killing it and

The summoning of a demon by a ritual magician. Illustration from the title page of Christopher Marlowe, *Dr Faustus* (1636).

offering its remains 'as a Christian carcass'. The charges against the men alleged that this fraud had succeeded and they had thereby acquired a 'vast treasure'.[10] Such confidence in the limits of demonic power, and the capacity of people to manipulate it, underpinned the practice of invoking spirits in both learned and popular magic in medieval England.[11]

Comic Depictions of Satan

The assumption that the devil's powers were limited helps to explain another characteristic of the tale of the Suffolk player, which appeared in many other contemporary works. The devil was presented in a humorous context. While he was not depicted as a figure of fun, he was apparently regarded as a suitable subject for comedy. Thus the revelation that the phantom on horseback was only a man in disguise was an occasion for 'myrth and desport'; the incident was not presented as a warning against sin or a call to virtuous living. The same tendency was evident in another tale published around 1530. This told the story of a man who dreamed one night that he met the devil, who led him into a field to dig for gold. When they uncovered the treasure the man wanted to take it away, but his companion would not allow it:

'Thou canst not carye it awaye nowe, but marke the place that thou mayste fetche it another tyme.'
'What marke shall I make?' quod the man.
'Shyte over it', quod the devyl, 'for that shall cause every man to shunne the place.'

The unfortunate hero took the fiend's advice, and when he awoke he found that he 'had foule defyled his bedde'. Undeterred by this catastrophe, he got up and prepared to seek out the riches that had been revealed in the dream. The story ends with a wonderfully gratuitous touch: 'he putt on his bonette, wherein also the same nighte the catte hadde shyt . . . Thus his golden dreame turned all to dyrt'. Here the devil's mischief provided an opportunity for vulgar entertainment, and no attempt was made to extract a moral from the tale. In a slightly different context, the devil's name was uttered mockingly in the punchlines of early sixteenth-century jokes. When a widow discovered that her potential suitor was impotent, she exclaimed that he could 'go to the dyvell'. A man condemned to hang was granted one last wish by the aristocrat responsible for his execution, and he requested that the lord should kiss him 'on the bare arse'. To this 'the lorde answered: "The devyll kysse thyne arse", and so let him go'.[12] Again, the use of the devil in these tales was purely comic, and indicates that he could be treated as an object of mirth as well as a figure of dread.

The scatological humour associated with the devil in 'merry tales' was also found in some medieval drama. *The Temptation of Christ* in the Chester mystery cycle, for instance, included a passage in which Satan, having been vanquished by Christ, bequeathed his excrement to the audience as his last will and testament. The comic possibilities of the fiend were also explored in some versions of *The Harrowing of Hell*, which featured comedic exchanges between the devil and his minions before their kingdom was purged by Christ.[13] In this instance, the subject matter of the play, which portrayed Jesus' descent into hell to free the souls imprisoned there, probably helped to make the evil one a safe target for comedy. The humorous aspect of Satan was also captured in visual images. Perhaps the most striking example is a carving on a choir stall in the priory church of Malvern in Worcestershire, which also neatly conveys the devil's concrete reality and his limitations. It depicts a monk driving away the fiend by inserting the nozzle of a pair of bellows into the creature's anus. Other grotesque and comic depictions of the devil have survived in the bosses of Norwich cathedral, while the leering, feline carvings of the fiend on the nave columns of Gloucester cathedral emphasise his comic aspect as much as his malevolence. The same can be said of the mischievous demons which populate the stonework and wood carvings of many parish churches.

How representative was the image of the devil described so far? The 'merry tales' were probably collected from oral traditions and printed for a literate minority, which then passed them back into oral circulation. The potential market for such work was huge, and most likely encompassed many different social groups. An equally large and diverse audience probably existed for late medieval religious drama, which presented a version of Satan similar to that found in the tales. It appears that highly devout catholics as well as ordinary layfolk believed that the devil could appear in a physical form, though some theologians noted that, as a spiritual entity, he possessed no flesh of his own and needed to compose an earthly body from materials such as mud and dust. The fifteenth-century mystic Julian of Norwich claimed that she was awoken from sleep one night by the devil in the form of a red-headed man, who clasped his hands around her throat and pressed his face close to hers. Her contemporary, Margery Kemp, experienced frequent visions of Satan before she abandoned her husband to devote herself to a life of piety. Many highly religious individuals also believed that the devil's powers were strictly limited, and could sometimes treat the fiend with remarkable levity. When Satan first appeared to Julian, she 'laughed so heartily' at his pathetic weakness 'that it made those around me laugh too'; she wished that all Christians could 'have seen what I saw, that they might laugh with me'.[14] In the 1530s a similar optimism was expressed by the priestly author Richard Whytford, whose best-selling guide to religious living asserted that Christ had achieved 'vyctorie and mastery' over Satan for the benefit of humankind.[15]

Many late medieval ideas about the devil survived throughout the sixteenth and seventeenth centuries. Indeed, it is likely that the majority of the population subscribed to similar views in the early 1700s, despite the suppression of many of the ecclesiastical and cultural conventions which had supported them. The remarkable continuity of these beliefs is considered in Chapter Three. But the rest of this chapter will argue that traditional ways of understanding Satan were challenged significantly by the introduction of protestantism, and a strikingly different view of the devil came to be embraced by the minority of men and women who committed themselves devoutly to the new creed. For the members of this minority, who were described by contemporaries with the words 'godly' and 'zealous', the devil assumed a new importance in religious life. The reasons for this transformation will be considered below, but first it is necessary to describe the characteristics of protestant attitudes towards Satan.

THE PRINCE OF THIS WORLD

In his 1530 book *A Werke for Housholders*, Richard Whytford presented a brief exposition of the Lord's Prayer. This was intended as a guide for catholic layfolk to the essential meaning and relevance of the sacred text, and formed part of the author's larger purpose of providing a model for Christian living. His exposition made no reference to the devil. Even the words of the seventh line, 'Deliver us from evil', were interpreted without mentioning Satan: Whytford read them as a plea to God to 'kepe me & al thy people from al syn & offence' and to 'conserve & kepe us continually in the state of grace'.[16] It is revealing to compare this work with a commentary on the same text published by the protestant Thomas Becon some twenty years later. Becon began his interpretation of the second line, 'Thy kingdom come', with the following announcement:

> It is not unknowen howe great, how mightye, and of what puissance [great power] the kingdome of Satan is . . . There is no ravening wolfe that so earnestly seeketh greedelye to devoure his praye as this enemye of mankynde, that olde serpent, [who] hunteth and studyeth every moment of an hour howe he maye destroy & brynge to everlasting damnacion mortall menne.

Becon devoted his next two pages to a description of the devil's 'most ample and populous' earthly kingdom. The fiend's power could be seen in the palaces and armies of his many political allies, in the false church of Rome which had been consecrated for his worship, and, most horribly, in the secret and sinful desires of outwardly pious men and women. Only by reflecting on the terrible extent of Satan's kingdom, Becon asserted, could Christians appreciate the importance of praying 'that the kingdom of our heavenly father may come & rule over us'. This interpretation set the tone for the rest of his work. When he came to the line 'Deliver us from evil', he not only mentioned the devil but embarked on a lengthy exposition of the various ways in which he plagued the people of God.[17]

Satan's Dominion

The work of Thomas Becon was part of a general tendency among protestants to amplify the power of the evil one. While Martin Luther affirmed that the devil was ultimately constrained by the power of God, he described Satan as 'the prince and God' of the earth, and averred that 'the bread which we eat, the drink which we drink, the garments which we wear, yea, the air, and whatever we live by in the flesh, is under his dominion'.[18] The reformer's opinion was endorsed by the first generation of English protestants, who habitually described the devil as the 'prince of this world'. Luther's position was later elaborated by William Perkins, arguably the most influential English theologian of the late sixteenth century.[19] When the catechist William Chub observed in 1584 that 'the gates of hell are opened and the floodes of Satan hath overflowen the whole world', he was stating a opinion that few devout protestants would have disputed.[20] This pessimistic outlook has been noted by the historian of Satan, Jeffrey Burton Russell, who has argued that the emergence of reformed theology entailed a 'vast increase in the devil's powers'.[21] For committed adherents of the new faith, Satan was transformed from a limited, rather peripheral figure into a central actor in daily life.

The main way in which the devil's power was enhanced was through a massive extension of his sphere of influence. It was the central idea of protestantism that men and women could do nothing to earn the love of God: his mercy, together with the promise of salvation, was bestowed purely by his own will, irrespective of the merits of those to whom this gift was offered. Thus all human efforts to obtain salvation were ultimately futile; all one could do was place complete faith in God's goodness and mercy. This apparently benign principle could lead to some alarming conclusions. The most bleak interpretation of the doctrine held that people were incapable of performing any act that was pleasing to God. Most reformers followed Luther in arguing that humans were so deeply stained with sin that they could not, without divine assistance, keep any of the ten commandments. For the majority of protestants, and especially those influenced by the work of John Calvin in the second half of the sixteenth century, this meant that virtually all human actions were inherently bad. They were inspired not by God but by the devil.

In 1530 Richard Whytford had asserted that only the sins of pride, envy and wrath could rightfully be attributed to Satan. Other sins, such as gluttony, sloth and lust, resulted from the failure of people to live according to God's laws.[22] The English reformers, in contrast, made it clear that the sins of the flesh were directly inspired by the devil. Many took this idea further by suggesting that human flesh itself was part of Satan's kingdom. This view was expressed most succinctly in Perkins' catechism of 1590, which stated baldly that 'all men are wholly corrupted with sin through Adam's fall, and so are become slaves of Satan'. All human emotions were the devil's property: 'the affections of the heart, [such] as love, joy, hope, desire, etc. are mooved and stirred to that which is evill, to imbrace it, and they are never stirred to that which is good, unlesse it be to eskew it'.[23] Perkins' catechism was reprinted at least four times in the next decade, and went through several editions in the seventeenth century. It followed from these ideas that the devil was an intimate, lifelong companion; as a godly preacher put it in the 1630s, he 'builds his nest' in the human heart.[24] Thus the struggle to overcome Satan had to be fought every day, with one's own body and mind enlisted in the enemy's camp. In one of his daily prayers, the protestant martyr John Bradford described his own body as 'a foe to myself' which he could only overcome with the help of God.[25] In 1616 William Gouge, the author of a guide to religious living equivalent to that published by Whytford ninety years earlier, urged all Christians to fight against their own 'flesh & bloud, [which] is but Satan's instrument; he is the generall, he [is] the captain, he setteth flesh and bloud on worke'.[26]

The Devil as a Tempter and Deceiver

Many protestants combined the idea that the devil was the 'captain' of flesh and blood with an emphasis on his role as the source of personal temptations. Satan's most common manifestation was as a tempter who sought to exploit the innate depravity of human beings. He pursued this goal with ferocious relish: as an early seventeenth-century broadsheet warned, Christians should 'be always armed against temptations' which relentlessly assaulted the mind.[27] Since men and women could do nothing to resist this onslaught on their own, the only armour available was prayer and faith in God's mercy. The range of the devil's temptations was infinite. One of his favourite enticements was sexual lust, which was so prevalent that it was routinely cited by protestants as proof of Satan's dominion over the earth. Thus John Olde claimed in 1557 that the satanic nature of catholicism was proved by its adherents' love of 'whorish women and of fylthy and abominable sodomitical lustes'.[28] This claim was repeated endlessly in the second half of the sixteenth century. Another favourite weapon was greed. This point was illustrated in 1569 in the marvellous woodcuts created for Stephen Bateman's *Christall Glasse of Christian Reformation*. One of these depicts three riders approaching the devil, who holds in his hand a large net containing earthly riches. The first rider represents 'persons of gentility that are not content with sufficiency'; the second is a papist duped by superstitious promises of wealth; the third is a yeoman who, not content with his lowly station, seeks to rise from 'the dunghill to [become] a gentleman'. Each one is beguiled by the fiend's temptations to ride towards his doom.[29] More luridly, the same point was made by murder pamphlets in the seventeenth century, which described how killers were egged on to their crimes by the devil, who lured them with promises of financial gain. In the most compendious example of the genre, John Reynolds explained that murder was usually inspired by 'the fiery and bloudy darts of Satan's temptations', and cautioned his readers to avoid 'the snares and enticements of the devil'.[30]

As well as temptations, the evil one deluded Christians with a wide range of 'false' and heretical thoughts. This concept derived from the medieval belief that Satan sometimes deceived men and women with evil ideas disguised as revelations from God. It was well known that the fiend could appear as an 'angel of light'. Protestant divines, with their conviction that human reason was utterly corrupted, were sharply aware of the devil's capacity to trick people into false beliefs. According to John Olde, the devil won many followers with 'crafty persuasions, deceatefull and false illusions'.[31] It appears that this view was widely accepted in the early seventeenth century, when Gryffith Williams declared that 'it is the policy and practise of the devill, the father of lies, to lay siege against the truth of God'.[32] Ballads from the same period described Satan simply as 'the lyar'.[33] For committed protestants, the most common example of the devil's 'illusions' was the false belief that individuals could earn salvation through their own merits. This delusion underpinned the practices of catholicism and provided further proof that it was a satanic religion; it also dominated the thinking of most ordinary members of the Church of England, whose belief that they could obtain God's favour by doing good works meant that they were only nominal Christians. At the other end of the spectrum, Satan also tried to deceive godly protestants into believing that their faith was in vain. Since they were painfully conscious of their own spiritual unworthiness, they were susceptible to the terrible belief, inspired by the devil, that God had abandoned them completely. Such moments of despair were identified by Perkins as the most subtle and cruel of the devil's works.[34] This idea was expressed vividly in a godly ballad from 1587, which described how a

Christian was tempted to doubt God's mercy when she contemplated the greatness of her own sins. Her agony was relieved by the words of Christ:

> Believe not the devill, for all his delay!
> For his subtill sleight is to work thy decay.
> Think how I converted my apostle, St Paul,
> By mercy and favour, which I give to you all.[35]

Similar assurances of God's mercy to true Christians were offered in sermons and books of practical divinity throughout the period. While they provide a reminder that protestant ideas were not unreservedly gloomy, they also indicate the awful, sometimes unbearable pressures that reformed theology could place on its devout adherents.

The Devil's Agents

Satan's great power over individual men and women was combined in protestant thinking with his immense influence in society as a whole. Since human nature was fundamentally evil, all people who lacked true faith in God were the possessions of Satan. Perkins spelt out the implications of this idea with characteristic bluntness:

> Most of the common people thinke that good meaning will save them; but a man may professe any religion, and have good meaning, and yet not know one step to the kingdome of heaven, but remaine the vassall and slave of Satan. For a man may have outward civill justice and civill pollicie, and meane well, yet be the servant of the divell.

This idea, which was elevated to the status of one of the 'six principles' of Christianity in Perkins' best-selling catechism, enormously swelled the number of the devil's servants.[36] It was a truism among godly preachers that most of the world was occupied by Satan's forces. In the 1580s George Gifford likened them to a great 'armie', and Richard Sibbes later affirmed that the evil one 'never yet wanted a strong faction in the world'. Not only were Christians outnumbered by the devil's allies, but the fiend was constantly rallying his troops against them. As Sibbes explained, there 'hath ever bene . . . a continuall conspiracy of Satan and his instruments' against God's people, whose fate was to endure the hatred of the world.[37] This sense of persecution shaped the religious experience of many zealous protestants. The martyr John Bradford advised Christians to pray for protection from 'Satan and hys mychevous mynysters' whenever they left their homes.[38] The ideal of heroic suffering at the hands of Satan's creatures was exemplified in Foxe's *Book of Martyrs* (1563) and its many imitators in the early seventeenth century.

At a more personal level, Elizabeth Grymeston advised her son in 1604 that the profession of Christianity would bring him constant persecution from the devil's agents, but he could endure it all with the protection of God.[39] This sentiment was repeated in the autobiographies of godly men and women such as Robert Bolton, John Bunyan and Lucy Hutchinson.

Satan's earthly instruments were not a random, uncoordinated force; they were organised into powerful institutions. The most dangerous of these were the false churches established to rival and undermine the true worship of God. Thomas Becon noted that 'the Jewes, the Mahometanes, the anabaptists . . . wyth al the rable of heretikes & sectaries, have their churches also, but al those churches are the sinagoges of Satan, unpure, filthy, stinking, vile, abhominable, ful of al synne and wyckednes'.[40] The most terrible of the false religions, however, was catholicism. The doctrines and rites of the Roman church were expressly designed to exploit the sinfulness of human nature by promoting idolatry and fostering the belief that individuals could earn salvation by their own actions. Thus the preface to a catechism published in 1586 denounced the former pilgrimage site at Walsingham as the 'proude shrine of Satan'.[41] After his conversion from popery in the 1630s, Richard Carpenter realised that 'the invocation of saints is a by-way which the devill hath sought and found to divert man from the due and true service of God'.[42] More crudely, the woodcuts that illustrated godly pamphlets often depicted the pope and catholic priests as demonic figures, complete with horns and cloven hooves.[43] To underline further its satanic origins, catholicism was routinely associated with an impressive range of immoral and anti-social activities. In 1612 Thomas Adams preached that 'perjury, sodomy, sorcery, homicide, parricide, patricide, treason [and] murder are essential things to the new papacy'.[44] Such claims were apparently so familiar by 1642 that 'popery' could be invoked by both sides in the Civil War as a synonym for immorality and evil.[45]

Catholicism's status as a demonic anti-religion was confirmed by its association with the mythical figure of Antichrist. The idea of Antichrist, who was described as the 'man of sin' in St Paul's letter to Peter and the 'beast' in the book of Revelation, had been developed in theology and art during the Middle Ages. According to tradition, he was destined to appear and conquer the world in the period preceding the second coming of Christ. His tyrannical reign would be challenged by the 'two witnesses' named by St John the Divine, who were usually identified with the Old Testament prophets Enoch and Elias. In his final act of persecution, the beast would strike down the two witnesses, but their murder would be followed by the return of Christ, the destruction of Antichrist and the Last Judgment. While theologians were careful to identify Antichrist as Satan's viceroy, rather than the devil himself, he was always closely associated with the fiend. This tendency was maintained by protestant divines, who described the beast as 'the devel's vicar' and the 'mayster demon'.[46] Protestants diverged from their medieval predecessors, however, by defining Antichrist as an institution rather than a single man. Thus John Foxe argued in his *Meditationes in Apocalypsin* that the beast foretold by St John was not one individual but an anti-Christian organisation, and William Fulke affirmed that Antichrist was 'a whole succession of men, in one state of devilish government'.[47] This refinement allowed them to argue that Antichrist's kingdom had already been established, and the events preceding its fall were now unfolding, with the reformers themselves cast in the role of the two witnesses.

Most godly divines agreed that the whole catholic church was a kind of corporate Antichrist. John Olde attested that 'that malignant church and congregation [is] the misticall bodie of Antichriste', and added that 'the principall minister is called the chief Antichrist, as all other members of the same faction, ministrie and office, be also Antichristes'.[48] This rule was followed by John Bale in his account of the examination and death of the protestant martyr Anne Askewe in 1546, in which he described Askewe's interrogator as 'a verye full Antichrist'.[49] It was more usual, though, to attach this title specifically to the pope. In 1595, Perkins preached a detailed commentary on the book of Revelation which concluded 'that Antichrist should be a Romaine, and that the see of his tyrannie should be at Rome'.[50] A few years later, a godly ballad urged all Christians to unite against the papacy and 'drag that triple-crowned beast from out [of] his monstrous throne'.[51] Such apocalyptic images of the pope abounded in theological tracts, ballads and woodcuts throughout the seventeenth century. The identification of catholicism with the Antichrist appears to have served several purposes for devout protestants. It provided them with a historic role in the struggle against the devil, together with the certain knowledge that their final victory was assured. This was the implicit theme of the *Book of Martyrs* and an idea developed repeatedly in spiritual autobiographies. Thus Lucy Hutchinson identified herself and her husband with the 'faithful witnesses whom God raised up after the black and horrid midnight of antichristianism'. She knew that the work begun by the first reformers would shortly culminate in a glorious triumph for God's servants, 'notwithstanding all the attempts of Satan and his ministers'.[52] Such beliefs attached a cosmic significance to the daily struggle against the besieging forces of the devil, and probably offered a strong inducement to continue the battle despite the hardship it involved.

The Rejection of Medieval Beliefs

The sentiments of Lucy Hutchinson and her devout contemporaries left little room for the beliefs expressed in the 'merry tale' of the Suffolk player in 1526. For a start, protestant ideas tended to challenge the view that Satan was a material creature existing in ordinary space and time. This did not mean that protestants rejected the concept of a physical devil: indeed, many godly men and women experienced graphic and terrifying visions of the fiend. But their conviction that he operated mainly at the level of temptations and 'false beliefs' allowed them to internalise their confrontations with the evil one. Even those protestants, like John Bunyan, who described physical encounters with Satan acknowledged that their most intense and frequent battles with the enemy were fought inside their own minds.[53] Similarly, the idea that the devil commanded a legion of human 'instruments' against the servants of God tended to limit his direct interventions in earthly affairs. In many protestant texts he was presented as the infernal mastermind behind a vast conspiracy: a hugely powerful but generally invisible figure. Samuel Clarke's 1651 work *A Generall Martyrologie*, 'a collection of the greatest persecutions which have befallen the church of Christ from the creation to our present times', began by asserting that 'the first murderer and persecutor that was in the world was the divel'. But the fiend made no personal appearances in Clarke's history after his initial manifestation in the Garden of Eden, preferring to work through a vast army of infidels, princes and popes.[54] While this interpretation emphasised Satan's power, it also tended to present him as a rather abstract and impersonal force.

Protestants also challenged traditional beliefs about the ability of men and women to protect themselves from the devil. In part, this followed naturally from their view that Satan possessed great powers which could only be overcome by God. It also reflected their conviction that God's mercy did not depend on the performance of rituals or the use of sanctified objects. Many medieval protections against the devil, such as holy water, candles and Latin prayers, were intimately associated with the catholic church. In the late Middle Ages, there was such demand for blessed candles, which could be taken from parish churches and kept in private houses to afford protection from demons, that the practice was carefully regulated and restricted to special occasions like the celebration of candlemas. All such beliefs were condemned by protestants. In 1616 William Gouge castigated 'superstitious papists who thinke to drive the devill away with holy water, holy oyle, crosses [and] crucifixes'.[55] This sentiment caused some zealous protestants to oppose parish rogation processions, which continued in a modified form in the reign of Elizabeth and the early seventeenth century. In a similar vein, protestant exorcists such as John Darrel condemned their Roman counterparts for using holy water and crucifixes to expel demons, while they defended their own methods by claiming that they relied entirely on the power of faith.[56] The same argument was presented in more concrete terms in a pamphlet in 1612, which mocked a company of papists in Antwerp for trying to defend themselves with holy water when the devil set fire to their church.[57] For devout protestants, such actions were not only ineffective but positively dangerous. The idea that holy artefacts and rituals could offer protection from Satan was itself diabolical, since it prevented people from placing faith in God and encouraged them to support the false church of Rome, which was the principal representative of the devil's kingdom on earth.

Lastly, protestant ideas about Satan made it unacceptable to regard him as a comic figure. He was no longer a laughing matter. This resulted partially from the removal of the protections against demonic power afforded by the medieval church, which meant that it was considerably less safe to poke fun at the fiend. More importantly, the new theology gave the devil a prominent and central role in all aspects of Christian life. Once the proposition that all people were by nature 'slaves of Satan and guilty of eternal damnation' was accepted as a basic principal of religion, it was difficult to treat the devil in a trivial or light-hearted manner.[58] William Gouge summed up the views of many committed protestants when he condemned 'sottish worldlings' who thought so little of Satan that they made jokes at his expense, and resorted to music, games and laughter to divert themselves from his assaults.[59] Likewise, godly pamphlets and ballads warned of the dire consequences of swearing on the devil's name or jokingly calling on him for help.[60] By rejecting the view that Satan was a suitable subject for humour, devout protestants further undermined the medieval ideas described at the beginning of this chapter. Taken as a whole, their vision of the devil was considerably darker and more powerful, yet also more abstract, than the one accepted widely in the late Middle Ages. It is now time to consider the reasons for this transformation.

EXPLAINING PROTESTANT ATTITUDES

Historians have traditionally assumed that protestant beliefs about the devil were a consequence of reformed theology itself. In other words, they have argued that protestants tended to emphasise the power of Satan because this followed naturally from their wider religious beliefs. This approach has the considerable merit of conforming to common-sense assumptions about the history of ideas. It seems wholly reasonable to suppose that the theological insights of the Reformation led its supporters to reject traditional views about the devil, just as it caused them to repudiate many other aspects of medieval religion. Working on this assumption, scholars such as Jeffrey Burton Russell have produced elegant and persuasive explanations for the protestant preoccupation with Satan, which will be considered below. There is a danger, however, that this approach overlooks the political and social factors which encouraged devout protestants to regard the devil as 'the prince of this world'. The attitudes of such people were not shaped in a political vacuum, nor did they always flow inevitably from the central tenets of reformed theology. The rest of this chapter will suggest that non-intellectual factors played a major role in moulding protestant ideas about Satan, and were probably more important than purely theological considerations. In particular, the attitudes of most godly protestants were shaped by their experience of persecution and their perception that ordinary layfolk were largely ignorant of true religion. Before turning to these themes, however, it is necessary to consider the psychological implications of protestant theology, which might have encouraged its adherents to fear the great power of Satan.

The Theological Context

Jeffrey Burton Russell has highlighted the tendency of the Reformation to encourage an intensely introspective and personal style of devotion, stripped of the traditional comforts and communal support afforded by late medieval catholicism. Within this framework, the devil emerged as a powerful and terrible force:

> Earlier ages had seen the devil's opponent as God, Christ, or the whole Christian community. If attacked by Satan, you could at least feel part of a great army upon whose hosts you called for aid. But now it was you versus the devil; you alone, the individual, who had the responsibility for fending him off . . . Against biology, against the social nature of mankind, against Paul's mystical body of Christ, against the practice of the early Christian community, against centuries of Christian tradition, this individualistic emphasis on self-reliance and competition left the Christian naked on a black heath at night, exposed to the winter winds of evil.[61]

While Russell suggests that this new introspection influenced many sixteenth-century catholics as well as their protestant counterparts, he implies that it was particularly marked among the supporters of the Reformation. Those devout protestants who reviled the invocation of saints and mocked the idea of holy water, along with the traditional rites and recitations used against the devil by the medieval church, could find themselves exposed to Satan's power with no support except their faith in Christ. As Russell notes, this faith itself was often far from secure, and could only be won through a lengthy period of intense self-examination. The lonely struggle against the evil one could be made more terrible by the stark doctrine of justification by faith alone. Since men and women had no power in themselves to earn salvation, they were forced to rely entirely on God's mercy; they could not trust their own inclinations to help them overcome Satan, and could assume that their own bodies and minds were highly vulnerable to his temptations. Russell's image of the solitary Christian facing the devil in the dead of night, protected only by the hope of God's mercy, is certainly appropriate to the devout men and women whose experiences are described in Chapter Three. Indeed, this image is a literal description of the 'night terrors' endured by many godly protestants in the early modern period.

But protestant theology did not make this outcome inevitable. Indeed, the central tenets of the Reformation were consistent with a variety of different attitudes towards Satan, only one of which was the intense awareness of his earthly power, combined with a constant struggle to overcome it, which came to characterise English protestantism. The insistence on the absolute power of God could lead to the belief that the devil was a relatively weak figure with little influence over faithful Christians. This view was expressed in the fourteenth century in *The Cloud of Unknowing*. After asserting that men and women could do nothing to earn God's mercy, the text affirmed that a simple faith in His goodness was sufficient to overcome Satan: 'Have no fear, the devil cannot come near you. Sometimes he may arouse your will but even then only from a distance, no matter how subtly devilish he may be!'[62] Such optimism was a rare commodity in devotional works of the sixteenth century, but it was still possible for godly protestants to draw similar conclusions from the doctrine of justification by faith alone. Thus the pastor Richard Greenham advised a gentlewoman 'troubled in mind' in the 1590s that her trust in God was enough to protect her from Satan's wiles: 'while you are tender of conscience, afraid of sin, reverently perswaded to walke holily with your God, laugh at Satan's accusations . . . and set naught at the terrors of hell'.[63] The practical and positive tone of Greenham's advice probably explains why it was published as a broadsheet in 1618. Other devotional works affirmed that the faithful would ultimately triumph over the devil, though this message was usually given less space than calls for constant vigilance and struggle against him. Stephen Bateman's *Christall Glasse of Christian Reformation* included one woodcut depicting an armour-clad man,

representing all 'stedfast belevers', standing over the broken body of
Satan, 'being overcome by faith in Jesus Christ' (*see* Plate 2).[64] Similarly,
devotional tracts describing the deathbed experiences of devout
protestants always ended with the dying subject triumphing over the
devil, who had sought to steal away their soul.[65] Such messages did
little to counter the emphasis on Satan's power which characterised
protestant literature, but they demonstrate that a less pessimistic
interpretation was possible.

Even when protestants accepted the great extent of diabolical power,
it did not necessarily follow that they should devote themselves to an
intense struggle against it. The need for such a struggle was certainly a
prominent message in devotional literature and the central theme of
many godly autobiographies, but it was not the only option. One
alternative was for faithful Christians to avoid the kind of introspection
and self-scrutiny which, as Russell has noted, often heightened fears of
Satan. Greenham observed that the devil was happy to exploit such
practices by planting 'false and causelesse feares' in the mind to keep
Christians 'from the glorious feeling of their redemption'. Since Satan
was an infinitely ingenious and deceitful adversary, he suggested that it
was often wise to avoid confrontations with him altogether: 'dispute not
with God lest you be confounded, nor with Satan lest you be
overcome'.[66] A similar sentiment was expressed by Elizabeth Grymeston
in 1604, when she advised her son that 'it is better to flie than to fight
with Satan'.[67] In 1621, the physician Robert Burton noted that
religious introspection had terrified 'the soules of many' by provoking
unwarranted despair about their spiritual condition. He cited Luther's
advice that individuals should not 'torture and crucify themselves' over
the state of their souls, but rather try to cultivate a simple faith in God's
mercy.[68] It was, of course, impossible to evade the snares of the devil
completely by following this course; but it was equally dangerous and
unhealthy to focus intensely on the need to confront and overcome
him. While such an outlook was by no means typical of zealous
protestants in the early seventeenth century, it was quite consistent
with reformed theology.

At the level of individual experience, it is reasonable to assume that
many protestants developed an acute fear of the devil in response to the
doctrines of justification by faith alone and predestination, combined
with the introspective style of religion often associated with them.
Indeed, it was this tendency which occasioned Burton's warning
against the dangers of excessive self-examination and religious
'melancholy'. This tendency was perhaps particularly evident in the
first half of the seventeenth century, when many individuals were first
introduced to protestant theology through the works of William

Perkins. The Yorkshire gentlewoman Lady Margaret Hoby, for one, used Perkins' books to tutor her servants and local women, and also employed them in her daily regime of meditation and prayers.[69] Nonetheless, it is still necessary to explain why the expositions of men such as Perkins, with their particular emphasis on the need to overcome Satan's power, were generally favoured over the more optimistic but equally orthodox views of divines such as Richard Greenham. I believe that the answer can be found in the political and social circumstances of committed protestants in Tudor and early Stuart England. One of the dominant factors in the lives of such people was their experience of religious conflict, and this experience disposed them to accord the devil and his instruments a central role in their view of the world.

The Social Context

The political circumstances of the English Reformation ensured that committed protestants identified their religion with conflict and the threat of persecution for much of the sixteenth century. The suppression of reformed beliefs in the later years of Henry VIII, exemplified by the execution of Ann Askewe in 1546, was resumed with increased ferocity under the catholic regime of Mary Tudor. Unsurprisingly, the theme of martyrdom was extremely prominent in the devotional and polemical literature of the early Elizabethan church. The widely circulated works of authors such as John Olde and Thomas Becon, alongside posthumous publications by martyrs like John Bradford, espoused a style of religion characterised by heroic suffering and conflict with powerful enemies of the gospel. The protestant message was often expressed in overtly martial language. John Gough, for instance, addressed his translation of Erasmus' *Enchiridion* in 1561 'to all Christ's soldiers living in the camp of the world'.[70] This literature also exploited the apocalyptic tradition of the late Middle Ages by presenting religious conflict as a sign of the imminent fall of Antichrist. John Foxe concocted these ingredients into the epic narrative of the *Book of Martyrs* in 1563, and his work was subsequently sanctioned as one of the approved texts of the Church of England. The war against Spain probably intensified the idea that true religion involved a struggle with hostile forces, despite the efforts of a minority of pastors who advocated peace.[71] By the early 1600s, it appears that most devout protestants had accepted the struggle with Spain as a natural expression of their faith. Many would have endorsed the view of the courtier Andrew Marten, who believed that the conflict involved much more than a military struggle: it was a war 'against that horrible beast who hath received power from the dragon, against the princes of the nations which have entered into league with the whore of Babylon'.[72] Such sentiments survived well into the seventeenth century, and were revitalised by the outbreak of religious warfare in Germany in 1618. Zealous protestants expressed solidarity with their German fellows throughout the 1620s and 1630s: in the private prayers and meditations of gentry families such as the Newdigates of Nuneaton; in financial collections for the 'distressed ministers of the palatinate'; and in petitions and political campaigns for an aggressively protestant and anti-Spanish foreign policy.[73] Such activities suggest that the idea of religious warfare continued to shape the thinking and behaviour of devout protestants in the early Stuart period.

The general perception that religion involved a struggle against hostile forces was reinforced by the personal experiences of many protestants. The word 'puritan', which emerged as a term of abuse around 1560 and retained its pejorative sense well into the seventeenth century, was used to ridicule the minority of devout 'professors of the gospel' in many communities. In extreme cases, resentment of 'over-zealous' protestantism could lead to physical attacks. Thomas Wilson, the godly pastor of Stratford-upon-Avon, was threatened with castration by a mob in 1619.[74] His colleague in the neighbouring parish of Woolston 'walked not abroad without his rapier in his hand' to protect him from members of his flock.[75] Such hostility was not confined to the clergy. As a young man in Wales in the 1630s, Vavasor Powell was assaulted by two former friends when he 'reproved them for sin'; and the zealous constable of Brinklow in Warwickshire received 'sore & greevous blowes, thrusts, hurts and wounds' when he sought to reform 'vices & abuses' in his village.[76] While such violence was comparatively rare, it appears to have reflected a widespread popular antagonism towards the perceived excesses of committed protestants, notably their habit of denouncing the impiety of their neighbours. William Perkins observed sadly in 1605 that the 'contempt' felt by most layfolk for godly ministers was 'too obvious in ordinary experience to need spelling out'.[77] Twenty years later, Ephraim Huitt complained that 'the cause of Christ' was mocked 'in every towne if not family'.[78] The reason for this hostility was spelt out poignantly by the celebrated Essex preacher, Richard Sibbes: 'Because God will not have his children love the world, therefore he suffers the world to hate them. They are strangers here, and therefore no wonder if they finde strange entertainment from them that thinke themselves at home.'[79] Such rationalisations led devout protestants to regard persecution itself as a sign of godliness. Robert Harris declared in 1631 that 'every man that would be Christ's true disciple must look for persecution'.[80] A godly maxim from the same period affirmed that 'persecution is the bellowes of the gospel, blowing every sparke into a flame, and martyrs' ashes are the best compost to manure the church'.[81] The prevalence of such attitudes is indicated by the fact that they were parodied in seventeenth-century ballads like *The Mad Zealot*, which mocked an archetypal puritan for glorifying his own sufferings and aspiring 'to be one of Foxe's martyrs'.[82]

The sense of persecution experienced by devout protestants was probably increased by their failure to win over more than a handful of people to the 'cause of Christ'. Historians of the English Reformation have recently emphasised the inability of the clergy to convert their flocks to the most basic protestant doctrines.[83] In practice, this meant that many communities came to be divided between a minority of convinced 'professors' and a much larger body of layfolk whose religious convictions were considerably less intense. Understandably, many godly pastors in the late sixteenth century abandoned the hope of converting the whole nation and focused instead on the small groups of 'true believers' within their parishes. This trend was encouraged by the tendency of godly professors to form close networks of friends, often travelling together to hear sermons and meeting informally to discuss the scriptures. The division between the godly minority and the impious masses was a common theme in late Elizabethan sermons and devotional works. George Gifford lamented the woeful inadequacy of 'the religion which is [found] among the common sort of Christians'; and Perkins prefaced his catechism by listing thirty-two 'false opinions' which were commonly believed.[84] At a more personal level, the sense that true Christians constituted a distinct community surrounded by an ungodly world was expressed in the journals of many committed protestants. The diary of Margaret Hoby described a small network of pious friends and ministers, and recorded her disapproval of the more 'profane' society outside this circle. Following the successful outcome of a lawsuit against her neighbours in 1602, she noted 'the justice and mercie of God to his servants in manifestinge to the world, which little regardes them, that he will bringe downe their enemies unto them'.[85] In the 1630s, similar sentiments were expressed in the journals of Robert Woodford, the constable of Northampton, and the Warwick schoolmaster Thomas Dugard.[86] The close-knit social circles of these godly professors, combined with their distrust of the impious society outside, probably reinforced their view that religion involved a perpetual opposition between God's children and their many foes.

It is in this context that the attitudes of zealous protestants towards Satan can be best understood. The highly confrontational world-view of many godly men and women encouraged a preoccupation with the devil. At the level of high politics, Satan's influence was obvious in the attempts of catholic forces, both at home and abroad, to destroy the 'cause of Christ'. The papal Antichrist was intimately linked with the devil, and his supporters were 'like black incarnate fiends'.[87] The cosmic struggle between God's people and the furious hordes of the beast provided an ideal framework for understanding the religious conflicts of the age. Similarly, the power of the evil one could be seen in the widespread hostility towards God's servants in their own communities. This point was often made explicit in godly literature. Ephraim Huitt described scoffers of the gospel as 'vassals of hel in execution of the devil's offices', and protestant autobiographers routinely claimed that their enemies were 'stirred up' by Satan.[88] More generally, godly professors understood that 'as there are many devils that molest the people of God so there are also many men to second them herein', and persecution by such foes was an inevitable consequence and sign of their faith.[89] The great power of the devil was further demonstrated by the mulish refusal of most people to embrace true religion. Their addiction to falsehood and sin was so strong that it confirmed Satan's status as the 'prince of this world'. The devil's capacity to stir up the masses to impiety was described memorably by George Gifford in 1584: 'all whoremaisters, drunkards, dicers, railers, swearers and such like are the devel's armie, as on the other side such as professe God's word and live godly are his soldiers, and do fight under his banner'.[90] Military metaphors of this kind were recycled throughout the seventeenth century. Christ was a 'brave captain' whose soldiers, protected by the armour of faith, marched defiantly against a multitude of foes. Their war was fought publicly against catholics and 'worldlings' and internalised in the private struggle to overcome temptation and sin, so that religion was 'a daily fighting with inward fears and outward troubles'.[91] This perpetual conflict placed godly Christians in a terrible, but ultimately heroic role: as John Milton affirmed in 1641, they fought for God 'with the unresistable might of weakness, shaking the powers of darkness and scorning the fiery rage of the old red dragon'.[92] Their struggle was made endurable by the knowledge that victory was assured. The words of Elaine Pagel, inspired by her study of first-century Christianity, appear to be strikingly relevant to early modern English protestants:

> Christian tradition derives much of its power from the conviction that although the believer may feel besieged by evil forces, Christ has already won the decisive victory . . . The faith that Christ has conquered Satan assures Christians that in their own struggles the stakes are eternal, and victory is certain. Those who participate in the cosmic drama cannot lose.[93]

The appeal of this world-view in the political and social context of the English Reformation was entirely understandable. But its consequence was to elevate the devil to the leader of a vast army, whose influence at every level of human experience was a dreadful fact of life.

It appears, therefore, that the particular circumstances of the English Reformation encouraged devout protestants to emphasise those aspects of reformed theology which amplified the power of Satan. But this does not mean that their beliefs and fears were not sincerely and deeply held. The private writings and autobiographies of those individuals who committed themselves firmly to the protestant cause suggest that the devil could be a powerful and almost tangible presence in daily life, whose ability to inflict mental and physical torment could seem frighteningly real. The experiences of these men and women will be considered in the following chapter.

3
LIVING WITH THE ENEMY: PROTESTANT EXPERIENCES OF THE DEVIL

VISIONS AND NIGHTMARES

In 1652 an anonymous woman published her account of a nocturnal encounter with Satan. The visitation occurred as the woman, who styled herself simply E.C., was lying in bed and trying to say her prayers. Suddenly she felt 'strange temptations upon me to put God out of my mind, and I could not speake a word, nor scarce think of God'. This sensation was followed at once by the appearance of the fiend: 'Satan then appeared to mee in a most ugly shape, laughing and jeering at me, which did much affright me.' The woman's fear turned immediately to a sense of guilt and the realisation that her religion was shallow and false: she was an untrue Christian who lacked faith and 'had played the hypocrite with God'. As soon as this feeling struck her she appealed to Christ for help. She remembered that Jesus had overcome the devil by his death on the cross, and this knowledge empowered her to rise from her bed to confront the monstrous apparition. Strengthened by her newly restored faith, E.C. commanded the devil to fly from her bedside. The creature was so overwhelmed by the power of God that it obeyed her direction and 'departed from my sight'.

This encounter, which was described in a collection of 'spirituall experiences' compiled by the godly pastor Vavasor Powell, provides an exemplary account of a protestant vision of Satan.[1] The confrontation took place at night, a time when devout protestants were especially aware of the devil's influence. More significantly, the fiend's appearance was associated closely with the spiritual condition of his victim, who interpreted the whole episode in terms of her relationship with God. The fiend's manifestation was heralded by E.C.'s failure to compose her prayers, and the most dreadful effect of the creature's presence was to suggest that her commitment to Christ was weak and 'hypocritical'. It was only when her faith was renewed that she was able to confront and vanquish the demonic intruder, relying entirely on the power of God. Thus the incident was both a test of her faith and a demonstration of the Lord's mercy. The same themes were found in many other protestant autobiographies in the sixteenth and seventeenth centuries. These texts, which were published for the inspiration and instruction of members of the godly community, tended to present the devil as a constant companion throughout their subjects' lives, relentlessly trying to exploit their weaknesses and lapses of faith. He was 'that cruell murdering theife, our ghostly enemy who every houre watcheth to take advantage of us, for bringing us to utter confusion'.[2]

It is possible, of course, that the authors of these godly 'lives' sometimes exaggerated the devil's role for dramatic or educational purposes. The struggle to overcome him could provide an effective structure for their narratives, while the appearance of the 'father of lies' offered an opportunity to rebut objections to reformed theology. But there is no reason to doubt that the accounts were based on real experiences. Indeed, the unpublished writings of devout protestants like Margaret Hoby and Richard Newdigate suggest that the struggle against the 'ghostly enemy' was a central aspect of godly religion. For the most part, Satan manifested himself in the form of temptations and false beliefs, which will be considered in the second part of this chapter. The first part will deal with the less common but more dramatic experiences of individuals such as E.C., whose visions and 'night terrors' provide unusually vivid illustrations of the conflict between devout protestants and the devil.

Godly Apparitions

Satan appeared in a remarkable variety of forms in the visions recorded by godly protestants. Perhaps his most grotesque manifestations were witnessed by the preacher John Rogers, who was tormented by visions of hell as a young man in the 1640s. The fiend and his helpers presented themselves 'in severall ugly shapes and formes (according to my fancies) and sometimes with great rolling flaming eyes like sawcers, having sparkling fire-brands in the one of their hands, and with the other reaching at me to tear me away to torments'.[3] Rogers' apparitions recalled the horrors described by the physician Robert Burton in 1621 as symptoms of 'melancholy' induced by excessive religious zeal: his patients had been taunted by the devil, smelt brimstone and behaved as if they were 'in hell fire, already damned'.[4] It appears that such experiences reproduced medieval depictions of the afterlife, which had survived in printed woodcuts and godly sermons describing the sufferings of condemned souls. Other writers were apparently influenced by the traditional idea that the devil could disguise himself in human flesh. Thus when Hannah Allen heard the sound of 'two young men' in the yard outside her chamber one night in 1664 she perceived that they were 'devils in the likeness of men, singing for joy that they had overcome me'.[5] Others encountered the fiend in the guise of a stranger, who tempted them to sin or declared that their souls were lost.[6] Satan could also manifest himself in more ghostly and insubstantial forms. A particularly chilling example was described in the autobiography of Vavasor Powell:

> Being alone in my chamber late at night at prayer, and the door shut, I continued in prayer till the candle went out, and as I went on I sensibly perceived a strong cold wind to blow . . . It made the hair of my flesh to stand up, and caused all my bones to shake, and on the sudden I heard one walk about me, trampling upon the chamber floor, as if it had been some heavie big man.

Powell fled the room and cried for help from the rest of the household. The demonic visitor disappeared, but it continued to 'affright and terrifie' him in the weeks that followed, 'not onely by secret workings in the conscience but by visible representations and outwardly real apparitions'.[7] A similar haunting was recalled by John Bunyan in *Grace Abounding to the Chief of Sinners*, which described how the devil attempted to disturb the author's prayers by pulling invisibly at the clothes on his back.[8]

Despite the dramatic nature of these events, they were not presented by those who experienced them as particularly exceptional or strange. In part, this can be explained by the tendency of godly narrators to depict their lives as religious exemplars revealing the providence of God in every happening, however unpleasant or apparently bizarre. But it also reflects the authors' understanding that physical manifestations of Satan were part of a much wider pattern of religious experience. They were unusually concrete examples of the devil's influence in the world, which normally expressed itself in more subtle ways. Even the grotesque visions of John Rogers were only one aspect of the spiritual crisis that engulfed him as a young man when he became aware of his own sinfulness. Coming to this awareness, which involved an apprehension of the devil's sovereignty in the fallen world, was a normal stage in the process of conversion to true religion. Similarly, the torments visited on Powell and Bunyan were an extension of the devil's usual ploy of disturbing Christians in their prayers. This strategy was described in a guide to the practice of prayer by John Preston in 1629 : 'Satan . . . knows it is this duty which quickens every grace, it is the greatest enemy he hath, and if he can keepe us from prayer hee hath the upper hand of us, hee hath wrested the weapon out of our hands, hee hath disarmed us, and then hee may doe what he will with us.'[9] Preston assumed that the evil one normally diverted Christians from their prayers with 'fancies' and sinful thoughts, and the writings of Bunyan and Powell confirm that these were his preferred weapons. The physical phenomena they described were simply a variation on the fiend's usual methods, deployed to achieve his familiar goal of unsettling their relationship with God. A similar point can be made about the demonic presence which invaded the bedroom of E.C. In disrupting her prayers and reminding her of her own sinfulness, the devil was only pursuing his usual strategy in an uncommonly direct fashion.

At a psychological level, the visions experienced by godly protestants were probably an expression of the acute tensions imposed by the practice of godly religion. The intensely introspective nature of devout protestantism, combined with its assumption that the human mind was innately wicked, could make individuals vulnerable to depression and attacks of mental anxiety. This danger was particularly marked at those times of solitary prayer and meditation when the devil's appearances were most commonly reported. In this sense, there may be some merit in Robert Burton's argument that the puritan lifestyle itself was the main cause of 'religious melancholy' and its attendant delusions. Burton was especially critical of those 'thundering ministers' who inspired their flocks with an excessive sense of sin and the horrors of damnation, suggesting that they were the 'most frequent cause of this malady'. It is also possible, as the physician implied, that excessive fasting and lack of sleep might have deceived the senses of men such as Rogers and Powell.[10] Equally, the absence of reliable spectacles for the great majority of the population meant that poor eyesight, as well as anxious imaginations, might have contributed to some visions of the fiend. Whatever their origins, the apparitions witnessed by committed protestants were readily explicable within their own belief system, which allowed them to treat such phenomena as a natural consequence and even a confirmation of their piety. Since these encounters were only an extension of the normal conflict between God's children and the devil, there was no reason for those who experienced or read about them to question their authenticity.

Night Terrors

Protestant visions of Satan were closely related to a collection of phenomena described by contemporaries as the 'terrors of the night'.[11] These phenomena, which ranged from nightmares to nocturnal apparitions and the awareness of spectral presences, were often recorded in godly memoirs as expressions of the devil's power. It is not surprising, perhaps, that godly men and women were sometimes afflicted by such experiences, since the night was a time for private reflection and prayer, when individuals were especially vulnerable to spiritual anxieties. More prosaically, the effects of darkness and shadow made it easier for the senses to be deceived. Writing in the 1550s, John Bradford warned that the night was a time of particular danger for devout Christians, when they needed to arm themselves against 'the craftes & assaultes of the wicked enemy'.[12] One of the most common forms of 'night terror' was the perception, often intense and irresistible, that the devil was creeping towards the victim's bedside to snatch them down to hell. As a young man, John Rogers was 'afraid every night lest the devill should carry me away', and imagined that the fiend 'would tear me a pieces' in his bed.[13] One of the contributors to Powell's *Spirituall Experiences* related that one night she 'was fearfull to sleepe lest the devill should fetch me away'.[14] When she awoke, 'the devill appeared to me and stood before me, and did exceedingly terrifie me'. These torments were linked explicitly to 'terrors of conscience' and the fear of damnation, which were part of the protestant conversion experience. They also recalled the symptoms of a sleep disorder known to contemporaries as 'the hag'. This condition, which is still reported today, is a form of waking dream in which the subject is paralysed and perceives a malevolent presence bearing down on them. One victim of this experience was the puritan surveyor, Richard Norwood, who described it as a state 'wherein a man is neither quite awake or asleep'. As he recalled in the 1640s, one of the demonic apparitions he witnessed while in this condition was so real that 'I have sometimes taken a naked knife in my hand when I went to sleep, thinking to strike at it.'[15]

   While the experience of the hag afforded the most spectacular expression of satanic power, the devil sometimes chose to appear in ordinary nightmares. As a child, John Bunyan was 'greatly afflicted, while asleep, with the apprehension of devils and wicked spirits, who . . . laboured to draw me away with them'.[16] In 1653 Mary Burrill recorded that she 'had in my dreams two terrible conflicts with Satan, by which I have been much assured of God's love, for that I alwayes had the better, the victory'.[17] Nightly battles of this kind were experienced by Thomas Hall, the godly pastor of King's Norton, throughout his adult life:

> His sleepe was not rest (many times) but terrour . . . He said his bed should refresh him [but] he was scared with dreames & terrified with visions, so he observed Satan's hand helping forward the affliction & distres, for constantly he complained that his nights before the Sabbath or before a fast (though he used all meanes to prevent it) were his worst nights.[18]

As Hall's interpretation of his afflictions suggests, the 'night terrors' endured by protestants were an extension of their daily struggle to overcome the devil's power. Whatever the psychological or medical causes of their experiences, godly men and women assumed that Satan attacked them at night to catch them off guard in their perpetual battle against him. In their waking hours he pursued the same goal in more subtle ways, with falsehoods and illicit desires. Their response to these temptations is considered below.

SATANIC THOUGHTS AND TEMPTATIONS

It is perhaps misleading to suggest that godly protestants experienced their major conflicts with Satan 'inside their own minds'. This twentieth-century phrase does not allow for the many ways in which the devil was believed to affect the mental states of men and women in the early modern period. According to William Perkins, Satan was capable of implanting his own thoughts into the mind of a human being.[19] This idea was fleshed out in 1634 by Robert Bolton, who argued that satanic thoughts could be 'throwne into our imaginations like a flash of lightening, with such an unavoidable impression that they cannot bee prevented by any wit or strength of a man'. Bolton described the experiences of his godly companions whose minds had been 'injected' in this way:

> I have knowne some which have beene fearfully vexed and astonished in heart with horrible and blasphemous thoughts, which were Satan's owne immediate injections, and terrours even to nature itselfe. But when they have beene told and taught that [these thoughts] were none of theirs, and that if they did hate, abhorre and withstand them as the pure spight and malice of the fiend of hell, they should never be imputed unto them as their own sinnes . . . they have received great ease and comfort.[20]

A first-hand account of this phenomenon was recorded in 1643 in an anonymous pamphlet by a London stationer. The author was singing a psalm in church when he was overwhelmed by the desire to blaspheme the name of God: he claimed that Satan impressed this urge 'so vehemently on my mind that I had no power to resist him'. This mental hijacking was followed by a series of temptations which drove the victim to the edge of despair.[21] Similar attacks were described by Bunyan, whose prayers were disturbed when the devil cast unwelcome thoughts into his mind.[22] As a young girl in the 1650s, Hannah Allen found that 'the enemy of my soul . . . cast horrible and blasphemous thoughts and injections into my mind, insomuch that I was seldom free, day or night, unless when dead sleep was upon me'. Allen claimed that she was comforted during these troubles by reading the works of Robert Bolton, and it is tempting to surmise that the godly author encouraged her to believe that her own thoughts had demonic origins.[23] The accounts of Bunyan and Allen suggest a link between the state of temptation, which was experienced by all godly protestants, and the more extreme condition of demonic possession, in which the subject's whole mind was occupied by the devil. This connection will be explored further in Chapter Six.

The belief that satanic thoughts could be planted in the minds of men and women raised the obvious problem of distinguishing between one's own cognitions and those 'injected' by the evil one. This problem was made worse by the assumption that all human faculties, including the mind, were so utterly corrupted by sin that people often succumbed to irreligious ideas even without the direct intervention of Satan. Thus Perkins asserted that wicked thoughts could arise 'either by a man's owne conceiving or by suggestion of the divell'.[24] Individuals were only responsible for those evil conceptions which arose from their own minds. Bolton suggested that ideas of satanic origin could be detected by the nature in which they appeared: 'sinfull thoughts of our owne come upon us enticingly, by allurements, baits, and insinuations; but Satan's suggestions rush in violently, forcibly and furiously'.[25] He also implied that the content of these ideas, which were often extremely blasphemous or 'unnatural', set them apart from ordinary cognitions. It appears that these rules were applied by those godly writers who believed they had been visited by satanic thoughts, which usually occurred very suddenly and sometimes contained such extreme blasphemy or scepticism that they could only be attributed to Satan. Most authors assumed, however, that such 'lighting flashes' were comparatively rare: they attributed most of their sinful ideas to their own fallen nature, which inclined them to yield to the 'baits and allurements' of the ghostly enemy.

Before considering these 'baits and allurements' in detail, it is interesting to note the psychological implications of the belief that Satan could invade the human mind with alien thoughts. This meant that individuals could, in certain extreme circumstances, absolve themselves of responsibility for ideas inside their own minds. They could also express these ideas to an audience which accepted their satanic origin and assumed that their true author was the enemy of everything that their human recipients really believed in. As a result, devout protestants could safely give voice to any fears and anxieties they harboured about their faith, and express any hidden desires, in a context which acquitted them of responsibility and guilt. This process was apparent in the behaviour of some possessed men and women. It was also evident in the accounts provided by some godly protestants of the mental 'suggestions' they received from the devil. Perhaps the most striking example is found in the work of 'M.K.', one of the contributors to Powell's collection of godly lives in 1652. Her description of Satan's 'suggestions' deserves to be quoted in full:

> Fond foole (quoth he) why dost thou trouble thyself? Take thy pleasure, doe what thou likest, thou shalt never be called to an account for any thing; for as the wise man dyeth, so dyeth the foole, and both rest in the grave together. There is no God to save thee or punish thee, all things were made by nature, and when thou dyest there is an end of all thy good and bad deeds. Thou talkest of the scripture, and of a God and of a Jesus which thou hast heard of there. See thy simplicity now. How canst thou prove the scriptures to be true? Alas, they were made by men's inventions, there is no hold for thee to take there.[26]

The satanic ideas recorded by M.K. appear to describe her own most profound doubts and fears about the Christian religion, which she overcame only after a protracted and painful struggle. In 1653 another godly woman, Jane Turner, described how the devil had assailed her with similar doubts during the process of her conversion: 'Satan was ready to assault me, and set upon me with this horrid temptation, to question the being of God; and I remember it usually came upon me when I was alone, but especially as I was going by myself to hear the minister.' Recognising the diabolical nature of this thought, Turner 'did resist and labour against it, drawing arguments as I went in the fields from the very works of creation to confirm [to] myself that there is a God, and that it should not be in vain to serve him'.[27] Hannah Allen was also inspired by the devil to have 'hard and strange thoughts of my dear Lord' in 1664, though she demurred from describing the exact nature of these thoughts in her autobiography.[28] In less extreme cases, the 'suggestions' of Satan seem to have expressed the feelings of unworthiness experienced by devout protestants. Thus the pastor Richard Rothwel was tormented with anxieties about his ministry during an illness around 1600: the devil visited him with the idea that his preaching would be 'the scorn of religion, and every man would reproach it for his sake . . . that he should never preach more, but should blaspheme the name of God'.[29] It is possible that the attribution of such thoughts to Satan made it easier for these individuals to express and confront their own deepest anxieties. At the very least, it allowed them to articulate these thoughts in a context which absolved them from guilt and emphasised their own godliness.

The Struggle Against Temptation

While most zealous protestants accepted that Satan could manifest himself directly in the mind, it appears that his usual strategy was to exploit the innate weaknesses of the human body and intellect. It was commonplace in sermons and spiritual guidebooks that human flesh was inclined towards evil. As such, it was one of the 'confederates' of the devil. In his 1586 catechism, William Chub expressed the conventional view that it was the natural inclination of men and women to 'fall into al filthie conversation, lewde lust, abominable sin and devillish desires'.[30] In 1630 the Warwickshire lawyer, Richard Newdigate, noted the warning of a local preacher that Christians should be constantly vigilant 'to withstand the divell', who took every opportunity to exploit the 'originall corruption whereby our natures are tainted'.[31] It appears that such sentiments were taken to heart by many godly layfolk. As a young man in the 1640s, Bunyan overheard a group of pious women discuss 'how they were convinced of their miserable state by nature'.[32] Some forty years earlier, the same pessimistic idea had been expressed vividly in a meditation by Elizabeth Grymeston:

> What is life but a continuall battell and defiance with God? What have our eyes and eares beene but open gates to send in loades of sinne into our minde? What have our powers and senses beene but tynder . . . to feede the flame of concupisence? What hath thy body beene but a stewe of an adulteresse, but a forge of Satan?[33]

As Grymeston implied, the corrupted nature of humankind was apparent in both the body and the mind. It was a favourite pastime of godly divines to identify the particular temptations to which these two aspects of the human constitution were especially susceptible. Predictably, the body was usually associated with the 'fleshly' evils of fornication and adultery, along with a wide range of illicit urges grouped under the loose heading of 'sodomy'. Few puritan diarists were prepared to record their own experiences of sexual temptation, but those who did tended to ascribe it to a mixture of human frailty and satanic influence. In the early 1660s, Henry Newcombe described how his mind was 'basely poisoned' by sexual desires which he attributed to the devil. The Quaker leader, George Fox, observed in his journal that sexual dreams were 'the whisperings of Satan to man in the night season'.[34] The mind, in contrast, was especially prey to the temptation of 'evil self-love' or pride. According to William Gouge, this vice issued 'from the corruption of nature and is daily increased by the instigation of Satan for the destruction of mankinde'.[35] This tendency was encouraged by material possessions and the 'flattery' of the world. The only way to escape these inclinations was through faith in God. Thus godly preachers likened Christianity to the 'deliverance' of men and women from the tyranny of Satan, to whom they would otherwise be enslaved by their natural instincts. As John Woolton proclaimed in 1576, it was only through God's mercy that 'Christians are translated out of the power of darknesse into the kingdome of his dearly beloved sonne'.[36] Similarly, Perkins asserted in 1595 that 'the church of God is a companie of men taken out of the synagogue of Satan, the kingdome of the devill', where their sinful nature had previously bound them as vassals to the evil one.[37]

Unsurprisingly, devout protestants tended to view the temptations of Satan in terms of spiritual warfare. This outlook was expressed in typically martial language in 1641 by the catholic convert Richard Carpenter, who declared that 'when a temptation stands up in armes against mee, I will fight valiantly under the banner of Michael the archangel against the dragon'.[38] Similar sentiments were expressed in the godly broadsheet *Stand Up for Your Beliefe* (1640), which enjoined Christians to enter 'spiritual combat' with the fiend:

> First take this shield of faith to arme your hearts,
> And if this quench not Satan's fiery darts,
> (But frequent tempting blowes doth crush the shield),
> The Word's a sword, take that, if he not yeeld.[39]

Despite the availability of these spiritual weapons, the fact that humans were condemned by nature to succumb to temptation meant that one's own body was a potential adversary in the struggle for salvation. Protestant teachers since Thomas Becon had stressed the need to subdue one's own flesh in order to withstand the devil's assaults.[40] In 1639, a godly layman noted that his struggle to conquer temptation was constantly hampered by the 'treachery' of his own body, which Satan 'workes upon [for] any base or villainous advantage'. Only the power of God could 'cut off that traiterous corruption of nature' and give him 'strength against the fiery assaults of the tempter'.[41] The belief that one's own flesh was allied with Satan could lead to moments of despair and self hatred. In 1664 Hannah Allen fell 'under a sad melancholy', and confided in her journal that 'there is such a woful confusion and combating in my soul that I know not what to do'.[42] Similar agonies were described by Vavasor Powell, while the Warwickshire pastor, James Nalton, was known as the 'weeping prophet' because of the 'violent fits of melancholy' which he suffered throughout his career.[43]

These times of desperation were balanced, however, by moments of confidence in the mercy of Christ. Allen was lifted from her despair by

the realisation that the Lord would empower her to overcome the devil
and her own treacherous flesh, and Powell and Nalton drew strength
from the same source. As a godly pamphleteer declared in 1614,
Satan's powers 'are great [but] the mercy of God is greater, who never
faileth to send comfort in temptation if we accept thereof'.[44] The same
confidence was expressed by Jane Turner in the preface to her
autobiography in 1653. She published the book 'knowing I must expect
to encounter with Satan in relation to it [in] several wayes, but
believing that which way so ever he appears, whether to abase or exalt
me in my own thoughts, the Lord will not be wanting with strength to
withstand and resist him'.[45] For many protestants, the conviction that
God would give them victory over the devil's temptations provided the
counterpoint to their anxieties about their innate sinfulness. The
autobiographies of godly men and women often recorded their
oscillation between these two states of mind.

This pattern was illustrated most distressingly in the accounts of
suicide attempts in several godly 'lives'. Typically, the subjects were
driven to despair by contemplating their own sinfulness and distance
from God; this led them to consider taking their own lives, only to be
saved by the sudden understanding that Christ would save them despite
their unworthiness. Satan sometimes appeared in these narratives as
the tempter who told his victims that their lives were irredeemable and
urged them to bring them to a violent end, even 'leading' them to
places where they could perform the act. This role was hardly
surprising, as the devil was traditionally associated with suicide, and
protestant theologians insisted that his 'policy and practice' was to
remind individuals of their degraded nature and persuade them 'that
God will forget to be merciful'.[46] In the 1630s John Rogers faced 'the
forcible temptations of a furious devill . . . to murder myself', believing
that his life was worthless because he was already damned.[47] The fiend
told Vavasor Powell that 'the fewer sins I committed in this world, and
the shorter time I lived in it, the less would be my torment' in hell. He
was delivered from this temptation by the power of God, but later
succumbed to 'great fears as to my eternal condition, being often times
tempted by Satan to destroy myself'.[48] In other instances, Satan seized
on the guilt felt by individuals when they committed particular sins,
using it to remind them of their innate badness. One of the contributors
to Powell's *Spirituall Experiences* told a lie as a young girl which caused
her sister to be punished; she was subsequently oppressed by remorse
and convinced by the devil that God had disowned her. This led her to
attempt suicide by swallowing the feathers in her pillow, before she was
rescued by her parents. Satan tempted others to end their lives after
they succumbed to lustful thoughts or impulses which reminded them

of their innately sinful condition, but his designs were foiled when his victims remembered the mercy of God.[49] These experiences were extreme, but they followed the pattern of temptation and disillusionment, followed by the acceptance of God's mercy, which characterised the spiritual 'trials' of most committed protestants.

These trials were described further, albeit in a less dramatic context, in the journal of the Yorkshire gentlewoman Margaret Hoby. Hoby's reflections, recorded every night between August 1599 and July 1605 as part of her daily regime of spiritual devotions, offer an intimate record of one individual's struggle to overcome the devil's temptations. In common with other godly 'professors', Hoby's religion was characterised by the acceptance of her own sinful condition and reliance on the saving power of faith: 'findinge my corruption and receivinge strength' from God. Satan appears to have played a specific role in this scheme. She always represented him as a tempter, and never mentioned him in the context of her occasional bouts of illness: the sickness which caused her to miss church in July 1600, for example, was recorded as a judgement of God for her transgressions. When the devil appeared in her journal, he usually assumed the form of a difficult or troubling thought which diverted her from her religious duties. On the last Sabbath in August 1599 she noted that 'this day, as ever, the divell laboreth to hinder my profittable hearinge of the word and callinge upon God', and prayed that the Lord would 'strengthen his children to rissist and overcome' him. During a sermon in July 1602, she 'was provoked to have binne disquieted', but God gave her the strength to hear the preacher with 'comfort and profitt'; the following week, however, she noted that Satan returned and 'I felte his buffets'. In a few instances, Hoby linked the devil's influence to specific social situations. When she was obliged to chastise a member of the household in October 1601, she recorded that 'I ever take [this] to be a buffitt of Satan's malice'. It is perhaps significant that the devil's assaults increased markedly in the summer of 1602, during the final stages of her husband's lawsuit against the neighbouring Eure family, who had offended the Hobys with their drunken and 'impious' behaviour two years earlier. Throughout these and her other spiritual trials, Margaret Hoby maintained confidence in God's power to overcome the evil one. In May 1602 she reflected that 'howsoever justly God hath suffered Satan to afflicte my mind, yet my hope is that my redeemer will bringe my soule out of troubles, that it may praise his name, and so I will waite with patience for deliverence'. Elsewhere, she reflected on the spiritual value to be gained from facing the devil's temptations: she was comforted in July 1602 by the belief that 'my God will make them in the end profetable to me'. On another occasion, she explained that Christians should 'expect new temptations to humble us for our former negligence'. These sentiments appear to reflect the views of Perkins and the other godly divines whose works provided the basis for her devotional practices.[50]

While Hoby's diary dealt primarily with her own spiritual condition, it also expressed her feelings about the devil's activities in the wider world. Indeed, she appears to have perceived the legal conflict with the Eure family in terms of her struggle to overcome the evil one, with the devil employing human agents to open up a second front against her.[51] This perspective was common in godly circles. A decade later, Lady Anne Newdigate of Nuneaton was faced with 'sundry sutes & troubles' concerning the inheritance of her husband's estate. In a letter of October 1617, she expressed the hope that God would protect 'me & mine . . . from the devile & al his instruments' malice, & give me triumph & victorie over my enemies, as he hath done & I trust in Jesus Christ will do'.[52] Similar sentiments were voiced by her son Richard in a prayer composed in 1626. He thanked God for his 'many favours unto me, protecting mee in daungers [and] preserving me from Satan's tyranny and the malice of my enimies'.[53] In his assaults on Hoby and the Newdigates, the devil combined the spiritual weapon of temptation with the less subtle ammunition of his earthly 'instruments', and his victims drew strength from the Lord to overcome them both. The link between Satan's attacks on the mind and the social persecution suffered by God's servants was made explicit by William Gouge, who insisted that 'the forces of the Lord's soldiers' had to fight both 'inward' and 'outward' assaults from the evil one.[54] This connection was also stressed by Vavasor Powell, who claimed that the devil alternated between inward temptations and outward persecution in his attempts to destroy him. Thus Powell was first terrified by his own wicked nature and goaded by Satan to attempt suicide, and 'when these temptations failed then he began to raise up persecution against me'.[55] The same pattern was observed by Samuel Clarke, who suggested in 1642 that 'if we be not encountered with the world's opposition we shall be the more encumbered with the flesh's corruption'.[56]

The Devil at the Deathbed

The determination of Satan to torment God's people meant that he not only assailed them throughout their lives, but also visited them in the hours before they died. The special danger that the enemy posed at the end of one's life was noted by Perkins in *A Salve for a Sicke Man* (1595), which offered spiritual guidance on the art of dying. Perkins warned that the devil would make a last assault on the mind during the pangs of death, and advised his readers to ignore the fiend's suggestions and 'commend thy cause to God'.[57] A fuller discussion of the same theme was published by John Gerard twenty years later. The works of Perkins and Gerard continued the medieval tradition of presenting the deathbed as a place of combat between God and the devil for the soul of the dying Christian, while focusing on the particular 'vexations' of Satan associated with godly religion. Gerard identified no fewer than forty-six specific temptations, including 'weakness of faith', 'the want of the power to beleeve', and 'the doubting of the application of the benefits of Christ'. He dealt with each of these separately, concluding each section by advising the dying person to submit to the saving power of the Lord: 'it is Christ who fighteth for thee and in thee, beleeve the devill shall not be stronger than hee'.[58] The warnings in these books were apparently vindicated by the deathbed terrors of a number of godly professors. The Shrewsbury pastor Julius Herring was subjected to a 'furious assault' from Satan the night before he died in 1644. Another godly divine, John Dod of Northamptonshire, told one of the watchers at his bedside in 1645 that he 'had been wrestling with Satan all that night, who accused him that he neither preached, nor prayed, nor performed any duty as he should have done'. He died the next day after winning a 'great victory' over the enemy.[59] Lengthy reports were published of the deathbed confrontations of godly men and women with Satan, and at least one such account circulated in the form of a ballad in the seventeenth century.[60] It is unlikely that such dramatic conflicts were a common occurrence, but the genre was certainly popular, with works such as Philip Stubbes' *Christall Glasse for Christian Women* republished every few years between 1591 and 1650. Like the spiritual autobiographies collected by Rogers and Powell, these texts provided exemplars of the fortitude of God's children while reminding their readers of Satan's presence at every stage of life.

The conflicts between godly professors and the devil in the last hours of life centred on the condition of the dying person's soul. The fiend's usual strategy was to appear to his victims, either physically or in the form of mental 'suggestions', and tell them that they were so corrupted by sin that God would refuse to receive them in heaven. In 1601 Satan reminded Katherine Brettergh of 'the severity of God's justice and the greatness of her sinnes'.[61] Similarly, he whispered to Elizabeth Stretton of Leicester that 'thy sins will weight thee down to hell'. Both women responded by asserting the saving power of God despite their sins, a sentiment which was conveyed in the final verse of the ballad inspired by Stretton's death:

A Renaissance depiction of the 'art of dying'. The devil tempts the
dying man with riches.

God's mercy is above my sin,
Who did protect me from my birth.
My father knows where I have been,
Amongst vile sinners here on earth.[62]

The evil one also employed his familiar tactic of disrupting the prayers
of his dying victims. Brettergh tried to recite the Lord's prayer but was
'interrupted' by Satan when she reached the line 'Deliver me from
temptation'. She 'shewed much discomfort' and cried out to those
present that 'I may not pray, I may not pray.'[63] When Katherine Stubbes
made a deathbed confession of her faith in 1591 she was suddenly
confronted by the devil, who 'bid her to combat'.[64] The printed

The dying man overcomes Satan's temptations and his soul rises to heaven. The medieval tradition of deathbed confrontations with the devil was continued by zealous protestants in sixteenth- and seventeenth-century England.

accounts of these struggles suggest that their participants followed Perkins' advice to place their fate in the hands of Christ, who empowered them finally to vanquish the fiend. Thus Brettergh repelled the enemy with these words: 'Satan, reason not with me: I am but a weak woman. If thou have anything to say, say it to my Christ; he is my advocate, my strength, and my redeemer.'[65] The same approach apparently worked for Stretton and Stubbes. The final triumph of the dying professors was revealed by their spiritual rapture at the moment of death. Samuel Clarke described the blissful appearance of Julius Herring and John Dod once their struggles with Satan were concluded.[66] More dramatically, Philip Stubbes recorded the ecstatic last words of his wife: 'behold, I see infinite millions of most glorious angels stand about me, with fiery chariots ready to defend me . . . These holy angels, these ministering spirits, are appointed by God to carry my soule into the kingdome of heaven.'[67]

Perhaps the most striking feature of these confrontations was the martial tone in which they were presented. The language and imagery of the battlefield was especially pervasive in the deathbed narratives of Katherine Stubbes and Katherine Brettergh. At the end of her conflict with the evil one, Stubbes addressed him as a 'cowardly souldier', and commanded him to 'remoove thy seidge and yeeld the field wonne'. She declared that if he did not flee 'I will call upon my graund captaine Christ Jesus, the valiant Michael, who beat thee in heaven and threw thee downe to hell with all thy hellish traine and divelish crew.' As the fiend retreated, she turned to those at her bedside and asked: 'doe you not see him flie like a coward, and run away like a beaten cock?'[68] Likewise, when Brettergh overcame the ghostly enemy she announced that 'my warrefare is accomplished and my iniquities are pardoned'. Despite their extraordinary context, the words of both women reflected the conventional belief that Christianity was a form of spiritual combat, and their deathbed experiences can perhaps be viewed as an extension of the normal principles of godly protestantism. The idea of Christian warfare was taken still further in the published account of Brettergh's death, which presented her experience as a vindication of God's people in their struggle against Antichrist and popery:

> It must needes be a divine religion, and a truth comming from God, that thus can fill the heart and mouth of a weake woman at the time of death with such admirable comfort. And a wretched conceite, and meere Antichristian is that religion which so hateth and persecuteth this faith, which is thus able to leade the true-hearted professors thereof with such unspeakable grace unto their graves.

The author contrasted Brettergh's triumph over Satan with the fate of catholics 'who have dyed most fearfully indeede', suggesting that they 'shewed manifest signes at their deaths that their popish superstition was the condemnation of their soules'.[69] Thus her final encounter with the devil was related explicitly to the wider conflict between God's children and the Roman church, which itself was regarded as a demonic institution.

The experiences described in this chapter suggest that devout protestants often viewed themselves as an embattled minority, assailed by 'inward' temptations and the more obvious hostility of the impious

¶ The deſcription of

Couetouſnes.

Ariſtotle. { To delight in treaſure, is a daungerous pleaſure,
Seneca. { In a lyer doubtles, there neuer was goodnes.

¶ The ſignification of the picture.

THe deuil is Enuy, the ſwords in his hand betokeneth
miſchief, the purſe couetouſnes, the globe the world,
the man in fooles weede ſignifieth careleſſe couetouſnes,
a man being ouercome with Enuy and couetouſnes, may
be likened to a foole that is not able to rule himſelfe, and
ſo the ende is death.　　　　　　　　　　B.i.

1. The fool confronts the devil, from Bateman's *Christall Glasse* (1569).

Of Faith.

¶Of fayth and the wonderfull working of the same: and
stedfast beliefe of the fathers in olde tyme.

The signification.

THe man in armour signifieth all stedfast beleuers of the veritie, being armed with constant zeale of Christianitie, and
weaponed with the shielde of liuely faith, the spere of continu-
aunce, and the sworde of the word of God: The Diuil vnder him
is temptation, being ouercome by faith in Christ Iesus.

M.iiij.   Faith

2. The triumph of faith over Satan, from Stephen Bateman, *A Christall Glasse of Christian Reformation* (1569).

Of Enuie.

To Serpent like I may compare : those greedie wolues that lambes deuoure:
Awayting still to catch in snare : all such as gette they may by power.

The signification.

THe Dragon signifieth the enemie to all that professe the
worde of God : the Cardinall persecution, or a persecutor of the same : the Fryer murther : the sheepe which are a
killing, signifieth the professours of Christ, from the beginning of the worlde to these present dayes.

D.ij.   Enuie

3. The persecution of 'all that professe the worde of God', from Stephen Bateman, *A Christall Glasse of Christian Reformation* (1569).

True and Wonderfull.

A Difcourfe relating a ftrange and mon-
ftrous Serpent (or Dragon) lately difcouered, and yet
liuing, to the great annoyance and diuers flaughters
both of Men and Cattell, by his ftrong
and violent poyfon,

In Suffex *two miles from* Horfam, *in a woode*
called S. Leonards Forreft, and thirtie miles from
London, *this prefent month of Auguft.* 1614.
With the true Generation of Serpents.

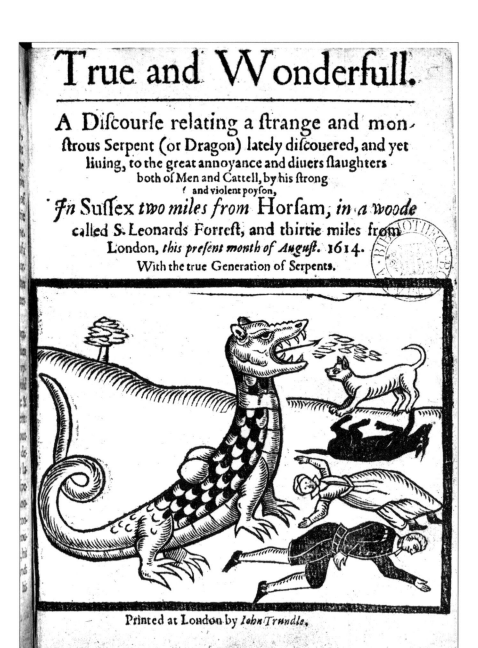

Printed at London by *Iohn Trundle.*

4. A 'monstrous serpent' reported in 1614. The text likened the beast to the dragon
described in the Book of Revelation, and warned that 'from the monsters of our sinnes,
the monsters of our punishment increaseth'.

The Miracle, of Miracles. 44

As fearefull as euer was feene or heard of in the memorie of M A N.

Which lately happened at *Dichet* in Sõmmerfetſhire , and ſent by diuers credible witneſſes to be publiſhed in L ondon.

Alſo a Prophefie reuealed by a poore Countrey Maide, who being dead the firſt of October laſt, 24. houres, 1613. reuiued againe, and lay fiue *dayes weeping, and continued prophefying of ſtrange euents to come, and ſo died the 5. day following.*

Witneſſed by M. *Nicholas Faber*, Parſon of the Towne, and diuers worthy Gentlemen of the ſame countrey. 1613,

With Lincolneſhire, Norfolke, Suffolke, and Kent their Teares For a great deluge, in which fiue Villages were lamentably drowned this preſent month.

T. I.

At London printed for Iohn Trvndle : and are to be fold at

5. The devil as a headless bear, from *The Miracle of Miracles* (1613).

The Witch of Edmonton :

A known true S T O R Y.

Compofed into

A TRAGI-COMEDY

By divers well-efteemed Poets ;

William Rowley, Thomas Dekker, John Ford, &c.

Acted by the Princes Servants, often at the Cock-Pit in *Drury-Lane,* once at Court, with fingular Applaufe.

Never printed till now.

Ho haue I found thee Curling.

Sanctabecetur nomen tuum

Mother Sawyer

Help. P I am Drownd

Cuddy Banks

London, *Printed by* J. Cottrel, *for* Edward Blackmore, *at the Angel in* Paul's *Church-yard.* 1658.

6. Title page from *The Witch of Edmonton* (1658).

Of Pride.

Sith witles braues doth alwayes frowne : and folishe errours will defend:
Such monster Satyre shooteth downe : all popishe relickes without end.

¶ The signification.

*T*He monster with the gunne, signifieth all Popish ceremonies : he which sitteth on horsebacke is mainteynance of
the same : the horse swiftnes : and his sworde persecution :
the Aungell standing with a burning sword, signifieth Gods
wrath agaynst all such persecutors of hys people.

       J.J.   **Be**

7. The demon with a gun firing popish trinkets, from Stephen Bateman, *A Christall Glasse of Christian Reformation* (1569).

8. The Roman Antichrist, *c.* 1640.

world. To some extent this perception was accurate. The demanding nature of godly religion meant that it could only appeal to a relatively small number of men and women; and the widespread denigration of 'puritans' in early modern England implies that zealous protestantism never established itself as a truly popular movement. It is hardly surprising, then, that godly ideas about Satan were not wholly accepted by the majority of the population. Instead, it appears that many medieval attitudes towards the evil one persisted in folklore and cheap literature throughout the sixteenth and seventeenth centuries, though these were intermingled with certain aspects of reformed theology. The result was an interesting mixture of protestant ideas and older beliefs concerning the devil, an outcome which probably typified the wider achievements and limitations of the English Reformation. This mixture of beliefs is considered in the next chapter.

4
THE DEVIL IN POPULAR CULTURE

THE SURVIVAL OF MEDIEVAL ATTITUDES

At the end of the seventeenth century, the Oxford historian John Aubrey described how two housemaids mistook a pocket watch for the devil. According to Aubrey, the incident took place in Herefordshire around 1620, when the mathematician Thomas Allen was visiting his patron John Scudamore. Allen left his watch, a machine which was then a 'rarity', in his chamber window before the maids came in to make the bed. The women, 'hearing a thing in a case cry tick, tick, tick, presently concluded that it was his devill, and tooke it by the string with the tongs and threw it owt of the windowe into the mote (to drowne the devill)'. Aubrey claimed that the string on the watchcase caught on the branch of an elder tree, 'so the good old gentleman gott his watch again'. The lucky preservation of the timepiece, however, only convinced the maids of the object's supernatural qualities and 'confirmed [to] them that 'twas the devill'. This peculiar tale reflects the tendency of learned men to mock the beliefs of uneducated people in late seventeenth-century England: the author characterised the outlook of the maids as 'vulgar' and 'ignorant', and criticised Allen himself for 'imposing on the understanding of beleeving people'.[1] If true, the story also suggests that early modern attitudes towards Satan did not always conform to the model developed by protestant theologians. The maids' belief that the fiend could assume the form of a small object on a window ledge, and their attempt to drown him in the moat, were hardly typical of protestant encounters with the 'prince of this world'. Instead, their behaviour provides a small illustration of the survival of distinctly unreformed attitudes towards the devil in the first half of the seventeenth century.

This chapter will argue that most of the English population retained essentially medieval beliefs about Satan throughout the early modern period. The appearance and attributes of the fiend in ballads, drama and popular books, as well as the legal records and medical notebooks which recorded the encounters of ordinary men and women with the evil one, owed more to pre-Reformation traditions than the work of godly authors like William Perkins. Traditional ideas of the devil not only survived but continued to flourish, influencing the depiction of new figures in popular literature like Faust and Mother Shipton. At first sight, the vitality of these ideas suggests that protestant doctrines were embraced by only a small minority of the English people, while the rest of the population remained largely untouched and unimpressed by them.[2] That was not the whole story, however. The second half of this chapter will argue that protestant ideas and the beliefs of the 'common sort of Christians', though different in many important ways, were rather less polarised than godly contemporaries imagined. Godly authors were prepared to exploit medieval traditions about Satan despite the compromises this involved, and some aspects of protestant thinking influenced people outside the community of zealous 'professors'. The partial assimilation of reformed doctrines meant that a diverse and ambiguous set of beliefs about Satan came to be accepted by the majority of the English population by the end of the seventeenth century. These beliefs were partly 'protestant', but they fell woefully short of the expectations of godly divines. Before describing this process, however, it is necessary to consider the persistence of older conceptions of the devil in the sixteenth and seventeenth centuries.

The Devil as an Animal

One of the most striking features of the devil in popular literature was his tendency to appear in the form of an animal. This characteristic was almost entirely absent in godly autobiographies, where his physical appearance was normally that of a man or a monstrous beast. In contrast, the first English edition of the Faust legend in 1592 depicted Satan as a squirrel with 'his tayle turning upwards on his back'. When Faust visited hell he encountered demons 'in the forme of insensible beasts, as swine, beares, woolves, apes, goates, antelopes, elephants, dragons, horses, lions, cats, snakes, toades, and all manner of ugly, odious serpents and wormes'.[3] Likewise, a ballad published in 1661 described the fiend's manifestations as a calf, a pig, a woman and a catholic priest.[4] The idea that the evil one could assume animal form was not confined to fiction. When Satan was mentioned by witnesses in witch trials he was often described as an animal: a deposition from Essex in 1565 recorded his appearance as 'a great dogge', and 'an evyll favoured dogge with hornes on his head'.[5] Similarly, when a young girl was asked to describe the devil in 1574 she replied that he was sometimes like 'a man with a gray bearde, sometimes lyke five cattes, sometimes [like] ravens and crowes'.[6] Two years later, a pamphlet announced the appearance of the fiend in the 'hideous and hellish likenes' of a monstrous dog in a Suffolk parish church:

The devil-dog, from *The Examination and Confession of Certaine Wytches at Chensforde* (1566).

There appeared in a most horrible similitude and likenesse to the congregation . . . a dog, as they might discerne it, of a black colour, at the sight wherof, together with the fearful flashes of fire which there were seene, moved such admiration in the mindes of the assemblie, that they thought doomesday was already come. This black dog, or the divel in such a likenesse . . . running all along down the body of the church with great swiftnesse, and incredible heate, among the people . . . passed between two persons as they were kneeling upon their knees, and occupied in prayer as it seemed, wrung the necks of them bothe at one instant clene backward, insomuch that even at the moment where they kneeled, they strangely dyed.[7]

Similar visitations were reported in the seventeenth century. In 1614 the devil appeared in Somerset as 'a strange thing like unto a snaile', then transformed himself into a bear.[8] The patients of Richard Napier in the 1620s reported sightings of the fiend in the shape of dogs, wolves, and even swarms of insects.[9] The precise origins of these beliefs are obscure, but the general reluctance of protestant writers to embrace them suggests that they emerged outside the influence of the Reformation. Equally, their persistence throughout the period indicates that they were largely unaffected by the advent of protestantism.

The belief that the devil could appear as an animal was probably linked to the idea that he always possessed cloven hooves when he assumed human form. Again, this notion was mostly absent from protestant descriptions of the evil one, and such a trivial and arbitrary limitation of his power was certainly inconsistent with reformed theology. In 1624 Elizabeth Jocelin noted that 'the common people beleeve the devill cannot alter the shape of one foot', despite his ability to appear in various human and animal disguises.[10] This belief surfaced occasionally in depositions and confessions from witch trials. A 'cunning man' from Dorset claimed in 1566 that he had summoned up an evil spirit 'something like a man in all proportions, saving that he had cloven feet', and the devil assumed the same appearance when he presented himself to witches in Essex in the 1640s.[11] In the late seventeenth century, the possession of cloven hooves signified the demonic origins of figures in cheap literature like Mother Shipton.[12] The persistence of this belief was demonstrated by its frequent appearance in collections of folklore compiled in the nineteenth century. A typical tale from Lincolnshire, recorded around 1880, described how a 'gentleman' asked a tailor to make him a suit on the sabbath, only to reveal a cloven hoof as the unfortunate man was taking his measurements.[13] Again, the longevity of this tradition suggests that it was largely unaffected by protestant conceptions of the devil.

The Power of Satan

The existence of different views concerning the physical appearance of Satan was less important than the issue of his power in the world. On this subject, it seems that godly protestants were fundamentally at odds with the rest of the population. In 1971 Keith Thomas argued in *Religion and the Decline of Magic* that popular religion in early modern England was based on assumptions and practices which were largely independent of official Christianity. Thomas' interpretation has been keenly debated in the last thirty years, with historians questioning both the distinction between popular and 'elite' culture and the supposed gulf between the religious practices of ordinary people and the activities of the church. Nonetheless, a consensus has emerged that many layfolk accepted the existence of a variety of supernatural entities, including fairies, imps and ghosts, as well as the orthodox figures of God and the devil. All of these beings were capable of influencing human affairs for good or ill.[14] Thus the cunning man who confessed to calling up the fiend in 1566 also described his dealings with fairies, and the deposition of a Leicestershire woman accused of witchcraft in 1619 described the activities of both fairies and the devil.[15] Richard Napier treated many patients who were 'haunted with fairies' and imps as well as those who

A witch and familiar spirits, from a manuscript of 1621.

reported encounters with the evil one.[16] Towards the end of the seventeenth century, the prevelance of fairy beliefs among the 'common sort' was noted by Joseph Glanvill and John Aubrey.[17] It seems reasonable to assume that the acceptance of such beings diluted the power of Satan by placing him alongside a host of other supernatural creatures. Indeed, it was even possible for the fiend himself to be relegated to the status of an 'old subtil elf', as he was described in a ballad printed in 1665.[18] The concept of the devil as a single, powerful entity was also compromised by popular beliefs about individual demons and wicked spirits. While protestant writers tended to attribute the actions of demons to the devil himself, and normally referred to Satan alone rather than his spritual minions, folk traditions continued to invest individual demons with distinct personalities and a degree of autonomy in their behaviour. This was most evident in depositions in witch trials, which focused on the activities of apparently demonic 'familiars' rather than Satan himself. The prominent role of familiars in English witchcraft, which is considered in detail in Chapter Six, suggests that the protestant image of the devil as a unitary force for evil was not accepted by a large part of the population.

While the existence of fairies and elves appears to have been widely accepted, it was common for devout protestants to dismiss them as 'old wives' tales' or reinterpret their activities as the work of Satan. This tendency was illustrated neatly in a godly meditation published in 1639. The author described how he was nearly killed as a baby by trapping his head between a bedframe and a wall, but was rescued when his parents heard him screaming. He later discovered that some local 'gossips' had interpreted this incident as the work of fairies. In their version, he had narrowly escaped being abducted by the creatures, who had planned to leave 'some elfe or changeling (as they call it) in my place'. This explanation was derided by the pious author, who argued instead that the assailant had been the devil: 'that attempt of stealing me away as soone as I was born (whatever the midwives talk of it) came from the malice of that arch-enemy of mankind, who is continually going about seeking whom he may betray or devour'.[19] As this vignette suggests, protestants tended to fill the gap left by their rejection of all spiritual forces except God and the devil by extending the powers of Satan. Conversely, the continued acceptance of beings such as fairies and elves outside godly circles meant that the devil's power was balanced by the influence of these other supernatural entities.

Satan's status as the 'prince of this world' was further challenged by beliefs concerning his physical limitations. The medieval idea that he could be bound by physical constraints appears to have survived throughout the early modern period. In 1574, a possessed woman claimed that the fiend had been trapped in a bottle before he took over her body.[20] As some godly contemporaries observed, the concept of possession itself seemed to impose an arbitrary restriction on the devil by placing him in the body of a single victim. Other ideas apparently limited his activities to certain times and places: it was often reported, for example, that the evil one was most active at night and haunted the sites of gallows and crossroads. The idea that the devil possessed physical weaknesses was presented most strikingly in popular fiction. One particularly robust tale from the late sixteenth century described how Satan, taking the form of a horse, attempted to carry a woman away to hell. His intended victim so 'kickt and prickt' his body that he had to cry out for mercy, and he finally abandoned the mission when 'she drew her knife and gave his eare a slit'.[21] A ballad printed in 1661 described how a baker castrated the fiend, and another from the same collection related how the devil, disguised as a calf, was slaughtered and sold 'for excellent veal'.[22] Satan's vulnerability was exposed less violently in other compositions which described how he broke his horns or choked on pieces of meat.[23] Several tales also suggested that the devil could be deceived. Typically, these stories began with the evil one presenting himself to a potential victim and offering to make a bet: the mortal would receive earthly riches as long as he or she performed a certain task, but the fiend would claim the person's soul if this task was not completed. The hero would then accomplish the feat by some ingenious means and escape from the bargain. One seventeenth-century ballad told how a poor man made a bet with Satan that he could find an animal that had never been seen before. After enjoying the 'cattel and corn' that the fiend delivered as his part of the deal, the man dressed his wife 'in feathers and lime' and pretended she was a strange beast. Satan was fooled, and the man 'went home with his wife, and they lived full merrily'.[24] Similar stories of 'the devil outwitted' were popular well into the eighteenth century.[25]

The fiend's power was also limited by the belief that he could only harm those who led outwardly wicked lives. This idea was linked to the common-sense assumption, frequently derided by godly pastors, that individuals could escape the torments of hell by practising good neighbourliness and trying to keep the ten commandments. In 1592 Perkins repudiated the notion that 'if a man be no adulterer, no thief, no murderer and do no harm' he would be safe from the devil, insisting that all those who held such beliefs were unwitting slaves of Satan.[26] But Perkins' position appears to have won little support outside godly circles. A very different perspective was offered by William Rowley, Thomas Dekker and John Ford in their 1623 play *The Witch of Edmonton*. In an early scene, the eponymous witch instructed the devil, who appeared as a black dog, to kill one of her neighbours. The creature refused and explained why:

> Though we have power, know it is circumscribed,
> And ti'd in limits: though he be curs'd to thee,
> Yet of himself he is loving to the world,
> And charitable to the poor. Now men

That, as he, love goodness, though in smallest measure,
Live without compass of our reach. His cattle
And corn I'll kill and mildew: but his life
(Until I take him, as I late found thee,
Cursing and swearing) I have no power to touch.[27]

The idea that Satan could destroy only those who were not 'loving to the world' persisted in drama and cheap literature throughout the century. Those whom he killed or dragged to hell were usually guilty of anti-social or immoral behaviour: they were often liars, hypocrites, thieves or cut-throats, whose cruel treatment of their neighbours implied that they richly deserved their fate. Thus a landlord who stole from his guests was devoured by the fiend in a tale published in 1642.[28] A chapbook from 1684 described how Satan murdered an avaricious money-lender, while a text from 1701 reported that he appeared to a 'lewd, notorious and wicked' prostitute, 'dragging her out of her bed and beating her black and blue all over her body'.[29]

As these examples suggest, the devil could execute dreadful punishments on wrongdoers. Popular literature tended to emphasise his physical attacks rather than the torments he inflicted in the mind, and stressed his capacity to destroy sinners in this world as much as the next. Even when malefactors were condemned to hell, they were usually dragged there physically, like the Coventry woman who was seized by two demons on her wedding day because she had broken her vow to marry someone else.[30] In a nasty variation on the same scenario, another woman who promised to marry a poor man then left him for a wealthier suitor was punished when her first child was carried away by the fiend. It was more usual, however, for the devil to murder his victims or treat them to horrible beatings. A ballad based on the Faust legend in the 1590s ended with the discovery of the magician's hideously mutilated corpse: his 'brains were cast against the wall', and the rest of his body was 'in pieces torn'. A slightly less gory fate befell a London wool spinner who attempted to defraud her employer: she was 'thrown down' by the devil in the shape of a man and then murdered in her bedroom. Another ballad described how Satan ended the 'wretched life' of a murderer by snapping his neck.[31] Each of these texts made it clear that the fiend's victims had brought about their own demise by their wicked behaviour, and presented the devil as a kind of supernatural avenger.

Comic Devils and Scenes From Hell

Despite Satan's horrible punishment of wrongdoers, the relative safety of those who led apparently good lives made it possible to present him in a humorous context. A light-hearted publication in 1606 described the evil one as 'that great tobaconist, the prince of smoake & darknes', and joked that he was illiterate despite attending 'all the universities in Christendome'.[32] In one early seventeenth-century ballad, 'old Beelzebub merry' visited earth to win the souls of gullible mortals by promising them eternal life. His plans were ruined, however, when he encountered the fishwives of London, who were so boisterous and noisy that they scared him away, vowing never to 'have dealing 'mongst women agen'.[33] While these texts mocked the fiend's limitations, others poked fun at the deserving victims of his wrath. The jocular ballad *The Feasting of the Devil*, which circulated in at least two different versions in the seventeenth century, described the scene at a satanic banquet. The devil's table was laden with such delicacies as 'a puritan poached' and 'a lawyer's head and green sawce', which he devoured with great relish. In one version, the meal ended with a dreadful 'fart from the devil's arse', likened to the stench of tobacco which 'hath foully perfum'd most part of the isle'.[34]

As this example suggests, comic tales about Satan continued the medieval tradition of scatological humour. This was prominent in the tale of a baker who 'gelded' the devil on his way to Nottingham market. To revenge himself of this outrage, the fiend promised to castrate the man if he ever returned to the town. With typical resourcefulness, the baker's wife put on his clothes and met the devil in his place, telling him that 'I was gelded yesterday'. When he demanded proof, she lifted her coats and 'let go a rousing fart'.[35] A similar wit characterised the late seventeenth-century tales of Mother Shipton, in which the devil punished the heroine's enemies by replacing their hats with chamber pots and making them break wind 'for above a quarter of an hour'.[36] In a slightly different vein, another ballad expressed the cheerful and distinctly un-protestant sentiment that 'when the devill comes for you, you need not care a fart'.[37] The devil also appeared in the punchlines of jokes. A jest printed in 1607 observed that the fiend was an 'asse' for failing to punish lawyers for their manifest sins, and the phrase 'Go to the devil' was aimed at lawyers, churchmen and unruly women in cheap print throughout the period.[38]

The same qualities that characterised popular images of the devil also flavoured descriptions of hell. In cheap literature, the infernal region was usually populated with men and women who had committed terrible sins on earth, and was not regarded as a place where all people were ordained to suffer unless they were saved by the mercy of Christ. The sufferings of the damned were depicted in intensely physical terms. Ballads reported the 'howling and yelling' of the fiend's victims and described the ingenious tortures they had to endure. The relationship between unneighbourly behaviour and damnation was emphasised by

Left: The punishments of hell, from *St Bernard's Vision* (*c.* 1640). *Right*: The torments of witches and a catholic priest in hell, from *The Most Wonderfull and True Storie of a Certaine Witch Named Alice Gooderige* (1597).

Punishments of the damned, from *A Booke Declaringe the Fearfull Vexation of one Alexander Nyndge* (1574).

the specific torments designated for particular crimes. Thus adulterers were tied to beds while their skin was flayed off with 'whips of glowing fire', and liars had molten lead poured down their throats. Usurers, thieves and murderers could all expect appropriately customised forms of torture. In 1596 the possessed youth, Thomas Darling, received a vision of 'the place of torments, where drunkards are hanged by the throats, swearers and filthy talkers by their tongues'.[39] Most of these horrors were taken from medieval depictions of hell, and the influence of pre-Reformation traditions was also apparent in pictorial representations of the afterlife. Seventeenth-century woodcuts often showed condemned souls trapped in the gaping mouth of a dragon, an image derived from medieval mystery plays.[40] The assumption that most well-meaning people would escape the pains of hell made it possible to depict the place, like its ruler, in a comical fashion. Thus Thomas Dekker joked in 1606 that hell is 'exceeding rich, for all usurers, both Jewes and Christians, after they have made away their soules for money here, meete with them there againe'. He suggested that Satan allowed no poets in hell because they would write libels against him, though he tolerated some 'ballad-makers' because their work was too poor to give offence.[41] Dekker's light-hearted approach was much closer in spirit to the *Merry Tales* of the early sixteenth century than the doctrines developed by protestants like William Perkins, who pronounced the word 'damnation' in his sermons with such emphasis that it 'left a doleful echo in his auditors' eares a good while after'.[42]

The 'Merry Devil' and Mother Shipton

Perhaps the best evidence for the vitality of the attitudes described so far was the emergence of new stories about the devil which contained distinctly non-protestant elements. The first English version of the Faust legend reflected traditional beliefs by locating the hero's initial encounter with the fiend at 'a crosse way' in a wood at night, and included comic touches quite incompatible with godly theology.[43] The story of Faust was imported from Germany, but other new tales about Satan originated in Reformation England. The Merry Devil of Edmonton, a play first staged around 1604 and revived frequently in the seventeenth century, was developed from an older tale about the legendary magician, Friar Bacon. In the earliest surviving text, The Famous Historie of Fryer Bacon, the hero used magic to rescue a young woman from an evil suitor who tried to marry her by force. The original plot contained no references to the devil, and these were presumably added in the course of the sixteenth century. In the play, the character of Bacon was replaced by 'the renowned scholler' Peter Fabell, nicknamed the 'merry devil' because of 'his fame in sleights and magicke', and it was made clear that his powers derived from a pact with Satan. Nonetheless, Fabell was presented as a good character who used his skills to perform 'pleasant pranks' and assist people in trouble. Moreover, he repeatedly outwitted the devil with ingenious ploys to prevent him from claiming his soul. In a chapbook version of the play in 1631 Fabell promised Satan that he could take his soul as soon as the candle in his study burned out. The devil assented and sealed the pact with an oath:

> As I hope to draw downe [a] thousand soules to the deepe abisse (the place of my abode), I will forbeare [to take] thee till that candle is burned. Then Maister Peter, presently after his hellish protestation, put the candle out and into his pocket. Looke heere (quoth hee), till this is burnt thou maiest not claime my soul. I'll keepe this safe enough from burning out . . . When the devill saw he was so cunningly deceived by Master Peter, with many bitter execrations he left him.

Unlike Faust, Fabell was not cast into hell at the end of the story. He promised the devil his soul if he was buried 'either within the church, without the church, in the church porch, church-yard street, field or highway'. The magician escaped the fiend's clutches by arranging for his body to be interred in one of the church walls.[44] Needless to say, the story of the 'merry devil' owed very little to the protestant concept of Satan, yet it emerged and flourished at the same time that this concept was being developed.

The limited impact of protestant ideas about the devil was demonstrated further by the emergence of the Yorkshire prophetess, Mother Shipton, as a popular figure in seventeenth-century literature. Like Peter Fabell, Shipton was based originally on a folkloric character who predated the Reformation, and the demonic aspects of her personality were added as her story was developed in print. The first version of Shipton's prophecies was published in 1641, and this basic text was augmented by the 'discovery' of new prognostications over the next thirty years. It was not until 1667 that Shipton emerged as a character in her own right, with a new edition of her works including the story of her nativity and the events surrounding her predictions. This text claimed that she was literally the daughter of Satan, who had taken her mother Agatha as his wife.[45] Shipton's diabolical credentials were confirmed in the following year, when a chapbook reported that she had cloven feet.[46] The acquisition of these features did not, however, turn the prophetess into a wicked or frightening figure. On the contrary, the author of the 1667 tract claimed that she was held 'in great

Illustration from *The Strange and Wonderful History of Mother Shipton* (1686).

esteem' by everyone who met her, 'and her memory to this day is much honoured by those of her own county'. In a bizarre reversal of the protestant insistence that Satan was the 'father of lies', Shipton's reputation rested on the truthfulness of her prophecies. Her alleged epitaph was 'Here lyes she who never ly'd'.[47] As well as her ability as a prophetess, the later editions of Shipton's life focused on the 'merry pranks' she played on her neighbours. These were often accomplished by diabolical means. In one story, she visited a mayor's banquet only to be ignored and insulted by the other guests. In retaliation, she 'run'd into the middle of the hall and sereeked out aloud, whereat a whole legion of devils instantly rose among them with terrrible thunder and lightening, who seized on every dish of meat and, walking orderly out of the hal with Shipton before [them], at the gate all vanished'.[48] A tract from 1686 described how 'her father the foul fiend' visited Shipton as an infant and played tricks on her nurse. These tales were presented as 'pleasant exploits' in which the devil was playful rather than malevolent.[49]

The adventures of the 'merry devil' and Mother Shipton indicate the strong appeal of Satan as a character in popular fiction. It appears, indeed, that the fiend was becoming more attractive in the course of the seventeenth century, since the earliest stories about Roger Bacon and

Witches and demons from *The Strange and Wonderful History of Mother Shipton* (1686).

the Yorkshire prophetess included few references to their satanic connections. But the demonisation of these characters did not turn them into unsympathetic figures, and their relationship with the evil one was strikingly inconsistent with protestant doctrines. Satan was gullible and limited in the tales of the magician of Edmonton, and he assumed a playful and comic role in the Mother Shipton stories. The success of these creations makes it easy to understand why godly pastors routinely castigated the ignorance and 'superstition' of ordinary people. It would be misleading, however, to assume that protestantism and popular culture were always in conflict. Ordinary layfolk were quite capable of appropriating aspects of godly religion, notably the link between popery and the devil, while ignoring the more harsh and demanding ideas propounded by men like Perkins. This process of partial assimilation led to some significant changes in the popular image of Satan, which will be considered at the end of this chapter. Equally, godly professors were prepared to exploit traditional images of the devil in order to reach a popular audience. This caused them to emphasise certain ideas more than others, and to play down some of the more difficult aspects of their theology, with results which were often ambiguous or misleading. This process is considered in the next section.

TRADITIONAL IDEAS IN GODLY TRACTS

It is tempting to view the English Reformation as a revolution 'imposed from above', in which an elite minority sought to refashion the beliefs and practices of the rest of society. This interpretation is valid in many respects. Almost certainly, the establishment of protestantism owed more to the decisions of the crown than any popular clamour for reform, despite the shortcomings of the late medieval church. It would be a mistake, however, to assume that the relationship between the new faith and popular culture was only a one-way process, in which traditional attitudes were gradually reshaped by the teachings of godly divines. On the contrary, it appears that the protestant message was often modified in order to meet the needs of a popular audience. In part, this reflected the willingness of godly proselytisers to exploit traditional themes and images for their own ends, despite the compromises this involved. It also demonstrated the problems inherent in translating difficult theological concepts into popular media. These problems were exacerbated by the fact that most of the population was semi-literate, which meant that the tenets of reformed theology had to be communicated in pictures as well as words.

Pictures of Satan

A woodcut printed in 1569 contained one of the most bizarre portrayals of the devil in the sixteenth century. It depicted the fiend as a bird-like creature with a peacock's tail, holding a gun in one of its misshapen hands. A stream of crucifixes and rosary beads issued from the gun's barrel, which was apparently aimed at a sword-bearing angel standing in the monster's path (*see* Plate 7). The illustration was included in Stephen Bateman's *Christall Glasse of Christian Reformation*, a picture book designed to introduce the central themes of protestant theology to a general audience. A brief text under the woodcut explained that 'the monster with the gunne signifieth all popish ceremonies', while the angel represented 'god's wrath against all such persecutors of hys people'.[50] The woodcut illustrates some of the obvious limitations of pictorial images in conveying the message of reformed Christianity. While it succeeded in linking the Roman church with the devil, it failed to explain that popery was satanic because it taught that salvation could be achieved through human actions. Indeed, it is difficult to imagine how this concept, which was the most fundamental tenet of the protestant faith, could have been conveyed effectively in pictures. The rosary-firing gun was an ingenious attempt to illustrate the satanic nature of 'works-based' religion, but the awkwardness of the image only indicates how difficult it was to reduce the idea to a simple, accessible picture.

This problem was encountered by all protestant teachers who attempted to convey their message in print to a large audience. In his ground-breaking work on popular propaganda in sixteenth-century Germany, Bob Scribner showed that the earliest reformers relied heavily on pictorial images to reach the non-literate majority of the population; he suggested that this material was enormously effective at exploiting grievances against the medieval church, but was ill-suited to communicate more complex and positive doctrines. Luther and his supporters plundered a range of familiar images and media to promote their agenda, but this process imposed inevitable limitations on the propaganda they created.[51] A similar process has been documented in England by Tessa Watt, who found that traditional imagery and genres were appropriated by protestants in their campaign to re-educate the population in the sixteenth and seventeenth centuries. Again, the use of traditional forms meant that certain messages could be communicated more successfully than others, and the purity of the original ideas was sometimes lost.[52] Protestant attempts to promote a new understanding of the devil present an interesting example of this general trend. Godly propagandists inherited from the medieval church a huge range of powerful and familiar images of the evil one, and the centrality of Satan to their belief system meant that they were bound to exploit them. The use of these images, however, imposed subtle restrictions on their work.

This difficulty was exemplified in Bateman's *Christall Glasse*. Fourteen of the book's forty woodcuts contained images of Satan, and he was a central figure in seven of these. These representations drew heavily on traditional images: the fiend often possessed cloven hooves and horns, and hell was depicted as the jaws of a dragon. Other figures were taken from popular drama: the first tableau, for instance, presented a man dressed as a carnival fool confronting the devil, who was tempting him with a bag of money. These symbols were employed to create some arresting and memorable scenes. In one, the devil in the shape of a friar watched approvingly through a doorway as a monk and a nun engaged in fornication. Another picture depicted two women, one riding a goat while the other held its beard and led it after a flying demon. Bateman's text pointed out that 'the goate signifieth lechery, the woman whoredom, she who leadeth the goate by the beard is . . . the bawde, and the devill [is] a blinde guide or deceavor' (*see* Plate 9). A later woodcut in the series represented the triumph of faith over temptation. An armoured man, holding a sword and shield, stood on the crumpled body of the devil. As the author explained, the figure 'signifieth all stedfast belevers of the veritie, being armed with constant zeale of Christianitie and weaponed with the shielde of lively faith . . . The devil under him is temptation, being overcome by faith in Jesus Christ.'[53]

In some ways, these images were strikingly effective. They underlined the demonic nature of catholicism and highlighted Satan's delight in sins such as lechery. But in other respects they were potentially misleading. By focusing on men and women engaged in specific sins, the woodcuts tended to support the popular view that only obvious wrongdoers were in thrall to the devil. While the identification of particular sins was essential for the pictures to make an impact, it also made it virtually impossible to convey the message that all people were slaves of Satan by virtue of their fallen nature. Equally, the pictorial representation of the devil emphasised his role as a physical threat rather than a source of temptations. Again, this problem was probably unavoidable. It is hard to imagine a visual depiction of the defeat of temptation through faith more effective than the one in Bateman's book; nonetheless, the picture does not really convey the daily struggle to overcome Satan's influence in the mind. It was for this reason, presumably, that Bateman supplemented the woodcuts with brief texts explaining their meaning. These tended to reinterpret the concrete images as abstract signs, and always presented the devil as a source of temptation rather than a physical creature. It is impossible to know how the *Christall Glasse* was received by its audience, but the work does reveal the problems involved in translating protestant ideas into a medium suitable for a largely illiterate population.

The same limitations were evident in other protestant woodcuts produced in the sixteenth and seventeenth centuries. These illustrations were generally successful at linking Satan with popery and specific sins, but failed to communicate the idea that he was the 'prince of this world'. Pictures of priests, cardinals and monks were often embellished with horns and cloven hooves, while the pontiff himself was commonly placed on the back of the dragon from the Book of Revelation. In 1616 the fiend appeared 'in Jesuited-angell shape', complete with cloven feet, on the title page of William Gouge's *Whole Armour of God*.[54] Later woodcuts showed him blowing instructions into priests' ears with a pair of bellows, and offering 'popish trinkets' to his earthly disciples.[55] In some cases, these images reinforced the more detailed content of the texts which accompanied them; but often they did little more than assert that catholicism was the devil's creed without explaining why.

Protestant propagandists also followed Bateman in linking Satan to specific sins: woodcuts depicting the devil encouraging blasphemy and fornication continued to circulate well into the eighteenth century. Likewise, protestant illustrations of the afterlife tended to populate hell with obvious criminals, usually including a contingent of cardinals and priests. More generally, all pictures of the devil tended to emphasise his physical presence rather than his role as a tempter. This could lead to some bizarre and inappropriate images. In 1683, for example, a godly broadsheet warning against the temptation 'to neglect learning and follow pastimes' was illustrated by a picture of Satan playing tennis.[56]

Satanic Retribution

The problems of communicating protestant ideas in pictures were probably greater than those posed by the exploitation of other media. Nonetheless, the attempts by godly professors to employ the conventions of story-telling also led to some interesting compromises. The idea that the devil would punish men and women for particular sins had an obvious appeal to godly pastors, who could use it to inspire fear in those layfolk who resented their ministry. The career of Hugh Clarke in Northamptonshire offers a good illustration of this point. Clarke's seventeenth-century biographer described the fate of a group of Sabbath-breakers in his flock in the 1580s:

> In the night, when they were retired to their several homes, there was heard a great noise and rattling of chains up and down the town, which was accompanied with such a smell and stink of fire and brimstone that many of their guilty consciences suggested unto them that the devil was come to fetch them away quick to hell. This so terrified and wrought upon them that they began to give better heed to the ministry of God's word, and to break off their profane courses for the greatest part, so that there was an eminent reformation wrought amongst them.

It appears that news of this event was actively disseminated by the minister as a warning to other malefactors in the parish.[57] The impact of the story on Clarke's flock is impossible to know, but the tale itself did nothing to challenge the popular wisdom that the devil troubled only those who were guilty of particular sins, just as God rewarded those who tried to keep his commandments. This problem was probably unavoidable. It was very difficult to describe the punishment of sin by the fiend without identifying individuals guilty of specific crimes, but this tended to undermine the idea that all people were by nature 'servants of Satan'. Equally, tales of 'exemplary punishment' relied for their impact on the sudden physical appearance of the devil rather than his insidious presence in the mind. These limitations were evident whenever protestants used the threat of the devil to promote moral reform. The sin of blasphemy, for instance, was often cited as the occasion for satanic retribution. A tale from 1631 related how a blasphemer was killed by the devil in the shape of a black dog.[58] A tract from 1642 described how a drunkard made a toast to the fiend and invited his companions to join him in the 'damnable' oath. When they refused, he called on Satan 'to come and doe it himselfe', and was visited by a terrible stranger who left him insane.[59] Despite their godly intentions, such tales presented the devil as a kind of otherwordly avenger very similar to his image in popular fables.

The same impression was conveyed in some protestant texts describing Satan's dealings with papists. One remarkable example, published in 1612, told how the devil exacted a horrible punishment on a catholic church in Antwerp. The author began by noting the altars, images and 'other idoletrous and supersticious relickes' which adorned the building, then described how the fiend appeared on the steeple and caused fire to rain down on the rest of the church. Holy water and crucifixes proved useless against the demonic arsonist, who proceeded to rampage through the church's interior. The fiend paid particular attention to an idolatrous picture hanging over one of the altars, which he 'spoyled & defaced . . . with his wicked nayles and clawes, [so] that he almost tore the same quite downe to the ground'. The moral of the story was made plain: 'God sendeth such . . . messengers unto the places wherein idolatrie and supersticious ceremonies are dayly used, thereby to give them warning to amend & leave all such wickednes and abomination'.[60] In a strange reversal of conventional protestant thinking, this tale portrayed Satan as the punisher of idolatry rather than its promoter. The same apparent contradiction was found in other anti-catholic works. As late as 1729, a ballad described how a papist was murdered by the devil for committing blasphemy 'and worshipping of stone'. The fiend declared that he would carry the man to hell to 'save the priests the trouble', then left him dead on a muckhill with his head 'turn'd behind, his eyes sunk in [and] his tongue swell'd out'.[61] Again, tales of this kind did little to challenge the idea that Satan attacked only obvious wrongdoers, even when his victims were members of the Roman church.

Godly Murder Books

While tales of satanic retribution for impious behaviour had limited value as godly propaganda, another popular genre appeared to be better suited for the task. This was the murder pamphlet, one of the staples of cheap literature in the sixteenth and seventeenth centuries. Works in this genre, which were the precursors of modern 'true crime' books and magazines, were written in grisly and sensational language and often accompanied by lurid woodcuts depicting murders and executions. Their appeal to godly proselytisers was that they offered an opportunity to depict Satan as a tempter, exploiting the weakness of human flesh to persuade men and women to commit terrible acts. Murderers could be presented as extreme examples of the depravity of human nature, and a warning to others to resist the ever-present temptations of the fiend. This message was spelled out in 1595 in the preface to A Most Horrible & Detestable Murder Committed by a Bloudie-Minded Man Upon his Owne Wife:

> How many most execrable murders have there beene done of late time, which hath bin published for our example to the world, thereby to put us in minde of our duties to God & withhold us from like trespasses . . . But so rageth the enemie of mankinde, day and night, restlessly with his temptations, that he ceaseth not stil to urge us to all mischiefe.

In an exemplary statement of godly ideals, the author enjoined his readers to take 'such firme hold on that anchor of faith, Christ Jesus, that neither pope or divell maye have power to harme us'. The rest of the book described how a Sussex miner was led by 'the ancient enemie of our salvation' to cut his wife's throat and leave her 'weltering in her owne goare', only to be caught and hanged for the atrocity.[62] Three years later, a similar publication described how Satan seduced a fisherman from Rye into poisoning his wife with ratsbane. In this case, the fiend exploited the man's desire to leave his spouse and begin a new life abroad, and lured him with the false hope that his crime could not be detected, 'til by his divillish practises he had brought him to the gallowes'. The devil's role as a master of deceit was underlined in a passage describing the fisherman's interrogation. When he claimed that he had bought the poison for the innocent purpose of killing rats, his examiner retorted that 'the devill is the father of lyers, and I feare thou art his sonne'. The text concluded by entreating God to allow others 'to withstand Satan's temptations and eschew his subtilties, that they be not led by his allurements nor intrapped by his snares'.[63]

Perhaps the most complete depiction of the protestant concept of Satan in a murder pamphlet was inspired by the case of Elizabeth Caldwell, who was hanged for killing one of her servants in 1603. A year later Gilbert Dugdale published a 'true discourse' on the crime, including Caldwell's letter to her husband from prison and the confession she made on the gallows. Assisted by her lover and two accomplices, Caldwell had attempted to poison her husband with ratsbane in oatcakes, but the food had been accidentally consumed by one of her maids. She confessed to the crime and implicated her partners, then experienced a conversion to godly religion in the months before her execution. The beauty of this story was that it provided a first-hand account of the devil's temptations and their appalling results, together with an affirmation of the saving power of God's grace. Dugdale stated at the outset that the case was a warning to others to guard against 'that uglie fiend (ever man's fatall opposite)', who had exploited the 'corruptible lives' of the protagonists. He noted that only Caldwell herself had been delivered through faith from Satan's dominion, while her accomplices remained servants of the evil one. In her letter to her husband, the murderess explained how the devil had taken advantage of her own wicked nature by sending 'his hellish instruments' to work on her mind, 'untill they made me yeeld to conspire with them [towards] the destruction of your bodie'. The rest of her letter was an appeal to all worldly people to admit their transgressions and fall on God's mercy. Caldwell expressed particular revulsion at the sin of sabbath-breaking, which was the 'certaine badge and liverie' of all 'servants of the devill'. The same preacherly tone pervaded her scaffold confession. After attributing her crime to her 'owne filthy flesh, the illusions of the devil and those hellish instruments which he set on worke', she exhorted her audience to keep the sabbath and resist the lure of adultery, asserting that these were her 'chiefe and capitall sinnes', although the world regarded them as 'a small matter'.[64]

The propaganda value of murder stories ensured that the form remained popular with godly authors in the seventeenth century. In 1657 a pamphlet described how a London apprentice was convicted of cutting the throat of one of his workmates, then experienced a conversion to godly religion before he was hanged. A similar tract from 1668 recorded the 'wicked life and shameful-happy death' of another penitent killer.[65] Like Dugdale's account of Elizabeth Caldwell, these texts focused on the pious deportment of the felons after their crimes, and presented their experiences as dramatic examples of Christians 'delivered out of Satan'. Other works concentrated on the devil's role as the instigator of murder. The most extensive publication in this tradition was John Reynolds' *Triumphs of Gods Revenge Against the Crying and Execrable Sinne of Willful and Premeditated Murder* (1635), which gathered together murder stories from the whole of Europe. Reynolds' preface explained that these tales were intended as warnings against 'the snares and inticements of the devill', though their lurid content meant that they probably attracted an audience much wider than the normal readers of godly literature. One typical story told how a French innkeeper conspired with a priest to poison a wealthy guest. The men were spurred on to the crime by Satan, who exploited their covetousness and turned their 'uncharitable contemplation into bloudy actions'. The crime was eventually exposed by divine providence: God sent a wolf as 'a minister of his sacred justice and revenge' to dig up the victim's body from the innkeeper's orchard, making sure that the beast 'never touched any part of his face' for the purposes of easy identification.[66]

Stories of this kind were perhaps the most effective genre for presenting protestant ideas of Satan to a general audience. They offered a racy and sensational context for the depiction of the devil as the source of temptations, and could even incorporate conversion narratives similar to those found in godly autobiographies. Nonetheless, the genre imposed certain limitations. By their very nature, murder pamphlets implied that the fiend had a special interest in the most extreme and violent forms of wrongdoing. This made it very hard for godly authors to communicate the message that all human actions were inherently evil unless they were inspired by true faith. This problem was reinforced by the tendency of many writers to depict murderers as unusually sinful before they committed their crimes: most were characterised by extreme covetousness or lust, and in some cases they were identified as papists. It was difficult to avoid the impression that only the most obviously wicked individuals were likely to fall prey to the devil's wiles. In practice, many authors quietly dropped the idea that all people without faith were unwitting 'servants of Satan', or relegated it to a slightly incongruous passage outside the main body of the text.

Satanic Murder in Coventry

Despite their tensions and ambiguities, godly murder books and tales of satanic retribution suggest the willingness of protestants to exploit popular themes for their own purposes. In 1642 this process was exemplified by Lawrence Southerne's *Fearefull Newes From Coventry*, a godly reworking of the ideas behind the stories of Faust and *The Merry Devil of Edmonton*. The tale described how a musician was visited on his deathbed by a handsome stranger who turned out to be Satan. The fiend murdered the man and vanished, leaving his widow to discover a chest full of gold which 'fell to dust' when she touched it. This false treasure turned out to be the prize for which her husband had 'sold himselfe to the devill, with whom he had made a contract for certaine yeares'.[67] Southerne's unpleasant tale reaffirmed many of the stereotypes of popular works on the same theme. The pretend gold was a motif in broadsheet ballads about the devil in the early seventeenth century, and recurred later in tales about Mother Shipton.[68] Similarly, the fiend's appearance was heralded by a 'mightie and tempestuous' storm like the one described in early versions of Faust. The tract also stressed the material presence of Satan in its grossly physical depiction of the musician's death: his carcass was found 'in his bed with his neck broken, to the terour of the behoulders'.

These elements were combined, however, with the principles of godly religion. Although the title page stated that the man arrived at his fate 'through covetousnesse and immoderate love of money', Southerne pointed out that the true cause of his damnation was his infidelity to God. He presented his grisly fate as a warning to others to fall on the mercy of Christ. At the very end of the story, he also introduced the sombre doctrine of 'double predestination', which held that the elect and the damned had been chosen by God from the beginning of time. To press home this message, the tale ended with a meditation on the torments of condemned souls in hell:

> O! The heavie doome of the just judgement of Almightie God, who as he hath not limited his mercies to his elect, so he hath not set or appoynted an end to the punishment of the reprobate, but so farr is their misery from ending that it is ever but beginning. Now then, let those damned soule-selling witches, conjurers and such like consider the miseries of eternall death. Consider it, I say, all you that forget God, lest suddainly his wrath breake out upon you and he teare you in peeces.[69]

Southerne's pamphlet can be read as a particularly sophisticated attempt to marry traditional ideas about Satan with reformed theology, and shows that protestant doctrines were not always set out in the terse and uncompromising language of godly catechisms and sermons. It is impossible to know, however, how such publications were received. Protestant arguments presented in popular forms could be easily misinterpreted or only partially understood, not least because of the compromises and ambiguities which they inevitably contained. There was a danger that traditional beliefs would be overlaid with a veneer of protestantism, which was not fully accepted or understood. This helps to explain the emergence in popular culture of an eclectic and inconsistent set of beliefs about Satan in the course of the English Reformation. It is now time to consider this peculiar melange.

THE REFORM OF POPULAR BELIEFS

Two ballads inspired by particularly nasty murders in the reign of James I provide a clue to the relationship between protestantism and popular culture. *The Wofull Lamentation of William Purcas*, composed around 1620, described how a man cut the throat of his own mother in a 'drunken fit'. In the other ballad, entitled *A Warning for All Murderers*, two brothers conspired to kill their uncle in order to inherit his property. Both texts assigned a prominent role to the devil. He was portrayed as a tempter who exploited the particular weaknesses of the murderers and goaded them to commit their crimes. Thus Satan enticed the two brothers 'to murder, death and blood, thereby to purchase to themselves their long desired good'. He took advantage of William Purcas' drunkenness to persuade him to take his mother's life. To reinforce this message, both ballads were accompanied by woodcuts depicting the fiend at the scene of the crime (*see* Plate 10b). In this respect, these works were similar to the godly murder pamphlets described earlier; but there is no reason to assume that they were written as protestant propaganda. Neither of the ballads took their bloody subject matter as the starting point for a wider discussion of the devil's temptations. It appears, rather, that the fiend was introduced simply to provide a motive for the outrages. Moreover, *A Warning for All Murderers* was primarily a revenge story rather than a religious tract: much of the text was devoted to an account of the killers' capture by their uncle's son, who was born shortly after his father had been slain.[70] It appears, then, that these ballads were not composed for the purposes of godly instruction, but they nonetheless presented Satan in a typically protestant role. They can be viewed as an amalgamation of godly ideas and popular entertainment.

The evil one appeared as a tempter in many other secular works produced for a popular audience. A song from 1632 described how he enticed an apprentice to speak disrespectful words about the king, an act which caused the poor youth to be hanged for treason.[71] In a later ballad, he persuaded a woman to defraud her employer by claiming she had spun eight pounds of wool when she had only done six. The fiend's 'subtil cunning game' led to the unfortunate woman's death.[72] A more cheerful song, entitled 'Fayre Warning', called on men and women to resist the temptation to cheat or slander their neighbours, and promised happiness and prosperity to all those who took this advice. Its chorus enjoined people 'to shun Satan's charmes'.[73] The devil's love of deception was acknowledged in other ballads which referred to him simply as 'the liar'.[74] All of these texts presented the fiend as a tempter and a deceiver, but they did not develop this theme at any length or link it to any wider religious message. It seems, rather, that the ballad-makers simply assumed that Satan was the originator of temptation and falsehood, and expected their audience to recognise him as such. This suggests that at least one aspect of the protestant concept of the devil was accepted outside godly circles, though it was placed in the context of a very different set of beliefs.

This impression is confirmed by other ballads and tales which combined the concept of satanic temptation with distinctly folkloric ideas. In one striking example, probably composed around 1620, a poor man from Essex met the devil disguised as a tall stranger wearing 'cole-black' garments, and was tempted to accept from him a purse of gold. When he returned home he discovered that the purse contained nothing but 'oaken leaves'. In despair, he returned to the stranger and fell into conversation with him. This time he was presented with a more dreadful temptation: the fiend told him to murder his 'children young and miserable wife' and then take his own life. The man ran home 'raging mad' and intent on bloodshed, but was prevented by one of his neighbours, who tied him to his bed and relieved his family's poverty 'with meat and money'.[75] In many ways, this bizarre narrative resembled folktales about the devil which had been in circulation since the Middle Ages: it included a typical meeting between a mortal and the evil one, and the promise of riches followed by disappointment. But it also echoed contemporary crime pamphlets which identified Satan as the originator of murderous thoughts. Interestingly, it combined the idea that the devil was the source of temptation with the popular convention of depicting him as a physical creature. The belief that the fiend appeared physically in order to tempt people was also recorded in other contexts. In 1600, a victim of witchcraft in Norfolk claimed that she was visited by 'a little black boy with glistening eyes, tempting her and speaking to her'. The demonic apparition tried to persuade her to drown herself.[76] The patients of Richard Napier described similar experiences. In August 1601, for example, Stephen Rawlings complained that 'the devill tempteth him often in his sleepe & appeareth to him'.[77] These curious episodes resembled the encounters with Satan described in godly autobiographies, but recast him as a corporeal being rather than a presence in the mind. In this way, they seem to represent an amalgam of protestant ideas and older beliefs.

While the idea of satanic temptation appears to have been widely accepted in seventeenth-century England, it is impossible to know if this was the result of godly propaganda. The devil had been depicted as a source of impious thoughts and desires in the late Middle Ages, though his importance in this role had been massively increased by the Reformation. It seems reasonable to assume that godly sermons and cheap print reinforced the idea that Satan was a tempter, without convincing the majority of the population that his power was as ubiquitous as protestant theologians claimed. In another area of popular belief, however, the influence of the Reformation was more obvious and direct. This was the demonisation of the Roman church. In their campaign to vilify popery, it appears that godly propagandists enjoyed remarkable success in exploiting and adapting traditional beliefs for their own purposes. In particular, they managed to promote the idea that the catholic church was the instrument of Antichrist. According to one godly observer in the 1640s, it was 'now so evident and notorious' that the pope was Antichrist 'that almost every child is able to assert it'.[78] This belief was closely linked to the assumption that popery was connected to the devil, an idea that appears to have been equally widespread in the seventeenth century.

The Roman Antichrist

The biblical figure of Antichrist, the beast which was to rule the earth for a thousand years before the second advent of Christ, was deeply rooted in late medieval religion. Derived originally from the Book of Revelation and the letters of Paul, the creature had become the subject of a rich collection of legends during the Middle Ages. In popular mythology, it was generally assumed that when Antichrist appeared he would be intimately related to the devil; some traditions predicted that he would be the offspring of Satan and a human bride, probably a prostitute. Medieval theologians, in contrast, assumed that he would be

The conception of Antichrist, assisted by demons, from a German pamphlet *Der Entchrist* (1475).

an uncommonly wicked man who would act as the devil's earthly regent.[79] English protestants challenged both traditions by arguing that the beast was an institution rather than an individual, and asserting that this institution, the Roman church, had already reigned on earth for nearly a thousand years. Despite these revisions, however, they tended to support the popular view that Antichrist was inseparable from Satan. Thus John Olde declared in the 1550s that popish beliefs were 'the doctrines of devyls', and the pope himself was 'the devel's vicar and successour, or els the devel himselfe'.[80] Likewise, John Gough asserted in 1561 that 'the devil now so rageth for that he seeth his kingdom and his eldest son (Antichrist of Rome) like to be overthrown'.[81] The protestant insistence that Antichrist was an institution was often blurred in godly sermons and tracts, which tended to refer to the pope as if he was the physical incarnation of the beast. This tendency was probably encouraged by the demands of popular propaganda, since it was much easier to present the pope himself as Antichrist, or indeed the devil, than to explain the Antichristian nature of the whole Roman church.

The identification of the pope with Antichrist was set out in a wide range of popular publications. A play by Nathaniel Woodes in 1581 had the devil refer to the pope as 'my eldest boy, in whom I doo delight', recalling the traditional idea that Antichrist was Satan's offspring.[82] A ballad from 1606 depicted the pontiff as 'that triple-crowned beast', assisted by fiends from the 'deepes of sulphur-flaming hell'.[83] In the following year, a chapbook account of a flood in Coventry included references to the machinations of the papal beast, who presided over 'false prophets, false prophecies, false miracles & false deceivers'.[84] The outbreak of the Civil War was accompanied by a deluge of cheap propaganda from both sides, much of which restated conventional views about the satanic origins of the papacy. In one satire from 1642, the pontiff addressed the devil as his 'partner in my see of Rome'.[85] Other texts purported to be letters from Satan to his papal viceroy, disclosing his latest plans for the spread of wickedness and superstition.[86] A parliamentarian ballad from 1645 asserted that catholics in the king's army were fighting under the banner of Antichrist.[87] In the same period, the assumption that the pope was one of the monsters described in Revelation 12–13 provided the basis for a series of printed prophecies. One of the best-sellers in this genre, *The Bloody Almanack: To Which England is Directed to Fore-Know What Shall Come to Passe* (1643), offered an interpretation of the struggle between God's people and the Roman beast, which had commenced when the Lord raised up 'his first ministers and servants, Luther, Calvin, Mellancthon and others, to preach out . . . the gospel publikely, which before was hid and obscured under the Antichristian reign'. The author described the defeat of 'the Antichristian and Spanish fleet' in 1588 as one of the 'marvellous indices' of the imminent return of Christ.[88] The same themes were recycled in prophecies printed throughout the rest of the century, which generally assumed that the Last Judgment would be preceded by the fall of the 'beast of Rome'.[89]

Anti-Popery and the Devil

As well as the papacy, the whole catholic church was routinely linked with the devil in popular literature. At its crudest, this involved the depiction of Satan as a member of the Roman clergy. In the earliest version of the Faust legend, the devil first appeared 'in the manner of a gray frier'. Subsequently, the magician instructed him always to assume this guise, 'that he might know of his certain coming'.[90] The motif of the devil as a friar recurred in seventeenth-century ballads. In *The Devil Transformed*, for example, the fiend took on a series of shapes before finally disguising himself 'in a fryer's old weed'.[91] In a variation on this idea, another ballad described a meeting between a friar and the evil one, in which they discussed which of them was the most wicked. The friar admitted that the fiend was his father, and described himself as 'a doctor of evil'.[92] The relationship between priestcraft and Satan was reinforced by claims that papists delighted in trafficking with demons. Elizabethan chapbooks affirmed that priests excelled in witchcraft and sorcery, and the legend that Pope Alexander VI had sold his soul to the devil was the subject of stage plays in the early seventeenth century.[93] This theme was revived in a bizarre chapbook in 1652. Purporting to be the confession of the murderer Giles Fenderlin, 'who killed his wife and sold his soul to the devil', this tract suggested that Fenderlin's crimes were initiated by a Jesuit, who persuaded him to make a compact with Satan in return for special powers. The priest 'drew up a covenant and delivered it to him in Latin', together with a magical ring which allowed him to travel invisibly over great distances. Unfortunately for Fenderlin, these powers lasted for only five years, and when they expired he was unable to renew his arrangement with the diabolical priest. He subsequently killed his wife and was committed to gaol, where he was tormented by the devil 'in the perfect shape of a bishop'.[94]

As these illustrations suggest, it was more common for the popish clergy to be vilified in this way than the religious community they served. On some occasions, however, the entire catholic population was depicted as satanic. Such allegations usually coincided with news of popish insurrections or threats from abroad. The defeat of the Armada and the discovery of the gunpowder plot were celebrated in anti-popish ballads, chapbooks and drama, which tended to emphasise the diabolical nature of the whole popish community. The latter event was commemorated with feasts and bonfires on 5 November, with Romish trinkets and effigies of the pope or the devil burned in many parishes. In the wake of the Irish rebellion in November 1641, which was accompanied by rumours of particularly vicious atrocities against the protestant settlers, a series of tracts declared the rebels' allegiance to 'his hellish majesty'. In one pamphlet, papists were described as 'obedient and well-affected children' of the devil, who took great care to preserve 'their church and ceremonies'.[95] Another text included a lament from Satan that 'the God the English serve' was too powerful for the rebels to overcome, and 'their beads and holy water can't protect them'.[96]

It is striking that many of the anti-catholic references in popular literature appeared in works that were not written primarily as attacks on the Roman church. The appearance of Jesuits as devils or black magicians was often incidental to the stories in which they occurred. The role of popery in the tale of Giles Fenderlin, for example, was peripheral to the main narrative of his crimes. Equally, demonic friars often had little more than walk-on parts in ballads and chapbooks, which were composed mainly as entertainments rather than anti-Roman propaganda. This suggests that the satanic nature of catholicism was sufficiently well known to be taken for granted: the theme could be dropped into popular texts of all kinds without any need for explanation. It is also notable that attacks on popery as 'the devil's creed' often appeared in works which displayed little sympathy for zealous protestantism. Some of the pamphlets which described the Irish rebels as Satan's army also mocked the excesses of 'puritan' religion. This was exemplified by *A Disputation Betwixt the Devill and the Pope*, which contained the following report from the devil to the pontif on the state of England in 1642:

> There all your bookes and beades are counted toyes,
> Altars and tapers are pulled downe by boyes . . .
> The cleane wash't surplice which our priests put on
> There is the smock of the Whore of Babilon . . .
> There, pope, you must expect a certaine losse,
> A taylor must not sit with leggs on crosse,
> But straight hee's set by th'heels, (It is a signe
> Of ceremony, only not divine).[97]

This text poked fun at the excessive zeal of puritan reformers – who allegedly condemned leg-crossing as an ungodly 'signe of ceremony' –

while affirming that the Roman church belonged to the devil. Such publications suggest that both godly protestants and their enemies accepted the kinship between popery and Satan by the middle years of the seventeenth century, and the idea was established as a motif in popular culture.

This did not mean, of course, that ordinary people accepted the protestant concept of Satan in its entirety. It appears, rather, that one aspect of godly thinking was assimilated into a pre-existing set of beliefs, which remained otherwise remarkably unchanged. This led to some fascinating contradictions. In some cases, popular texts combined the idea that popery was satanic with folkloric traditions about the devil. The ballad *The Devil's Oak*, for instance, began with the meeting between Satan and a friar described earlier; but its last verse described how the fiend was deceived by a crafty tinker, who caused him to fall down and break his horns.[98] Another song told how the devil was subjected to a series of humiliating assaults before he ran away in the shape of a friar.[99] Both these works presented the evil one as a subject of comedy rather than a powerful and terrible force, but they also accepted the diabolical nature of catholicism. In a rather different vein, *The Merry Devil of Edmonton* combined anti-popery with profoundly non-protestant sentiments. After making his pact with the evil one, the magician Peter Fabell proceeded to mock the hypocrisy and greed of the Roman church. In one story, he came upon a lecherous friar who had abandoned his 'booke and beads' to fornicate with a young woman. Fabell disguised himself as an angel and commanded the couple to perform a penance or 'live in despaire and die [as] damd wretches'.[100] This passage recalled the escapades of Marlowe's Faust, who also used demonic powers to play tricks on papists; but unlike Faust, Fabell repeatedly outwitted the devil and escaped damnation at the end of the play. The same elements were combined in an early eighteenth-century ballad, *The Wonder: or The Devil Outwitted*. In this curious text, a 'lover in distress' entered a pact with a demon in order to win the heart of a young woman. In return, he was obliged to keep the creature constantly occupied with tasks; if it ever fell idle he would lose his soul. The man sent the demon on a series of improbable missions, all of which were completed at lightning speed. He then sent it to Rome in the hope that it would be overwhelmed by 'holy water and the pope', but the creature returned swiftly to mock him with a parcel of useless 'bulls and pardons'. Eventually, the man's dilemma was solved by his resourceful lover, who gave the demon the never-ending task of looking after her hair.[101] Like *The Merry Devil*, this ballad mixed anti-popery with a comic depiction of Satan and the belief that he could be bested by mortals.

The Strange and Wonderful HISTORY
OF
𝔐𝔬𝔱𝔥𝔢𝔯 𝔖𝔥𝔦𝔭𝔱𝔬𝔫,
Plainly ſetting forth
Her prodigious Birth, Life, Death, and
Burial.
With an exact Collection of all her famous
PROPHECYS
More Compleat than ever yet before
published. And large Explanations,
shewing how they have all along been
fulfilled to this very YEAR.
𝔏𝔦𝔠𝔢𝔫𝔰𝔢𝔡 𝔞𝔠𝔠𝔬𝔯𝔡𝔦𝔫𝔤 𝔱𝔬 𝔒𝔯𝔡𝔢𝔯.

Printed for *W. H.* and ſold by *J. Conyers* in *Fetterlane*.
1686.

Title page of *The Strange and Wonderful History of Mother Shipton* (1686).

Perhaps the most curious example of the combination of anti-popery with popular beliefs was provided by Mother Shipton. Despite her close acquaintance with the devil, the Yorkshire seer was credited with a series of robustly anti-Roman prophecies in the second half of the seventeenth century. According to a tract in 1667, she successfully foretold the sufferings of protestant martyrs 'under the bloody hands of Bonner, bishop of London'. She also predicted the defeat of the Armada, 'a victory so remarkable that [neither] time nor age will ever wear the remembrance thereof away'. As the same text affirmed, these landmarks in England's protestant history were foreseen by a woman who was fathered by Satan and widely regarded as a witch, despite the 'great esteem' in which she was universally held.[102] It was noted earlier that the demonisation of Mother Shipton showed the continuing vitality of medieval attitudes towards the devil; equally, the anti-popish elements in her legend suggest that hatred of catholicism had struck deep roots in English culture. This peculiar outcome tends to support the conclusions of recent research on the English Reformation as a whole. Christopher Haigh has argued that the majority of churchgoers were not converted to protestantism by the end of the sixteenth century, but they could not be defined as catholics either: they were 'de-catholicized but un-protestantized'.[103] In a similar way, it seems that traditional attitudes towards the devil were overlaid with anti-Roman sentiments in the early modern period. The set of beliefs that emerged from this process was neither wholly catholic or protestant, but a remarkable melange of apparently incongruous ideas. The mixing together of traditional assumptions and protestant teaching has been noted by another historian of the Reformation, Tessa Watt. She has advised historians to be mindful of the capacity of cultures 'to absorb new beliefs while retaining old ones, to forge hybrid forms, to accommodate contradictions and ambiguities'.[104] By the end of the seventeenth century, it appears that a diverse and contradictory collection of ideas about Satan was accepted by most of the English population. These ideas might have made little sense to godly theologians, but they apparently suited the needs of ordinary men and women.

5
WOMEN AND THE DEVIL

The high profile enjoyed by Satan in the sixteenth and seventeenth centuries was reflected at every level of English society, and appears to have transcended the confines of academic theology. The fiend pursued a lively career in the theatre and cheap literature, and played a prominent role in politics and contemporary anxieties about witchcraft. This did not mean, however, that the protestant image of the devil was universally accepted. As we have seen, popular representations of the evil one often departed wildly from the views of godly divines, though they were strongly coloured by anti-catholic sentiments. The reception of protestant ideas depended largely on pre-existing cultural factors, which meant that the ideas themselves were refashioned to meet the needs of different social groups. The same process ensured that women's perceptions of Satan were not identical to those of men: they reflected the pervasive influence of male assumptions about female nature, and they were adapted to the particular life experiences of early modern women. It is beyond the scope of this book to account for the variety of religious experiences available to women in Elizabethan and Stuart England, and any generalisations about them must be advanced with a good deal of caution.[1] Nonetheless, there is sufficient evidence to suggest that women's perceptions of the devil were distinctive in several ways: they tended to focus on traditional female 'weaknesses' such as vanity, and were often connected with domestic relationships. For godly women, moreover, the 'voice of Satan' could express the anxieties and temptations which often arose from the practical circumstances of family life, and which were otherwise denied any legitimate expression.

The first part of this chapter deals with contemporary perceptions of the relationship between women and the devil, and draws largely on literature produced by men. These perceptions, which combined traditional assumptions with the insights of protestant theology, provided the context in which many women conceived of the evil one. The power of these ideas is apparent in the writings of godly women, which are considered in the second part of this chapter. These suggest that many conventional assumptions were internalised by female authors, giving a distinctive flavour to their conflicts with Satan. Their references to the devil also indicate the tensions which could emerge between wives and their husbands, and show that religion could offer a psychological resource for coping with these problems. The final part of the chapter considers the impact of the Reformation on 'charismatic' women, who claimed to possess special gifts from the Holy Spirit. It argues that the claims of these women were normally rejected by protestant churchmen, who preferred to understand their behaviour as symptoms of demonic possession. This tendency effectively suppressed a tradition of female spirituality which had flourished in the late Middle Ages, and placed visionary women under the control of men.

REPRESENTATIONS OF WOMEN AND THE DEVIL

An anonymous tract printed in 1655 carried the enticing title *The Reign of the Devil*. This was not, as one might expect, another protestant commentary on the depraved state of humankind under the earthly rule of Satan, but a description of the unruly behaviour of women. The 'devil's reign' of the title was illustrated by a series of grisly domestic murders committed by women, and explained by the volatile and treacherous nature of the female mind. A few years later, another pamphlet warned men against a different but equally terrible threat posed by the opposite sex: 'the pox' or venereal disease. This depicted the female body as one of the snares of Satan, and delighted in the title *The Devil Incarnate*.[2] As these texts suggest, the connection between women and the evil one was well established by the middle of the seventeenth century. It was even possible to depict Satan himself as a woman, particularly in the guise of the whore of Babylon, who combined the traditionally feminine traits of 'proud attire' and sexual lust.[3] The proliferation of such imagery was hardly surprising in the context of English protestantism, with its emphasis on the innate sinfulness of human desires. It appears that many godly men identified the demonic temptations of the flesh with a rapacious model of female sexuality, epitomised by the image of the 'Romish whore'. The fear that lustful women could entice men to Satan was summed up by Nicholas Breton in 1616: 'a wanton woman is the figure of imperfection, an ape in quality, a wagtaile in countenance, a witch, and in condition a kinde of divell: her beck is a net, her word a charme, her looke an illusion, and her companie a confusion'.[4]

In the light of such publications, it is hard to dispute Jerome Friedman's observation that discovering seventeenth-century texts that castigate women 'is only a little more difficult than finding shells at the seashore'.[5] It is surprising, therefore, to find that the protestant theology of Satan was not entirely hostile to women. Indeed, it actually provided a theoretical argument for equality between the sexes. This argument, which proved to be decidedly limited in practice, will be considered below, followed by a more general discussion of the representation of women and the devil in popular literature.

Satan and the Social Role of Women

The protestant argument for sexual equality was based on the bleak premise that men and women were so utterly depraved by sin, and enthralled by nature to the power of the devil, that there was no spiritual difference between them. Luther himself argued that Adam and Eve were equally culpable in the fall of humankind; and this idea was taken up by several English theologians under Elizabeth and the early Stuarts. Some writers, such as the catholic convert Richard Carpenter, went so far as to argue that 'the greatest fault' should be attributed to Adam, since he was persuaded to disobey God by a mere mortal, whereas Eve had been deceived by the more formidable powers of Satan himself.[6] These rather esoteric ideas were complemented by a more practical consideration: godly religion obliged both sexes to join in 'spiritual combat' with the evil one. According to William Gouge, 'neither ministers nor people, poore nor rich, male nor female' were exempted from this duty. This presumption was reiterated in his best-selling guide to 'domesticall duties', which insisted that both 'husbands and wives ought to be carefull to keepe one another from the temptations of Satan, that is, from sinne, whereunto all his temptations tend'. In extreme situations, this obligation could even be used to justify wifely disobedience: Gouge asserted that women should defy their husbands if they asked them to commit obvious sins, such as visiting the theatre or going 'garishly and whorishly attired'.[7]

There is some evidence that these ideas created opportunities for women to escape from the social conventions which normally restricted their behaviour. Certainly, it appears that godly women among the gentry were prepared to condemn the actions of impious or 'superstitious' men. During a visit to York in 1600, Margaret Hoby noted in her diary that one of the town's beneficed ministers had preached 'false' doctrine; on another occasion she expressed her distaste for the views of Thomas Bilson, the anti-puritan bishop of Winchester.[8] For women such as Hoby, the practice of godly religion entailed an involvement in the kind of theological and political debates which were traditionally reserved for their male superiors. The implications of this were most obvious during the fierce religious disputes of the early 1640s, when many godly women were outspoken supporters of the campaign to 'purify' the English church. In her autobiography, Jane Turner recalled that she was repelled by the ungodly 'innovations' promoted by Charles I during the 1630s, and driven by her religious convictions to support Parliament at the outbreak of the Civil War.[9] Writing to her daughter in 1640, Anna Temple rejoiced that the parish churches of Warwickshire were being stripped of their popish trappings, and looked forward to the abolition of 'idolatry and superstition' throughout the land. To Temple, the campaign for church reform appears to have been a natural extension of her faith: she concluded her letter by noting that 'sin was growen to a great height, but let it be our care to keepe our harts close to God in the use of his ordinances, and to avoide everie sin, and seeke to him to keepe us from the temptations of Satan'.[10] Since educated and reasonably wealthy women such as Turner and Temple were able to leave their own records, their political activities are relatively easy to reconstruct. It is much harder to discover the practices of godly women from lower social ranks. There is a clue, perhaps, in the fact that women generally outnumbered men in the religious sects which emerged in the 1640s and 1650s. At least one woman, Martha Simmonds, assumed a prominent role among the early Quakers, and appears briefly to have challenged the position of George Fox as the leader of the movement.[11] The prominence of women within the sects suggests that the concept of spiritual equality could sometimes overcome traditional assumptions about female inferiority, and implies that this phenomenon was not confined to members of the gentry.

Despite these considerations, however, there are good reasons to assume that the protestant theory of sexual equality was strictly limited in practice. First, committed protestants made up only a small part of the population, and most people were probably untouched by the theological arguments developed by men such as William Gouge. Second, godly divines were careful to limit their arguments for equality to the spiritual sphere. Thus Stephen Geree asserted in 1639 that women were equal to men in matters pertaining to salvation, and could even acquire the masculine qualities of 'sharpnes of apprehension and soundnes of judgement' when they were assured of their redemption through Christ; but in all other respects they were inferior to men.[12] Other English divines followed Luther in arguing that women were inferior by nature: they had been created by God for the specific purposes of child-raising and home-making, and were constitutionally incapable of more manly pursuits. In practice, this allowed writers like Stephen Bateman, Philip Stubbes and Gouge to reaffirm the traditional female weaknesses of vanity, inconstancy and intellectual dullness, while preserving the idea that women were spiritually equal to men. Bateman characterised the sin of pride as a peculiarly feminine trait, while Stubbes devoted a whole chapter of his *Anatomie of Abuses* (1583) to 'a particular description of the abuses of women's apparell'. He noted

Consumed by vanity, a woman is unaware of the trap laid by the devil. From the English edition of Sebastian Brant, *The Ship of Fooles* (1570).

that face paints were 'the devil's inventions to intangle poore soules in the nets of perdition', and observed that looking glasses were 'the devil's spectacles to allure us to pride'.[13] Likewise, Gouge argued that the natural limitations of women meant that they should normally be subject to their husbands' will.

The distinction between 'natural' and 'spiritual' qualities was a helpful device for preserving male authority, but it was a rather ambiguous and difficult position to maintain. On one hand, it was not easy to draw the line between spiritual and secular affairs, particularly given the protestant insistence that religion should be paramount in every area of life. This left open the possibility that women could assume a leading role in the religious duties of the household, and even participate in public controversies when these touched on matters of faith. On the other hand, some thinkers were tempted to assume that women's natural limitations could affect their relationship with God and the devil. Stephen Bateman, for instance, illustrated the sin of pride with a woodcut depicting a woman holding a looking glass, resting one foot on a skull, while the devil stood behind her and mocked her vanity (*see* Plate 13b). His text explained that 'the woman signifieth pride, the glasse in her hand flattery or deceate, the devil behinde her temptation, the death head which she setteth her foote on signifieth forgetfulnes of the life to come, whereby commeth destruction'. The implication of the print was that women's natural weaknesses made them more vulnerable to the temptations of the fiend.[14] The same tendency was apparent when protestant authors addressed the tricky subject of witchcraft. In theory, both sexes were equally subject to Satan's powers, but the predominance of women in witch trials led some theologians to claim that they were especially susceptible to the devil's wiles. Most famously, James I argued that 'that sexe is frailer than man is, so it is easier to be intrapped in these grosse snares of the devill'.[15] Similar views, including the belief that women's vanity and sexual insatiability made them easy prey for the evil one, were repeated in godly texts throughout the early modern period.

The careers of godly women reflected the ambiguous and limited opportunities created for them by protestant teachings. Margaret Hoby and Jane Turner were prepared to express strong views on issues of religious controversy, but also acknowledged the 'natural' frailities of their gender and generally deferred to their husbands in secular matters. Hoby privately condemned the falsehood of anti-puritan preachers, but appears to have confined her own evangelising work to the servants in her kitchen. Turner defied the religious censorship of the 1630s to track down godly books that had been condemned by her parish minister, but she delayed the publication of her autobiography in 1653 because she feared that Satan would use it to 'exalt me in my own thoughts'.[16] Similarly, the sectarian women of the 1650s rarely emerged as religious leaders in their own right, and even Martha Simmonds had been marginalised by the male hierarchy of the Quaker movement by the end of the decade. It was, of course, always unlikely that protestant doctrines would undermine deeply entrenched conventions of sexual inequality, even among the most godly members of society. They appear to have made even less impact outside the puritan community, where popular literature routinely challenged the view that men and women were equally sinful before God. It is to this literature that we now turn.

Women and the Devil in Cheap Print

Encounters between women and Satan were one of the staples of popular literature in the sixteenth and seventeenth centuries. The most common accounts can be divided roughly into three types. The first genre was 'judgement' tales, which focused on the miraculous punishment of individuals guilty of particular sins. Despite their salacious and unpleasant content, these stories often purported to convey a serious religious message, which made them a useful medium for the kind of protestant propaganda described in the previous chapter. The second genre was accounts of witchcraft, usually precipitated by actual cases and drawing to some extent on the records of trials. Finally, comic stories depicted meetings between resourceful women and the evil one, normally framed within the conventions of folklore and presented in merry ballads. Each of these genres tended to emphasise the traditionally feminine qualities of pride, inconstancy and sexual desire, though the comic tales also presented women as guileful actors who were capable of outwitting the fiend.

A typical judgement story, published in 1600, related the sad experiences of an unnamed 'young maiden' from Colwall in

Herefordshire. She pledged herself to marry a youth from the village but broke off the engagement, then 'fell a lusting' for one of her cousins with whom she worked as a servant in her uncle's house. As a result of their illicit union, she gave birth to a 'monstrous' child which died soon after its delivery. The role of the devil in this tragedy was made clear at each stage: first, it was 'Satan, the enemy of all goodnes, [who] by his instigations and instruments wrought so in the minde of the maiden' that she broke off her match; subsequently, he 'so blinded the eyes' of the woman and her new lover 'that they lay together and she was gotten with child by him'. The author also noted that the woman's natural weaknesses made her peculiarly vulnerable to the snares of the fiend:

> Such is the lightnesse and inconstancy of a great number of this sexe . . . [that] they are many times in extreames: for, either they will not at all bee ruled by their parentes and friends in marraige, or else, when with their parent's and friend's consent, they have assured themselves, and entangled the mindes of younge men, yet upon some sinister course they will flit off againe; yea, and sometimes get a great bellie by some such match, and so breake off, with all the shame that may be.

While the tract offered a brief warning to young men that they could also expect punishment from God for fornication, it made no reference to the fate of the cousin and failed to link his sin to the 'inconstancy' of his gender. The tale concluded by enjoining young women to practice 'fasting, praier, modesty in apparell, lookes, gesture and countenance'.[17]

The same didactic tone was adopted in another tale about a 'monstrous birth', *God's Handy-Worke in Wonders* (1615). This thoroughly nasty text concerned the benighted relationship between a woman and her debauched husband. When she found herself to be pregnant, she begged her spouse 'to tarry at home' and abandon the company of prostitutes and his wicked friends. He refused to do so and cursed her, causing her to exclaim that she would rather give birth to 'the devill of hell' than continue to live in the 'woe and miserie wherewithall thou dost so vex me'. Having thus sealed her fate, she gave birth to a hideously deformed child. Again, the author depicted the woman's sin as typical of her gender, and hoped that her fate 'may be a looking glasse unto every wedded woman, whereby to refraine [from] casting out such unadvised words'. The tract entreated wives to have patience with their husbands 'and commit all matters to almighty God'.[18] A similar message was conveyed in *A Good Warning for all Maidens*, a broadside ballad telling how the devil deceived a young woman into betraying her lover, then stole away her child on the 'wofull night' that it was born.[19] Tales of God's punishment of evil women were particularly abundant in the decade after the Civil War. In one well-publicised incident in 1645, the birth of a deformed child in Leicestershire proved not only the immorality of the unfortunate mother but the wickedness of the whole region, since 'no other part of England hath had so many witches'. The ultimate cause of such dreadful judgements was spelt out in a pamphlet in 1653, which observed that women were the 'instruments and immediate causes of murder, idolatry and a multitude of other heinous sins'. They were, the author concluded, faithful servants of 'their great lord and master, Lucifer'.[20]

The image of evil women presented in judgement books was complemented by cheap tracts about witchcraft. The role of women in English witch trials has been the subject of intense debate over the last thirty years. Most recently, Jim Sharpe has argued that women played an unusually active role in the prosecution of witches: they furnished allegations against suspects, appeared as witnesses in trials, and sometimes acted as searchers for incriminating marks on the bodies of the accused.[21] This interpretation has been challenged by Clive Holmes, who suggests that men normally took the lead in initiating prosecutions, with women providing only supporting evidence.[22] Whichever of these views is correct, there can be little doubt that women were much more likely than men to appear as defendants in these cases. They were also far more prominent in popular accounts of the crime. The assumption that witchcraft was a female vice was shown most strikingly in those texts which presented entirely fictitious accounts of the activities of witches. For example, Rowley, Dekker and Ford's play *The Witch of Edmonton* placed a woman in the title role. Similarly, a chapbook in 1643 presented the imaginary tale of a witch 'standing on a small planck board and sayling on it over the river of Newbury'. The accompanying text and woodcut illustration made it plain that the witch was a woman.[23] Conversely, fictitious female characters such as Mother Shipton were sometimes transformed into witches as their stories were elaborated in successive editions.[24] The assumption that witches were usually female was also noted by sceptical observers of the beliefs of the 'common sort of people'. Reginald Scot, for instance, observed in 1584 that those most often suspected of the crime were 'women, which be commonly old, lame, blear-eyed, pale, foul, and full of wrinkles'.[25] That this cultural assumption was as influential in the prosection of real witches as it was in their fictional image is suggested by a list of 'presumptions against witches' drawn up for

Yorkshire justices of the peace in the 1590s: the first presumption was that 'they are moste comonly weeke women'.[26]

While it is easy to demonstrate that ordinary people regarded witchcraft as a typically female vice, the connection between witches and the devil is a bit more problematical. Since the pioneering work of Alan Macfarlane and Keith Thomas in the early 1970s, historians have tended to argue that accusations of witchcraft in England focused primarily on the practice of harmful magic, and lacked the elements of diabolism which characterised allegations in Scotland and mainland Europe. In recent years, however, this view has been challenged by historians, who have called into question the supposed peculiarities of the English experience.[27] The implications of this new work for early modern perceptions of Satan are considered in Chapter Seven. Here, it is sufficient to note that popular accounts of witchcraft frequently linked the crime to the devil. In 1565, the first printed description of the trial and execution of a witch claimed that the accused woman had named her familiar spirit 'Satan'.[28] A

A late fifteenth-century depiction of Satan seducing a woman. The idea that the fiend seduced his female disciples resurfaced in English witch trials in the 1640s.

chapbook report of a witch trial in Windsor in 1579 claimed that the accused had performed magic with the help of 'a wicked spirit' and 'the devil'. Ten years later, another pamphlet described a witch 'invocating upon Satan' and offering her soul to the fiend.[29] In *A Newe Ballad of the Life and Deaths of Three Witches* (1589), three women hanged for witchcraft in Chelmsford were described as 'Satan's fiends', who 'cried the devil's name'.[30] The satanic nature of witchcraft had become a commonplace in cheap print by the middle of the seventeenth century. In 1653 a chapbook recorded how Ann Bodenham, a witch from Salisbury, caused her followers to write their names in blood 'in the devil's book'.[31] Later that year, another pamphlet reported that a Cornish witch was obliged every month 'to send the devil on some destructive errand'. By this period, the links between women, witchcraft and

Satan were entwined in the lurid fantasy that the fiend enjoyed sexual intercourse with his female disciples. As a newsbook explained in 1645, 'the female being the weaker sexe, and the inclinations of the flesh being prone unto lust, the devill maketh choyce by that way most to oblige his servants, which by nature most they are addicted to'.[32]

A much lighter and slightly more positive portrayal of women was offered in comic ballads describing the devil's misadventures on earth. Typically, these songs described how the fiend's plans to destroy some unfortunate man were thwarted by the unexpected intervention of a woman. In *The Devil Gelded*, for instance, a quick-thinking baker's wife saved her husband from being castrated by Satan, while the heroine of *The Wonder* prevented her young lover from losing his soul to a demon.[33] In these and other tales, women rescued men from apparently hopeless situations in which they had trapped themselves, normally by making foolish bets with the devil. It is tempting to view these ballads as celebrations of the intelligence and courage of their female protagonists, but this would probably be a mistake. First, it is quite likely that the strong roles given to women in these tales were designed for comic effect: they represented a jocular reversal of normal social expectations, and served to underline the haplessness of the male characters. Viewed in this way, the ballads actually reinforced conventional assumptions about women. Second, the female characters in comic ballads often defeated the devil by behaviour that was perceived as typical of their sex, and was regarded as a vice rather than a virtue in most other contexts. Thus a ballad from the 1620s described how the fiend was driven from London by 'the poore women that cry fish and oysters', whose sharp tongues and unruly conduct were more than he could endure.[34] Similarly, the fiend was overwhelmed by the unquenchable vanity of the heroine of *The Wonder*, and ended the tale working as her hairdresser.[35] Finally, the punch-line of some *Merry Tales* was that women were actually worse than the devil. This was exemplified by a sixteenth-century ballad about a man who was so abused by his wife that he asked Satan to take her away. The evil one accepted his offer, but returned her after she had given him more pain than 'a hundred years in hell'.[36] In sum, it seems that comic depictions of women and the devil did not really challenge prevailing ideas about the weaknesses of the 'fair sex', and probably confirmed many conventional beliefs about female behaviour.

THE PERCEPTIONS OF GODLY WOMEN

The cultural assumptions described above provided the context in which religious women experienced 'spiritual combats' with the devil. The idea that women were particularly sensitive to the presence of the evil one predated the Reformation, and was apparently confirmed by the mystical experiences of pious women in the fifteenth century like Julian of Norwich and Margery Kempe. The opening pages of Kempe's Book, which is generally regarded as the earliest autobiography in the English language, describe her encounters with the fiend and tempestuous visions of hell, where she saw 'devils opening their mouths all alight with burning flames of fire, as if they would have swallowed her in, pawing at her, sometimes threatening her, sometimes pulling her and hauling her about both night and day'.[37]

Kempe's acute awareness of the devil was echoed by many women in the early modern period. During the 1630s, John Bunyan overheard some 'poor women' in Bedford describe their own less dramatic, but equally intense confrontations with Satan. His account presents a remarkable vignette of the beliefs of ordinary women inspired by zealous protestantism, and deserves to be quoted at length:

> They talked [of] how God had visited their souls with his love in the Lord Jesus, and with what words and promises they had been refreshed, comforted, and supported against the temptations of the devil; moreover, they reasoned of the suggestions and temptations of Satan in particular, and told each other by which they had been afflicted, and how they were borne up under his assaults: they also discoursed of their own wretchedness of heart, of their unbelief, and did condemn, slight and abhor their own righteousness, as filthy and insufficient to do them any good.[38]

Bunyan's text suggests that the protestant theology of Satan provided some women with a framework for understanding and describing their spiritual experiences, and shows that these experiences could be the topic of lively discussions amongst them. Frustratingly though, it reveals nothing about the content of the devil's 'temptations', and offers no clues that they were significantly different to those endured by men. It is possible, however, to discover the nature of Satan's 'assaults' in the numerous spiritual autobiographies and meditations composed by women in the seventeenth century. These suggest that godly women internalised conventional assumptions about the limitations of the female mind, and perceived themselves to be especially vulnerable to the devil's attempts to exploit these weaknesses. They also show that women often experienced their most intense struggles with the evil one in the context of difficult family relationships. It seems that Satan was most likely to rear his head when women were unhappy with their domestic circumstances, and their efforts to overcome him can be viewed as attempts to come to terms with the practical frustrations of their lives.

Satan and the Sin of Pride

The tendency for women to internalise the idea that they were particularly vulnerable to the sin of pride was not confined to the godly. Margaret Cavendish, the fiercely anti-puritan duchess of Newcastle, wrote in 1653 that vanity was 'so natural to our sex' that it would be abnormal if she did not suffer from it.[39] At the opposite end of the social spectrum, a woman executed for murder in 1655 ignored the godly chaplain who entreated her to repent before she went to her death, but 'only cryed out against pride, saying that that was the cause that brought her to this miserable end, and desired that all women take warning by her example thereof'.[40] Similar sentiments were expressed in the confessions of female witches in East Anglia in 1645.[41] For godly women, however, the daily struggle to overcome the devil's temptations meant that the conquest of pride assumed a particular importance. In a recent essay on the 'puritan deathbed', Ralph Houlbrooke has observed that dying women were more likely than men to engage in lengthy combats with the devil in their final hours, and speculated that their heightened awareness of his presence was 'because of the impression made on them by Eve's fall'.[42] This point can be taken further, perhaps, since it appears that many of these women believed themselves to be especially guilty of the original sin of pride. This was most explicit at the deathbed of Katherine Brettergh, who 'accused herselfe of pride, that shee had delighted too much in her selfe and her beautie'. She exclaimed that she 'wished that shee had never beene borne, or that shee had beene made any other creature, rather than a woman'. Despite her acute sense of her own vulnerability, Brettergh overcame Satan by telling him 'to reason not with me' but with Christ, who intervened to save her from the fiend.[43] The belief that women had a peculiar susceptibility to pride was also expressed by Elizabeth Jocelin in *The Mother's Legacie* (1624), a collection of spiritual advice addressed to her unborn child. Jocelin implored her offspring to shun the vanity of 'new fangled fashions' in dress, 'whether thou be [a] son or daughter'. She added, however, that 'if a daughter, I confesse thy taske is harder because thou art weaker, and thy temptations to this vice greater'. For Jocelin, this meant that her daughter would be more exposed to the temptations of the enemy, who 'is alwaies busie and ready at hand to draw thee away from God'.[44]

It is, of course, impossible to know how women's awareness of pride affected their daily lives, but a tantalising clue is provided in the diary of Lady Margaret Hoby. In January 1600, Hoby chastised herself for speaking 'of something not so as I ought', and resolved to be 'more watchfull hereafter that I so grossly offend not my God'. The next day she was assaulted by the 'malice' of Satan, but found comfort in her private prayers and the devotional writings of Thomas Cartwright. Three weeks later, another entry in the diary hinted strongly at the nature of her previous sin: she had spent the afternoon discussing parish affairs with her husband and the minister, Mr Rhodes, 'yet thouge I were with all the companie, it pleased God to free me from sundrie temptations wherunto I had before beene subject'. It appears that Hoby had suppressed her desire to speak inappropriately in the presence of her husband and the minister, and that she had previously succumbed to a similar temptation. If this interpretation is correct, it is reasonable to assume that her earlier struggle with the devil had been occasioned by her proud behaviour in speaking 'not so as I ought', and her victory over temptation had prevented her from committing the sin again.[45] Hoby's diary provides an insight into the social pressures which shaped the religious experiences of godly women, and suggests that satanic temptations could arise from the practical limitations imposed on their lives. In turn, the conquest of these temptations could restore women to their 'proper' role within the household. This process was demonstrated most explicitly in situations of extreme domestic tension, which are considered below.

Satan and the Troubled Household

The connection between Satan and domestic strife was not invented by the protestant Reformation. Some of the most memorable passages in Margery Kempe's autobiography described how her 'combats' with the evil one arose in the context of her troubled marriage, which ended when she admitted that she 'would rather have eaten and drunk the ooze and muck in the gutter' than have sex with her husband.[46] Many more accounts of this kind were written, however, by protestant autobiographers in the early modern period. A small number of godly men linked Satan's temptations with their anxieties about domestic life, such as the London apprentice who noted in 1643 that 'Satan followed me and suggested unto me that it were best for me to leave my wife and children.'[47] But it was much more common for women to describe the work of the tempter in this way, a fact which probably reflected their greater investment in family life and the particular restrictions that it imposed upon them.

Unsurprisingly, the devil made his most dramatic appearances at times when wives were very unhappy with their spouses. In 1652 a woman described as 'M.K.', one of the anonymous contributors to Vavasor Powell's collection of 'spirituall experiences', told how her husband comported himself 'with some company which did not only cause much time to be spent in idlenesse, but almost all of our means'. After he befriended a particularly offensive drunkard, M.K. implored him tearfully 'to refraine [from] that man's company, or at least not to suffer him to come so often home to our house'. When her entreaties proved to be futile, 'the devill set his foot into my heart' by suggesting that she should murder her husband's friend. She was immediately overwhelmed by guilt, and managed to overcome the temptation through strenuous prayer. In the days that followed, however, she was assailed by satanic thoughts and visions of hell, imagining that demons 'waited in every corner, and behind every doore to snatch me away'. Her torments reached a climax one night when a 'little dogge' jumped on her bed and she 'thought it was the devil who was come to take me away'. This episode was apparently the catylist for her spiritual recovery: it forced her to throw herself on the mercy of Christ, who empowered her to resist the fiend's temptations and patiently accept her lot.[48] A similar pattern was evident in the brief memoir of Mary Burrill published in 1653. Burrill confessed that 'I have been infinitely troubled by my marriage to my second husband, and have been afflicted in conscience about it very much, til my Lord gave me comfort within that my sins were forgiven mee.' During her period of affliction, Burrill experienced in her dreams 'two terrible conflicts with Satan', which ended in her victory over the enemy through the power of 'God's love'.[49]

As well as overt conflicts between wives and their husbands, periods of frequent or prolonged absence between spouses could create tensions for the devil to exploit. In the most spectacular, if not the most typical case of this kind, Elizabeth Caldwell succumbed to the fiend's temptation to kill her husband in 1604. In a letter to her intended victim written after her conviction for attempted murder, she invited him to 'remember in what a case you have lived, howe poore you have many times left me, howe long you have beene absent from mee, all which advantage the devill tooke to subvert mee'. She described how Satan 'continually wrought upon my weaknes, my povertie, and your absence', until she was driven to contemplate murder.[50] Less dramatic but probably more common was the experience of Hannah Allen, who recalled how 'the devil had the more advantage' of her during her marriage in the 1650s, 'occasioned by the oft absence of my dear and affectionate husband, with whom I lived present and absent about eight years'. Allen was afflicted with further 'great strugglings' with the devil after her husband's death at sea in 1663.[51] For Allen and some other godly women, the death of their spouse appears to have occasioned an intense spiritual crisis, accompanied by particularly vicious assaults from the devil. This experience was described vividly by a woman in 1647, who agonised over the fate of her husband's soul and her own responsibility for his possible damnation. She wondered 'what would become of me that had made him worse by my perverse words to him, when he was faulty'. Her sufferings culminated one morning when she awoke to a terrible vision: 'I suddenly flew out of my bed into the midst of the room; and a voice said within me to my heart: "Thou art damn'd, thou art damn'd". I felt the smell of brimstone.' In this case, the tormented widow found some solace in the unconventional ministry of the prophetess Sara Wright, who assured her that Christ would 'show mercy'.[52]

Other domestic situations could also create feelings of intense guilt, which left some women vulnerable to Satan's malice. A particularly dramatic and tragic case, recorded by the physician Richard Napier in 1602, concerned a woman who confessed that she had helped one of her serving maids to terminate an unwanted pregnancy. Napier observed that she was overwhelmed by guilt and 'distracted of her wits'; she wanted 'to kill [and] make herself away, being tempted (as she sayth) thereunto by the tempter'.[53] It appears that the devil could also exploit family conflicts between women. In 1634, Napier's nephew described how one of his patients, Joan Fellow, was afflicted with 'night terrors' during a dispute with her mother-in-law, who 'hath used her very unkindly'. He noted that Fellows had slept badly for nine nights, 'and in her slumbers feares somebody will kill her'. The exact nature of the conflict between the two women was not recorded, and we can only speculate about the psychological pressures which caused Fellow to experience these nocturnal visitations. It seems reasonable, however, to accept the doctor's assumption that they were linked in some way to tensions within the household.[54]

Most of the women described in this section experienced feelings of temptation or guilt arising from domestic situations that were largely beyond their control. They appear to have understood these feelings as the 'buffets' of Satan, which had to be endured and overcome through Christ before they could be restored to spiritual health. The implications of this belief were deeply conservative: it encouraged women to concentrate on defeating the devil within them instead of attempting to change their material circumstances. Even Elizabeth Caldwell ended her life as a penitent sinner on the scaffold, publicly renouncing her proud and lustful behaviour and imploring others to resist the snares of Satan. The conservative consequences for women of belief in the devil can be shown in another, very different area of religious experience. By emphasising the power and ubiquity of the evil one, the English reformers effectively suppressed a tradition of female mysticism which had thrived in the late Middle Ages and the first part of the sixteenth century. It is now time to consider this process, and the related phenomenon of demonic possession.

THE END OF PROPHECY

'The end of prophecy' is the phrase coined by the Italian historian Ottavia Niccoli to describe the suppression of religious visionaries by the forces of the Counter-Reformation in the early sixteenth century. Until about 1530, she argues, prophetic visions were accepted at all levels of Italian society, and the recipients of these divine revelations, most often women, were treated with great admiration and respect. From the 1530s, however, this situation was transformed. Faced with the challenge of protestantism, the Roman church adopted a much more sceptical attitude towards ecstatic religious experiences, believing that they could give encouragement to the kind of heresy that was flourishing in Germany. Subsequently, women who claimed to receive revelations from angels or St Mary were subjected to a regime of close examination by their confessors, who sought to persuade them that they were deluded or, worse, the victims of demonic possession. Niccoli cites the case of one woman, Christina della Rovere, who was so affected by this pressure that her rapturous visions of 'a most handsome young man with blond hair, dressed in white', were replaced by apparitions of a monstrous, fire-breathing dog. More generally, she argues that 'women who seemed to enjoy particular charismatic gifts' were often accused of delusion or 'affected sanctity', arising from their pride and hypocrisy or the seductive wiles of the devil.[55] These conclusions have been confirmed by research in other European countries, which suggests that similar pressures were responsible for transforming women's visionary experiences into cases of demonic possession.[56]

There is good reason to assume that the same process was encouraged by the English Reformation. As Niccoli's study suggests, the theology of protestantism itself was not primarily responsible for the suppression of visionary women, just as the doctrines of sixteenth-century catholicism did not lead inevitably to this outcome. Rather, the political interests of the crown and the clergy created a situation in which all forms of charismatic religion were treated with extreme scepticism. Like the papacy, the English crown was inclined to take a dim view of any activities which threatened to promote heresy. This concern was heightened by the creation of the Church of England, which made any open expression of religious dissent a potential challenge to the state. Equally, protestant pastors had good reason to be cautious about claims of divine inspiration: not only were they anxious to avoid the promotion of unpredictable and potentially heretical 'fanatics', whose actions could bring discredit on the godly community, but they were wary of sanctioning alternative sources of religious authority, which could undermine their own role as the leaders of God's people. These political interests were complemented perfectly by the emphasis on the power of Satan which characterised English protestantism: since the evil one delighted in falsehood and sought constantly to undermine the true church, it was only to be expected that he would assail God's people with false prophets who appeared as 'angels of light'. While a number of male visionaries were cast in this unfortunate role, the effects of the new climate of scepticism were felt most strongly by women: the experience of divine inspiration was a traditional aspect of female piety, reflecting the conventional belief that women's passivity made them unusually receptive to the power of God.[57] This tradition of female spirituality was effectively suppressed by the second half of the sixteenth century. As a result, women who attempted to take on the role of prophets were usually dismissed as charlatans or hysterics, or presumed to be possessed by the devil.

From Prophecy to Possession

The prohibition of women's visionary experiences was illustrated neatly in a case from Huntingdonshire in 1629. This concerned the activities of Jane Hawkins, a self-proclaimed prophetess from the village of St Ives, who experienced religious ecstasies and 'uttered verses in rythm' during a period of prolonged illness. Her revelations were apparently accepted as genuine by some members of the local community, and were recorded in a book by the curate. When news of these events reached the Bishop of Lincoln, John Williams, he instigated an investigation which concluded that Hawkins was a fake: her performance was 'stark juggling' which abused the name of God, 'as if those notions came from God which came from fraud, and from Satan'. The parish minister was obliged to denounce the prophetess from the pulpit, and to apologise for the part he had played in giving her credence. In a later account of the story, John Hacket offered an explicit acknowledgement of the political motives behind the bishop's move: Hawkins' verses were 'full of detraction and injury to the authority of the bishops, to the church-way of England in the liturgy, and not sparing some occurences of the civil government'. It is impossible to test this assertion against Hawkins' own words, since Williams' intervention proved so successful that no copies of her work have survived. Whatever their content, Hacket had no doubt that they had a wide appeal 'among the rural hobs'. He noted sadly that they 'would have spread into fairs and markets, and been sung by fiddler's boys, if it had not been prevented'.[58]

While the devil was implicated indirectly in the ecstatic experiences of Jane Hawkins, he was given a leading role in the story of other women who attempted to play the role of religious visionaries. In 1621 Helen

Fairfax, the eldest daughter of a gentry family from Fuyston in Yorkshire, fell into a series of trances in which she received visions of the devil and local women believed to be witches. Her condition was accepted as a genuine case of possession by her father Edward, who later wrote an account of the episode, and the godly clergy in the region. After a few weeks, however, the symptoms of Helen's condition changed dramatically, and she began to receive heavenly visions conveying messages from God:

> She fell into a trance in the hall, and then one in bright clothing appeared to her, a man of incomparable beauty, with a beard, and his apparel shining: upon his head [was] a sharp high thing, from which, and from his mouth, and from his garments, streamed beams of light, which cast a glorious splendour over him. He spake unto her and said that he was God, come to comfort her; that the devil had troubled her by God's sufferance, but she was so dearly beloved of God that he was come to comfort her.

Helen engaged in conversation with the divine apparition, which promised to relieve her afflictions and assured her of a place in heaven. She joined it in reciting the Lord's Prayer. When the spirit departed, 'she was persuaded [that] this was God or some angel sent to comfort her', and would probably have persisted in this view had it not been challenged by her father and his friends. Despite her strong opposition, they were convinced that the vision was a subtle attempt by the devil to seduce her mind. According to Edward Fairfax, they spent the rest of the night trying unsuccessfully to convince her of this, 'but next morning, with some difficulty, we persuaded her . . . by such reasons and scriptures as our small knowledge could afford'. The effect of this intervention was dramatic. Three days later, Helen fell in a trance and 'saw the same glorious apparition again'. This time, however, she confronted the angelic figure with her knowledge of its true identity, declaring that 'God did not reveal thee unto me, and will rebuke thee for taking his name upon thee.' At this, 'she saw many horns begin to grow out of his head, and his beauty and glorious light were gone, and he changed into a most terrible shape'.[59]

Like the Italian visionary Christina della Rovere, Helen Fairfax appears to have abandoned her claim to divine inspiration in the face of persistent male scepticism, and convinced herself that her ecstatic experiences were demonic in origin. One can only speculate about how her condition might have developed in a more sympathetic context, but her initial dogged refusal to accept that her angelic visitor was the devil suggests that she would have continued to receive heavenly revelations.

The crucial role played by social factors in shaping the experiences of charismatic women was shown after the Civil War, when the collapse of the church courts and the proliferation of religious sects created an atmosphere much more receptive to the claims of 'inspired' individuals. In these new circumstances, visionary women like Anna Trapnel and Sara Wright were freed to pursue brief careers as prophets. In a striking reversal of the experience of Helen Fairfax, Trapnel admitted in 1654 that she had once suspected that her visions were signs of demonic possession, but later decided that this was 'but a fancy'.[60] Despite these new opportunities, however, women who displayed signs of inspiration still came under intense pressure to accept that they were really possessed. Around 1645, Joyce Dovey of Bewdley in Worcestershire was affected by convulsions and 'fits' after attending a godly sermon. These symptoms, which were 'observed especially to take her in the time of private prayer or performance of pious duties', were entirely consistent with the signs of the Holy Spirit; but this possibility was closed off by the intervention of an army chaplain who 'strongly imagined that shee was possessed'. Subsequently, Dovey began to manifest the conventional symptoms of demonic possession, which reached a climax when the fiend seized control of her voice to declare that 'my power is over all the world, and my kingdome is the greatest'.[61]

Satan and the Expression of Female Authority

One of the consequences of the suppression of divine inspiration was to deny women the respect and power which traditionally accompanied the role of prophet. But while this option was largely closed off in the period before the Civil War, some women managed to exploit other extreme spiritual experiences to assert a measure of authority that would normally have been denied them. The most obvious examples occurred in cases of demonic possession. In 1593 Joan and Jane Throckmorton, the daughters of a gentry family from Huntingtonshire, were possessed by evil spirits which caused them to suffer convulsions and experience terrible visions. Towards the end of their ordeal, however, the girls were allowed to deliver religious speeches to the adult members of the household. According to one observer, 'the heavenly and divine speeches of these children' were such 'that if a man had heard it he would not have thought himself better edified at ten sermons'.[62] These performances, which were presumably attributed to the Holy Spirit, allowed the Throckmorton girls to enjoy some of the privileges of divine inspiration without relinquishing their role as victims of the devil. An alternative way for women to express spiritual authority was by confronting and overcoming the devil in public, an opportunity normally associated with the protestant deathbed. Thus

Katherine Stubbes assumed the manner of a godly preacher as she addressed the evil one in front of the audience gathered to witness her final hours:

> But what sayest thou now Satan? Dost thou aske me how I dare come to him for mercy, he being a righteous God, and I a miserable sinner? I tell thee, Satan, I am bold through Christ to come unto him . . . Christe's armes were spred wide open, Satan, upon the crosse (with that she spread her owne armes) to embrace me and all penitent persons: and therefore, Satan, I will not feare to present myselfe before his foot-stoole, in full assurance of his mercy, for Christ his sake.[63]

This kind of behaviour went beyond the passive submission to Christ recommended in protestant guides to the art of death, but was apparently accepted by godly men such as Philip Stubbes, Katherine's husband and biographer. The privileges of the deathbed were exploited more ostentatiously by Sara Wright in 1647. At the age of sixteen, Sara took to her bed with a mysterious and apparently terminal illness, which left her blind, deaf and unable to eat. During her sickness she embarked on an epic struggle with Satan, who fought with her 'as he did with Michael and the angels'. She periodically interrupted this conflict to offer words of religious comfort and advice to the audience at her bedside; and eventually, when she had overcome the final onslaughts of the fiend, she devoted herself entirely to this more tranquil role. After spending several weeks in the role of a semi-conscious spiritual adviser, Sara recovered her health and retired to Highgate.[64]

As these accounts suggest, it was possible for women to express the kind of authority traditionally associated with female mystics in religious experiences involving the devil. Such opportunities were decidedly limited, however, and they imposed severe restrictions on the individuals involved. Even in the relatively favourable circumstances of the 1640s, Sara Wright was obliged to endure a lengthy and debilitating illness for her prophetic status to be acknowledged; and she relied heavily on the support of a Baptist minister, Henry Jessey, to authenticate and publicise her experiences. Other women, such as Katherine Stubbes, enjoyed their brief moment of preacherly authority only at the very end of their lives. For the victims of possession, the conventions surrounding the condition imposed strict limits on their behaviour and made the expression of divine inspiration extremely problematical. The 'inspired' experiences of Helen Fairfax and Joyce Dovey were denied by their male interpreters, while the 'heavenly speeches' of the Throckmorton children were accepted only at the end of their affliction, when the Holy Spirit was working to free them from the devil's grip. Moreover, the logic of possession dictated that its victims would eventually be restored to health through the ministry of godly men, who thereby asserted their own authority over religious affairs. This was, perhaps, one of the factors which encouraged zealous protestants to accept the existence of demonic possession and the practice of exorcism. This strange subject is considered in detail in the next chapter.

6

POSSESSION AND EXORCISM

THE IDEA OF POSSESSION

In April 1593 Alice Samuel was hanged at Huntingdon assizes for sending devils into the bodies of five young girls. In the course of her trial for witchcraft, she had made a full confession of her crimes to the Bishop of Lincoln, which included a remarkable statement of the physical reality of demonic possession. Asked about the unclean spirits that she had visited on the girls, Samuel asserted that they had departed from her victims and gone into her own body instead: they had 'now come into her, and are now in the bottom of her belly, and make her so full that she is like to burst'. Reinforcing the point, she claimed that the demons inside her 'caused her to be so full that she could scant lace her coat, and that on the way as she came [to be questioned], they weighed so heavy that the horse she rid on did fall down and was not able to carry her'.[1] Despite the bizarre details of Samuel's confession, her understanding of possession in these grossly physical terms cannot be regarded as isolated or eccentric. Other accounts suggest that the phenomenon was often perceived in this way, with the invading spirit viewed as a kind of bodily parasite. During the possession of Edward Dinham of Somerset in 1621, witnesses described something 'beate up and downe in his stomacke and belly'.[2] Jane Slade, one of the patients of Richard Napier in 1635, claimed to feel 'something stir in her body with a rising up & downe'. She suspected that the creature had been sent to torment her by her neighbours. In the same year, another of Napier's patients was 'conceited that there is something within [him], which came into him on Whitsun's eve in the night'.[3] The physical location of the possessing demon was sometimes revealed when it spoke from the body of its victim. According to Stanley Gower in 1651, the spirit possessing a man in Nottingham was heard 'with an audible voice in him, which seemed somtimes to be heard out of his belly, somtimes out of his throat, and somtimes out of his mouth, his lips not moving'.[4] Less dramatically, it was commonly claimed that possessed men and women spoke without moving their lips, with the words issuing from the upper part of their body or the back of their throat.

111

The intensely physical nature of possession was underlined by accounts of how unclean spirits invaded their hosts. In some instances, they were ingested directly into their victim's bodies. In a highly publicised case from Lancashire in 1596, Edmund Hartley was accused of breathing demons into the mouths of five children and two housemaids when he kissed them. It appears that this crude procedure was essential for the possessions to succeed, since Hartley failed to infect one of his intended victims, Joan Smith, when she avoided his attempts to kiss her.[5] A similar technique was described in Leicestershire in 1618, when a witness at a witch trial described how a 'spirit' had been blown into her mouth.[6] The belief that a demon needed to be in close proximity to its potential host meant that observers at exorcisms sometimes perceived themselves to be in danger. During the dispossession of Thomas Darling of Burton in 1597, for example, some of the spectators were alarmed when one of the demons inside the boy threatened to 'enter into some of these here'. The concrete reality of unclean spirits was further emphasised when the victims of possession claimed to have actually seen the creatures as they entered or departed from their bodies. Thus Darling attested that a devil had come out of his mouth in the shape of a mouse. His claim was apparently confirmed by some of the witnesses at his exorcism.[7] A similar belief was expressed by the accused witch, Margaret Mixter, who claimed that Satan 'came like a mowse' to possess her in 1645. She thanked her examiners for forcing the foul creature out of her body.[8]

It is difficult, of course, to take these accounts at face value. The confessions of Alice Samuel and Margaret Mixter were produced under extreme psychological pressure, and most printed narratives of possessions were probably embellished by their authors, who normally had good political or commercial reasons for doing so. This tendency was particularly marked in the late sixteenth and early seventeenth centuries, when the practice of exorcism provoked sharp controversy within the established church. As a result, the original circumstances of many alleged cases of possession will always remain elusive. But despite these problems, it appears that contemporary accounts reflected a fairly consistent set of assumptions about the phenomenon. Both sceptics and believers acknowledged that possession involved the physical manifestation of the devil in the victim's body, though they disagreed about the genuineness of the symptoms in specific cases. Similarly, popular accounts tended to emphasise the corporeal presence of the devil or demons in the body of the afflicted person. These physical symptoms, it seems, were part of a widely accepted set of beliefs about possession in early modern England.

This prompts some intriguing questions about the impact of the Reformation. It was argued in Chapter Four that many late medieval ideas about the devil survived throughout the sixteenth and seventeenth centuries, though they often challenged the beliefs of the minority of devout protestants. The grossly physical concept of possession sketched out above appears to fit into this pattern. In the context of early modern Germany, Lyndal Roper has recently argued that protestants were more sceptical about demonic possession than their catholic counterparts. For Roper, this scepticism was based ultimately on their rejection of the link between spirituality and physical objects. She notes that the reformers 'denied that divine forces could be captured in the physical, whether representations of saints or saint's relics, or even, as the radical Zwinglian position had it, in the host itself. The holy could not therefore be manifest in parts of the human body, a theological position which widened the gulf between things of the divine world and matters of the flesh'. This outlook inclined protestant divines to be sceptical about demonic possession; they were generally reluctant to perform exorcisms and keen to denounce their popish rivals for doing so.[9] It would be tempting to apply Roper's argument to the godly 'professors' described in this book. Given their view of the devil as an immaterial, spiritual force, it would have been entirely appropriate for English protestants to eschew the belief that Satan could occupy the physical bodies of men and women. Moreover, the notion that the evil one could manifest himself in the bodies of particular individuals tended to undermine the idea that all people were by nature 'slaves of Satan'. It is surprising, therefore, to discover that zealous protestants were the most active supporters of the concept of possession in England. Indeed, godly pastors played a prominent role in many of the cases described above.[10] By the early years of the seventeenth century, the practice of exorcism was associated strongly with the most 'godly' members of the English clergy, and it was the more conservative elements in the church hierarchy who challenged the practice, and were sometimes accused of popery for doing so.[11]

How can this be explained? The answer, I think, is that the idea of demonic possession is a particularly good example of the mixing together of protestantism and popular beliefs already described in Chapter Four. In this case, it appears that godly protestants deliberately appropriated traditional ideas about possession, despite the apparent contradictions that this involved. As Jim Sharpe has suggested, there was 'a widespread cultural dispersion of notions of possession' in early modern England. Although much of the surviving evidence comes from godly sources, it seems that both devout protestants and their less zealous neighbours accepted the basic conventions surrounding the condition.[12] These conventions, and the social context in which they were understood, will be explored in the first part of this chapter. The second part will argue that the godly community endorsed the idea of possession for two main reasons. First, the practice of godly religion made its adherents, and those living under their influence, particularly susceptible to the affliction. This made it very difficult for godly pastors to dismiss the phenomenon. Secondly, the performance of exorcisms provided zealous ministers with a remarkably effective platform for promoting their political and religious objectives. It was primarily for this reason, rather than any theological objections to the concept of possession, that the church hierarchy sought to suppress the practice of exorcism in the early seventeenth century.

The Symptoms

Historians have often noted the strongly theatrical elements found in many cases of demonic possession. Apart from the obvious trappings of the stage, such as the presence of large audiences at some of the most famous incidents, it seems that both the possessed and their spiritual doctors were acting out socially determined roles. These roles, which they performed either consciously or unconsciously, had the effect of confirming the legitimacy of the victim's affliction. In the earliest stages of the drama, both sides relied on a standard repertoire of symptoms and responses, and the behaviour of either party could determine the eventual diagnosis. It appears that the assumptions of those around a potential victim could shape their perception of their own condition, causing them to accept it as a 'natural' illness, a religious experience, or a true case of demonic possession. In the 1620s John Hall, a physician from Stratford-upon-Avon, treated a woman who had fallen suddenly into 'a grievous delerium' and 'was most angry with those that formerly she most loved, yet her talk was very religious'. Though her condition displayed some of the typical signs of possession, Hall regarded it as a physical malady. As a result of the doctor's attentions, 'she was happily cured' in the space of a few days.[13] In other cases, the initial assumption that patients were suffering from 'natural' disorders was revised when their symptoms grew worse or they failed to respond to medical treatments. Both Thomas Darling and the Throckmorton children were diagnosed with physical ailments before the supernatural cause of their suffering was identified. Even when patients were convinced that they were possessed, the true nature of the invading spirit was sometimes unclear, and the behaviour of those around them could determine whether they believed themselves to be divinely inspired or possessed by the devil. As we saw in the previous chapter, both Helen Fairfax and Joyce Dovey were persuaded by others that they were the victims of demonic possession, despite their initial conviction that they were inspired by God.

Once a case of possession was recognised, the repertoire of symptoms was remarkably consistent. The patient, or 'demoniac', almost always showed physical signs of the devil's presence, often in the form of swellings around the throat. Thus Catherine Wright was so afflicted in 1586 that 'her body and necke were swollen twice as big as they were wont to be'.[14] Thirty years later, a possessed woman from Worcestershire had 'something arising big in her throat'.[15] In some cases, like those of Alice Samuel and the patients of Richard Napier, it was also claimed that these swellings could move around the body. In 1599 the godly exorcist John Darrel insisted that this symptom was displayed by William Sommers, who was 'seene to have a certaine variable swelling or lump . . . swiftly runing up and downe betweene the flesh and skinne'.[16] The appearance of swellings was often accompanied by grotesque bodily contortions. Thomas Darling, another of Darrel's subjects, bowed his body so violently that his stomach was raised above his head, and the possessed victims of Edmund Hartley in Lancashire were tormented with many 'strange and sore fits'.[17] A chapbook from 1641 reported that a possessed woman from Durham 'was shaken with such force that the bed and the chamber did shake and move', causing her family to hold 'her downe violently in her bed'.[18] In numerous other cases, victims of possession appeared to be thrown against walls or down onto the floor.[19]

As well as their physical symptoms, the behaviour of demoniacs was highly stereotyped. They almost always communicated or received visions in a state of trance or 'bewitchment', in which many of their normal faculties were suspended. In 1621 the daughter of Edward Fairfax 'sunk down in a deadly trance' before witnessing a parade of bizarre apparitions. She described what she had seen only when she 'came to herself'.[20] Similarly, a chapbook account of the possession of Anne Styles of Salisbury in 1653 described her as 'lying in trances' for most of the ordeal.[21] In several cases, this enchanted state allowed the possessing spirit to take control of its host. Again, the conventions surrounding this process were strikingly consistent. When the devil spoke through its human vessel, its voice was characterised by its difference from the victim's normal tones, and often described as uncommonly deep or shrill. The voice of the devil in Edward Dinham in 1621 was 'deadly and hollow', while the spirit possessing Joyce Dovey in 1647 had 'a bigger and grosser tone than her ordinary speech'.[22] In cases of child possession, the voice was usually larger and more adult than that possessed by its host. The alien nature of the speech was sometimes emphasised by claims that it issued from unusual places in the body, or occurred without the subject moving their lips.

The actions attributed to possessing spirits also conformed to certain familar types. When a demon spoke or acted through the body of its host, it normally expressed a repugnance of religion and a delight in blasphemy. This was often directed at particular forms of pious behaviour, such as churchgoing or prayer, or religious texts like the Bible. A fairly typical account of the irreverent conduct of a possessed child was presented in *The Most Strange and Admirable Discoverie of the Three Witches of Warboys* (1593), which recounted the behaviour of Elizabeth Throckmorton:

> She was very quiet and well until motion was made of prayers, all which time it seemed as though it would have rent her in pieces, with such screeching and outcries and vehement sneezing as that it terrified the whole company; but prayers being ended she was quieted, but still in her fit. Then Master Pickering, and others that were acqainted with the manner of it, said that if any should read the Bible or any other godly book before her, it would rage as before so long as they read; but because it was a thing very strange and therefore hardly believed, one did take a Bible and read the first chapter of Saint John, the first verse. At the hearing whereof she was as one besides her mind; when he that read held his peace she was quiet.[23]

In this instance, it seems that the actions of the possessed girl and those around her had settled into a familiar pattern, with both sides feeding off the responses of the other. The reading of the verse from St John's gospel, which had been used as a protection against evil spirits since the late Middle Ages, also suggests that they were drawing on popular traditions about the devil. A similar pattern was evident in the behaviour of William Sommers and the observers of his possession, who repeatedly read him the Lord's Prayer, which he interrupted at the line 'Lead us not into temptation'.[24] In 1621 Edward Dinham was thrown into a fit of convulsions and blasphemy when he was handed a prayer book.[25] Likewise, Joyce Dovey cast a Bible into a fire in 1647, though witnesses claimed that it was miraculously preserved.[26]

As these illustrations suggest, the drama of possession depended on the interplay between demoniacs and those around them, with both sides exploiting a traditional repertoire of beliefs and actions. This was exemplified by the 'dumb show' performed by William Sommers in 1597, in which the possessed man appeared to mime a catalogue of sins in front of the audience gathered for his exorcism. The idea that demons mimicked human vices was a commonplace in late medieval religion: it was expressed in depictions of hell and printed guides to the art of dying, such as the fifteenth-century *Ars Moriendi*, which presented the sickroom of a dying man as a stage for devils acting out the seven deadly sins.[27] The persistence of this idea was acknowledged in 1641 by the pastor Richard Carpenter, who noted that 'many teach that the devils in hell shall mock the troubled imagination of the damned person with the counterfeit imitation of his sinnes'.[28] It was in the context of these beliefs that Sommers' extraordinary performance made sense to his audience, who perceived his gestures as representations of various criminal and ungodly acts. As his exorcist later recalled, the precise interpretation of these gestures was determined by the crowd as a whole: 'no one man especially, but many confusedly did interpret the dumb show'.[29] A similar process of interpretation was probably at work in those cases in which demoniacs appeared to speak in foreign languages. It was widely assumed that the ability to speak in a foreign tongue, unknown to the afflicted person, was a sign of possession. This belief sometimes caused observers to interpret the utterances of demoniacs as imperfect pronunciations of foreign words. In 1621, for example, those present at the possession of Edward Dinham believed they heard the spirit inside him cry out the Latin word 'laudes', or 'praise', though the context of Dinham's speech suggests that he actually said 'ladies'.[30] In this case, it appears that the reaction of the witnesses was at least as important as the behaviour of the possessed man in establishing the symptoms of his condition.

Just as the symptoms of possession conformed to certain recognised types, the cause of the affliction was understood in highly conventional terms. In most cases, the victims attributed their sufferings to another person, who had bewitched them or sent demons into their body. Sometimes, as in the case of the Fairfax children, this information was obtained through visions induced by the bewitchment itself; in other instances, it was apparently revealed by the possessing spirits.[31] The subjects treated by John Darrel in the late sixteenth century usually described meetings with sinister strangers that preceded their afflictions. Thomas Darling had encountered an aged woman in a wood, who cursed him before he succumbed to the first of his fits. He later identified Alice Gooderidge, who was tried and convicted for witchcraft.[32] Likewise, William Sommers was accosted at a coalpit by 'an old woman (as he thought), who asked where he dwelt, and wither he was going'. She demanded money and forced him to eat a piece of bread, which apparently conveyed a demon into his body.[33] In the case of the Throckmorton and Fairfax children, the possessed were tormented with visions of the witches responsible for their sufferings, together with the familiar spirits they employed. Once a suspect was identified, meetings between them and their alleged victim usually agitated the symptoms of bewitchment, sometimes inducing spasms or hallucinations. The strong connection between witches and their victims was underlined in those cases, such as that of Alice Samuel and the Throckmorton children, in which the symptoms of possession were only relieved once the supposed perpetrator had been punished.

The stereotypical nature of possession was demonstrated most clearly in cases of fraud. It appears that those individuals who confessed to faking bewitchment were exploiting a ready-made and widely recognised set of behaviours. In several cases, their deceptions were only uncovered after they had convinced large numbers that their afflictions were genuine. Sometimes, as in the case of Thomas Darling and William Sommers, allegations of fraud were strongly contested even after the demoniacs had apparently admitted to fabrication. This does not mean that the men and women who believed in these 'possessions' were unusually credulous: they were simply accepting the symptoms of a condition that was widely accepted as real, and that went completely unchallenged in many other instances. An early example of counterfeit possession occurred in London in 1574, when two young girls, Rachel Pinder and Agnes Briggs, confessed to Archbishop Parker that they had simulated the condition. Pinder's performance as a demoniac involved a faithful imitation of all the major symptoms. When the devil spoke through her body, her 'lypps moved with no suche moving as coulde pronounce the words uttered, the eyelids moved, but nott oppen, she had greate swellinge in hur throte, and abowte the jawes, and the voyse was somwhat bygger than the child's voice'. Likewise, Briggs 'disfigured herselfe with divers straunge countenaunces, faigning divers straunge voyces and noyses'. Both girls attributed their affliction to a witch, Joan Thornton, though they were unable to provide her address.[34] Fifty years later, Katherine Malpas from West Ham admitted the fabrication of identical symptoms. Among other signs of her affliction, she had a 'rising up in her stomach to the bignes of a halfe penny loafe', and she cast aside bibles and prayer books when they were handed to her. Before she admitted her deception, she accused two of her neighbours of sending spirits into her body.[35] The main interest of these cases is not that they prove the existence of fraudulent possessions, but that the false demoniacs knew exactly what was expected of them in order for their conditions to be accepted. They were deliberately acting out a socially sanctioned role which, in other cases, was probably performed sincerely by the victims of 'genuine' possession.

The Social Functions of Possession

According to the indictment against them, the family of the fake demoniac Katherine Malpas had instigated her fraud for financial gain: they had hoped to attract charity from people moved by her pretended distress. In most other cases of possession, however, the behaviour of the alleged victims is much harder to explain. The undoubted existence of fraud, and the observation that possession involved the acting out of socially constructed roles, does not mean that all demoniacs can be dismissed as counterfeits. As Clarke Garrett has argued in the context of divine inspiration, 'to say that the possessed are performing culturally determined roles is not to say that they are faking – at least not often. There are too many accounts from too many cultures which insist that the experience of divine possession is real, overwhelming, and unforgettable for those who undergo it'.[36] It appears that the best way to explain the actions of early modern demoniacs is to explore the social functions of the performance in which they were engaged. In some instances, the drama of possession probably offered an explanation for physical symptoms which might, in different contexts, have been diagnosed in medical terms. For victims of the 'falling sickness', or epilepsy, the notion of possession offered one option for understanding and controlling a condition that was notoriously difficult to treat. In 1691, Richard Baxter recorded the case of Nathan Crab, a possessed youth from Exeter, who was apparently diagnosed with the falling sickness for over a year before anyone suspected that his illness might have a supernatural origin.[37] As well as explaining physical ailments, the idea of possession offered a framework for interpreting certain types of mental disturbance. Roy Porter has suggested that the diagnosis of possession in early modern Europe allowed some individuals, including those who suffered the symptoms of conditions later understood as forms of 'neurosis' or 'schizophrenia', to make sense of their experiences and obtain support from religious authorities, who fulfilled a role similar to the psychiatric profession in the nineteenth and twentieth centuries. In some cases, like that of the German demoniac Christoph Haitzmann, their treatment at the hands of the exorcists produced 'cures' at least as successful as those achieved by later psychiatric techniques.[38]

As well as providing a context for the understanding and treatment of illness, the role-play involved in possession conferred authority on its supposed victims. As the main players in a spectacular and engrossing drama, they were provided with a large, attentive audience, which often included leading figures from the local clergy and magistracy. Their words were treated with uncommon respect, and those spoken at the behest of possessing spirits were also expressed with complete impunity. For these reasons, the experience of possession provided an occasion for relatively disempowered individuals to address their social betters from a position of lofty, if precarious authority. It is hardly surprising, therefore, that women and young people appear to have been particularly susceptible to the condition. The two London girls who feigned possession in 1574 were able briefly to reverse conventional hierarchies of gender, age and social rank. Speaking through the voice of Satan, they asserted their great power and demanded gifts from their elders and social superiors; they compelled the adults around them to listen seriously to fantastical tales of witchcraft, complete with bizarre details about the antics of familiar spirits. At one stage, they commanded the attention of some of the city's most respected ministers, including the celebrated martyrologist and preacher John Foxe, whom Rachel Pinder threatened to 'tear in pieces'.[39] A similar role reversal was effected during the possession of the Throckmorton children in 1592. In this case, which was generally accepted as genuine by contemporaries, the entranced children abused and commanded the adults in the household and successfully accused a local woman and her daughter of causing their affliction. They subjected the women to a series of interrogations, in which they addressed them with 'hard words' and gestures quite inappropriate for their age.[40]

By providing an outlet for 'satanic' behaviour, the experience of possession allowed its victims to articulate thoughts and desires which were otherwise socially unacceptable. Indeed, the expression of these sentiments was not only safe, but actually reinforced their forbidden nature, since they were attributed to demonic beings which were believed to be utterly opposed to true religion and morality. Demoniacs were thus allowed to 'speak the unspeakable'. As Jim Sharpe has noted, the words ascribed to possessing spirits contained surprisingly few intimations of sexual desire, though certain communications described as 'immodest' or 'indecent' might have contained sexual elements.[41] This was possibly the case with William Sommers, whose speech was 'many times filthy and uncleane, [and] very unfit to be named', and whose gestures included a simulation of 'whoredom'. In a small number of cases, it appears that possessed individuals also took the opportunity to express economic grievances: Sommers, for instance, referred repeatedly to 'the unsatiable desire of gaine, or raising the price of corne in corne men'.[42] Much more common, however, were blasphemous or irreligious statements. Demoniacs commonly expressed contempt for Christian texts and doctrines, and asserted the overwhelming power of Satan. When the devil took possession of a man in Berwick in 1645, he declared that his hold on his victim's soul was so great that he could never be saved by Christ; he mocked the attempts of the godly exorcist, Robert Balsom, to lead prayers for the man's salvation, and promised that 'I will never give over blaspheming so long as thou stayest in the roome.'[43] Occasionally, possessed individuals expressed heterodox or sceptical religious opinions. In 1573, for example, Alexander Nynde

The exorcism of William Sommers in 1598, from the 1641 edition of John Darrel's *True Relation of the Grievous Handling of William Sommers of Nottingham, Being Possessed with a Devill.*

declared that Satan was a 'disciple' of God.[44] More boldly, William Sommers asserted that 'there is no God' in 1598, and three years later a possessed maid from Hockham in Norfolk announced that 'God is a good man and I can do as much as he.'[45] Though it is impossible to trace the development of these beliefs in the individuals who expressed them, it is reasonable to assume that the 'voice of Satan' provided possessed men and women with an outlet for their religious anxieties and doubts. Similarly, exorcisms offered a public opportunity to overcome these anxieties and affirm the saving power of God.

POSSESSION AND GODLY RELIGION

The fake possession of Rachel Pinder and Agnes Briggs in 1574 led to the mockery of those who had been deceived by the children's antics. In particular, the printed account of the case singled out those members of the London clergy who 'had the matter in handling, being, as they professed themselves, godly men, plentifully adorned with fayth, and sent of God to disturbe the devill'.[46] The association between godly protestants and possession has already been noted in Chapter One. Following the trial of John Darrel in 1599, the church hierarchy placed new restrictions on the practice of exorcism, which obliged clergy to obtain licences before attempting 'by fasting and prayer to cast out any devil'.[47] Despite this, the practice was endorsed by many puritan pastors in the decades before the Civil War, and became common in the 1640s and 1650s. The acceptance of demonic possession by zealous protestants can be explained by two factors, which will be considered in detail in the rest of this chapter. First, the beliefs and experiences related to the concept can be viewed as natural extensions of the godly style of religion, with its intense focus on the need to confront Satan in one's body and mind. In many ways, the godly attitudes towards the devil described in the first half of this book predisposed those who accepted them to take possession seriously, and encouraged psychological experiences which could be easily perceived as its symptoms. Second, the practice of exorcism presented zealous pastors with an extraordinary opportunity to assert their authority, to consolidate the community of 'God's people', and to educate the public at large. It was never likely that they would allow this opportunity to slip, despite the theological compromises it required them to make.

Temptation and Possession

For Robert Burton, the pioneering English psychologist, demonic possession was one of many forms of 'religious melancholy' inspired by the 'thundering ministers' of the early seventeenth century. Burton suggested that over-zealous protestantism encouraged a morbid obsession with sin and damnation, which could lead to visions of hell and imaginary encounters with the devil himself. The doctor's position was hardly surprising: he developed his theories at a time when his prospective patron, James I, was determined to rein in the excesses of 'over-hot' ministers in the English church, and his claim that religious fanaticism was a source of mental illness was broadly consistent with government policy. Nonetheless, Burton's suggestion that possession experiences were linked to protestant zeal was probably correct. The most obvious connection was the belief, advanced by godly pastors like Robert Bolton, that Satan could implant impure thoughts directly into the minds of normally pious men and women. Such satanic cognitions were reported by earnest protestants throughout the seventeenth century. In Burton's view, this belief was a delusion akin to the idea of possession itself: he noted that some sufferers of religious melancholy believed that the devil 'is within them, as they thinke, and there speakes and talkes as to such as are possessed'.[48] Following Burton's lead, it seems reasonable to view the 'demonic' thoughts which assailed godly protestants as a kind of possession experience. This is certainly how they were described by those who received them: Hannah Allen referred to satanic 'injections into my mind', while Bunyan claimed that the devil's ideas were 'cast into' him.[49]

As we saw in Chapter Three, the notion that the devil could intervene directly in a person's mind was only the most dramatic example of the godly assumption that Satan was responsible for impious thoughts and feelings. Such direct interventions were normally unnecessary, since human nature was already inclined to serve the devil.[50] The struggle to overcome one's own sinful desires represented a daily conflict with the evil one. As John Woolton noted in 1576, God's children were engaged in 'a greevous and dayly battell which is never ended before the daye of death, for . . . the devyll rusheth upon us with great vehemency, and undermyneth us with a thousand temptations'.[51] In this sense, the practice of protestantism was a kind of ongoing personal exorcism. This idea was reflected in the Book of Common Prayer, which abolished the catholic rite of exorcism in the service of baptism: instead, the reformed ritual simply required the godparents to renounce Satan on the child's behalf, until the infant 'come of age and take it upon himself'.[52] According to John Milton in 1641, the act of baptismal exorcism was an example of the 'frippery and ostentation' which characterised the Roman church, and had been swept away by the 'bright and blissful Reformation'.[53] In practice, the commitment of devout protestants to renounce Satan throughout their adult lives placed them in a role similar to that of an exorcist. Indeed, the methods they used to overcome their personal temptations, such as prayer, fasting and meditation on the scriptures, were often identical to those described in accounts of godly dispossessions.

The similarity between possession and exorcism and the more conventional piety of zealous protestants was particularly striking in the case of Hannah Allen. Allen never believed herself to be possessed, but the experiences she recorded in her journal in the early 1660s were very similar. In April 1664 she was so assailed by temptations that she felt a 'woful confusion and combating in my soul'; on another occasion, she told her aunt that 'I am just as if two were fighting within me, but I trust the devil will never be able to overcome me.' From her childhood, she suffered from 'horrible' thoughts, which seemed to be 'cast in' her mind against her will. These included the urge to hate God and to blaspheme against Him. These symptoms, which echoed the experiences of earlier demoniacs such as Edward Dinham and the Throckmorton children, were taken by Allen as signs of her constant struggle to overcome the devil, and this interpretation was reflected in the title of her autobiography, *Satan, His Methods and Malice Baffled*. She managed to 'baffle' the devil through a daily round of prayer and Bible-reading, diligently assisted by members of her family and a number of godly pastors. In sum, Allen's whole religious life resembled a series of exorcisms, though the incursions the devil made against her were never so great that he succeeded in completely taking over her body.[54]

In some cases of fully-fledged possession, the similarities between the phenomenon and the conventions of godly religion were equally marked. In 1596, the demoniac Thomas Darling sought relief from his condition by reading the Bible and offering prayers to God, which were joined by the crowd witnessing his affliction. He also embarked on lengthy dialogues with the demon possessing his body, in which he appeared to draw strength from the scriptural account of Christ's temptation by Satan. At the climax of one such exchange, he rebuked the devil by asserting that 'I care not for all that thou canst do unto me: in the Lord is my trust, who will deliver mee when his good pleasure is.'[55] One of the spectators at Darlings's possession, Jesses Bee, later described these spiritual 'combats' as exemplars of the power of faith and scripture to overcome the fiend, and noted their salutary effect on those who saw them. Darling's own protestant zeal was expressed during his dispossession, when he voiced his desire to become a godly preacher if he survived the ordeal. Six years later, he was sentenced to lose his ears for libelling John Howson, the aggressively anti-puritan vice-chancellor of Oxford University.[56]

The similarity between possession and the everyday struggle of the godly against Satan was also evident in the two accounts of successful exorcisms in Samuel Clarke's *Generall Martyrologie* (1651). In the first, which involved a 'godly man' from Berwick around 1646, the possession was directly preceded by a period of mental 'affliction', in which he was 'much weakened and worn out by the violence of temptation'. Once it was established that he was possessed, the dialogue which ensued between the unclean spirit and the exorcist, Robert Balsom, covered topics familiar from godly literature and sermons. At one point, the devil announced that his victim was so consumed with sin that he could never be saved, allowing Balsom to offer the standard reply that 'the blood of Jesus Christ cleanseth us from all sin'. The whole confrontation recalled John Gerard's guide to the protestant deathbed, *The Conquest of Temptations* (1621), and Thomas Becon's sixteenth-century book *The Christian Knight*, an imaginary dialogue between a godly man and Satan, which was intended to fortify its readers in their daily struggle against temptation. Clarke's second account followed a similar pattern. The exchanges between the devil and the exorcist, Richard Rothwel, echoed the language and sentiments often expressed in godly meditations and prayers. Tellingly, Rothwel likened the plight of the possessed man to his own struggles to overcome the evil one. Speaking directly to the possessing spirit, he declared that 'thou hast oft beguiled me, [but] I hope God will in time give me wisdom to discern, and power to withstand thy delusions; and he it is that hath delivered me out of thy hands, and will I doubt not also deliver this poor man'.[57] In both cases, it appears that the spirits inside the demoniacs' bodies were similar to the 'devil in the mind' described by godly autobiographers. They interrupted prayers and disturbed attempts to read the Bible, they raised objections to points of protestant doctrine, and they blasphemed against God. The main difference was that godly Christians normally internalised their struggle with Satan. The demoniacs described in Clarke's book succumbed completely to the devil's power, so that their exorcists played the role of the Christian conscience struggling to overcome him.

As well as providing a religious context in which individuals could easily make sense of demonic possession, godly religion created social circumstances in which the affliction was likely to occur. This came about in two different ways. First, the community of godly 'professors' was generally receptive to the idea of possession itself, a factor which was important since the condition depended largely on the behaviour of those around its supposed victims. It is likely that networks of devout protestants, who shared an intense awareness of the devil's presence in the world, provided an ideal audience for potential demoniacs. In some cases, it seems that the initial diagnosis of possession came from a zealous minister. When Robert Balsom was called to treat the man 'afflicted with temptation' in Berwick, he tried first to counsel him with comforting words from the scriptures. This approach appeared to work, but the man fell back into mental anguish within a couple of days. The pastor returned, and again tried to comfort the man with the promise of God's free grace to all faithful Christians. When this failed to relieve his distress, Balsom tried a different tack:

Perceiving that no words of comfort would fasten on him, he whispered to him in his eare to this purpose: 'I doubt there is something within, that you should do well to discover.' Whereupon immediately the man's tongue swelled out of his mouth, insomuch that he was not able to speak. Master Balsom continued speaking to him, till at length, to the astonishment of those in the roome, being many, and some of them persons of quality, a shrill voyce was heard, as from out of his throat (having not any use of his tongue) to this purpose: 'What dost thou talking to him of promises, and free grace? He is mine.' Master Balsom, apprehending it to be the voice of the devill, replyed: 'No Satan, thou dost not know any man to be thine while there is life in him.'

In this dramatic instance, it appears that the minister's suggestion that the man might be possessed was the catalyst for the definitive symptoms of the condition. As soon as these symptoms appeared, Balsom confirmed the diagnosis by acknowledging the devil's presence in the victim's body.[58] Similarly, Joyce Tovey only displayed the signs of possession in 1647 after she had been examined by a godly pastor, who 'strongly imagined' that her fits were caused by the devil.[59] Once the condition was identified, members of the godly community provided a supportive audience for the drama of possession. During the affliction of Alexander Nynde in 1573, a crowd of 'twenty persons and more fell downe and saide the Lord's prayer' to assist in his exorcism.[60] Some thirty years later, the possession of a young boy from Northwich in Cheshire attracted godly pastors and layfolk from across the region, who participated in a series of fasts and prayers for the boy's deliverance.[61] It is reasonable to assume that such gatherings, which were typical at godly exorcisms throughout the period, provided a social environment in which the phenomenon of possession was likely to flourish.

The second way in which zealous protestantism created a social context conducive to possession experiences was very different. In recent years, historians such as Anthony Fletcher and Lyndal Roper have drawn attention to the impact of reformed religion on family life. They have argued that many protestant households adopted new standards of religious discipline during the sixteenth century, with fathers assuming some of the responsibilities for spiritual instruction previously undertaken by priests. Since godly protestantism relied heavily on education, devout parents were obliged to provide an appropriate regime of theological and moral instruction for their children and servants.[62] The conduct books of the seventeenth century suggest that these regimes were often repressive: Richard Baxter was typical in warning the heads of households to keep their charges from 'cards, dice and stage plays, play books and love books, and foolish wanton tales and ballads'.[63] In the context of these restrictions, the drama of possession provided a drastic but socially acceptable outlet for youthful rebellion. Jim Sharpe has suggested that this helps to explain the possession experiences of adolescents in godly households, such as the Starkeys and the Throckmortons in the 1590s, which were characterised by a violent rejection of the religious values of the adults around them.[64] In a slightly different context, the antics of possessed youths like Thomas Darling, William Sommers and Thomas Harrison of Northwich can be viewed as rebellions against the spiritual values promoted by the godly pastors in their communities. If this interpretation is correct, the demands of zealous protestantism created some of the psychological pressures which gave rise to possession experiences, while the godly community itself provided a supportive context in which these experiences could be acted out.

Possession, Religious Ecstasy and the Deathbed

The links between possession and zealous protestantism can be illustrated further by a brief discussion of two related phenomena: the behaviour of godly Christians on their deathbeds, and the experience of religious ecstasy or 'inspiration'. In both situations, devout men and women displayed symptoms similar to those manifested by demoniacs, but their actions were understood differently by those around them. They were acting out socially sanctioned alternatives to possession, with a different set of rules and expectations governing their performances. During their deathbed struggles with Satan, godly protestants often entered a trance-like state, and spoke 'idle' and incoherent words in the manner of demoniacs. Once the conflict began, however, they assumed for themselves the role of the exorcist.[65] Like godly dispossessions, their actions were witnessed by large gatherings of sympathetic observers, who identified with the symbolic struggle and offered prayers to support them. These audiences also played a crucial role in the interpretation of events, ensuring that they were placed within the framework of conventional ideas about a 'good death'. The witnesses at Katherine Brettergh's bedside, for instance, noticed that she was 'once or twice troubled with vaine speeches', but ignored them because they 'saw that these things proceeded of weaknes, emptines of her head, and want of sleepe'.[66] Such observations suggest that the actions of dying protestants, like those of demoniacs, were interpreted selectively, according to a repertoire of conventional assumptions. The parallels between the two conditions are revealing, and indicate that they performed a similar function within the godly community: they both dramatised the conflict between Christians and the devil, and offered a public demonstration of the ultimate triumph of Christ.

Other spiritual phenomena described by godly protestants were also reminiscent of possession. In 1653 John Rogers recalled a remarkable 'judgement of God' from his youth, which he likened explicitly to a possession experience:

About 1637 . . . at Messing in Essex, I was playing with children (my fittest companions then) . . . [when] I threw out vain words, and crying 'O Lord!' (which we were not suffered to do), my heart was suddenly smitten upon it, and I was suddenly set a running as if I had been possessed (by I know not what power or spirit), not having any strength to stay myself . . . untill I was headlong carried through a little gateway, where (as plainly to my thinking and in my appearance as ever I saw anything by the sunshine) there was set a naked sword, glistering with a fearfull edge . . . I ghastly screeched, and yet had not the least power to stay or stop my precipitant course.

Rogers claimed that he passed through the terrible blade and thought himself to be dead; but when he recovered his wits, he found that the sword had vanished and he was completely unhurt. He interpreted the episode as a warning from God against his breach of the third commandment, but acknowledged its affinities to the experiences of demoniacs. By admitting that he knew 'not what power or spirit' had taken over his body, he even left open the possibility that Satan, rather than the Holy Spirit, had been the immediate cause of his affliction.[67]

While Rogers' enchantment could be explained as a divine judgement, another possession-like experience was more problematical. This was the state of 'rapture', or spiritual ecstasy, in which a person's body was apparently overwhelmed by the Holy Spirit. As we saw in the previous chapter, godly pastors were generally sceptical about the phenomenon; but it seems to have occurred quite frequently among devout protestants, possibly because of their strong emphasis on the personal experience of God's grace. Thomas Darling received spiritual ecstasies as well as demonic temptations during his possession in 1596.[68] During a period of illness in Newcastle in the 1630s, Jane Turner felt herself to be 'in a continual converse and exchanging love with God, as it were lodging and living in the bosome of Christ'.[69] In the decade that followed, ecstatic experiences of this kind were common among the members of religious sects, and later emerged as one of the defining features of the Quaker movement. The practice was always controversial, and provoked allegations from critics that those who claimed to be 'inspired' were either charlatans or unwitting demoniacs. Richard Baxter, for instance, declared that Quakers were 'enthusiasticks that Satan hath notoriously deluded by pretended angelical revelation'.[70] Despite their polemical motives, critics like Baxter were probably correct to identify a connection between demonic possession and 'inspiration'. The symptoms of the two conditions were similar, with inspired men and women experiencing involuntary spasms, seeing visions, and sometimes speaking in unfamiliar voices or foreign languages. Thus the prophetess Sara Wright 'spoke as with a new tongue' in 1647; and John Robbins, the leader of a small group of 'shakers' in 1651, proved the genuineness of his ecstasies by speaking in Hebrew, Latin and Greek.[71] In a small number of cases, the words that inspired individuals ascribed to the Holy Ghost resembled the utterances of demoniacs. Most notoriously, Abiezer Coppe was moved by the Spirit to blaspheme, declaring in 1649 that 'what goes for cursing and swearing' in those blessed by God 'is more glorious than praying and preaching in others'. He later suggested that his mystical experiences caused him to be 'infected' with a 'plague of swearing'.[72] The parallels between religious ecstasy and possession meant that the two conditions could be confused. In an arresting episode from Kendal in 1647, a Quaker convert, John Gilpin, was moved by the Spirit to 'a great rapture of joy'. He and his companions initially accepted this experience as genuine, but began to suspect that its source was diabolical rather than divine. After much uncertainty, Gilpin eventually concluded that he was a victim of possession, and attempted to exorcise the devil from his own body.[73]

As this incident suggests, the diagnosis of religious ecstasy was largely a matter of interpretation, and individuals susceptible to the condition could be perceived as victims of possession in different circumstances. It seems reasonable to assume that the willingness of godly pastors to accept the existence of demoniacs, and their general reluctance to acknowledge cases of divine inspiration, normally encouraged such individuals to act out the drama of possession in the period before the Civil War. Subsequently, the proliferation of religious sects in the 1640s created new opportunities for men and women to experience spiritual raptures, despite persistent allegations that they were really possessed by Satan. Throughout the reign of Elizabeth and the early Stuarts, protestant divines had good reason to favour the diagnosis of possession over that of inspiration: individuals touched by the Holy Ghost could command a spiritual authority to rival their own, whereas demoniacs were viewed as victims of the devil's malice, whose deliverance depended on their ministry. Broadly speaking, the professional concerns of the godly clergy inclined them to dismiss the phenomenon of inspiration while promoting its demonic alternative. Similar interests encouraged some pastors to take up the practice of exorcism, an activity which is considered below.

The Politics of Exorcism

The performance of a godly exorcism was viewed by many contemporaries as a form of religious education, akin to a particularly dramatic and instructive sermon. Like a sermon, a successful dispossession advertised the authority of the minister who performed it, and afforded an opportunity to instruct those present in the essentials of the protestant faith. Unlike many sermons, it was also likely to attract a large and attentive audience. The appeal of such demonstrations to godly pastors is best understood in the wider context of the English Reformation. The introduction of protestantism encouraged the emergence of the parish clergy as a professional class, whose university training increased both their social status and financial expectations. Paradoxically, the same process undermined their institutional position, since reformed doctrines stripped the church of the magical power of the mass, the control of holy relics, and the authority to offer help to the souls of the dead. As a result, many ministers came to identify themselves primarily as leaders of the Christian community, whose authority derived mainly from their knowledge of the Bible and fidelity to Christ. The performance of exorcisms was ideally suited to this role: it provided a vivid demonstration of their leadership among God's people, and confirmed the idea that the true church was a gathering of believers rather than a physical institution. These points have been noted by Stephen Greenblatt, who has observed that English exorcists made it clear that their practices 'did not depend upon a state-sponsored ecclesiastical hierarchy'.[74] Exorcists such as John Darrel stressed that their work depended more on their personal faith and knowledge of scripture than the institutional power of the church. As Darrel averred in 1597, his ability to cast out demons derived entirely from his faith in Christ, and did not imply that he possessed any 'speciall or greater gift . . . than the rest of my brethren'.[75] For godly ministers, exorcisms provided a perfect means of validating their authority and confirming their reputation as faithful servants of God.

This process was neatly illustrated by the lengthy dialogues which often took place between protestant exorcists and the devil. In 1593, George Gifford warned Christians not 'to talke and question' with Satan when he spoke through a possessed person, suggesting that they should only 'intreat the Lord to show mercy and to expell him'.[76] This advice was admirably consistent with protestant theology, but it appears to have been frequently ignored. The advantages of disputing with the fiend were demonstrated in Richard Rothwel's exorcism of the possessed man in Nottingham. The dialogue between Rothwel and the devil, speaking through his victim's body, took the form of a learned debate in which the pastor was able to overcome Satan through a combination of biblical expertise and personal faith. The devil 'quoted many scriptures out of the Old and New Testament, both in Hebrew and Greek, cavilled and played the critick, and backed his allegations with sayings out of the [church] fathers'. Happily, the exorcist 'was mightily enabled by God to detect the devil's sophistry', and so confounded the fiend that he forced him to surrender the man's body. At the end of the struggle, Satan candidly admitted that his cause was lost: 'What [chance] stand I talking with thee? All men know thou art Bold Rothwel, and fearest no body, nor carest for words. Therefore I will talke to thee no more.'

Gower reports that this incident secured the reputation of his friend, who was subsequently known among members of the godly community as 'he the Devil called Bold Rothwel'.[77]

As well as establishing the credentials of zealous ministers, cases of possession offered them opportunities to fulfil their role as religious teachers. Public exorcisms were a powerful weapon in the battle against popery. First, they allowed pastors to rebut the popish lies that the devil expounded through the mouths of demoniacs. In 1573, for instance, the demon possessing Alexander Nynde announced that it was good for Christians to offer prayers to St Mary, only to have these idolatrous words condemned by a godly exorcist. The falsehood of the spirit's claim was eventually proved when it was forced to depart from the man's body.[78] Secondly, successful exorcisms could be an effective tool in the campaign to win converts from the Roman church, especially in regions with large recusant communities. Thus John Darrel claimed in 1599 that some catholics in Lancashire had promised to 'forsake the church of Rome' if his dispossessions were genuine, since the ability to cast out devils was a sign of the 'true church of Christ'. Accordingly, he condemned those members of the ecclesiastical hierarchy who objected to his activities as 'secret friends of Rome'.[79] In this respect, godly exorcisms appear to have played a similar role to the deathbed struggles with Satan experienced by zealous protestants like Katherine Brettergh, which were used to validate their beliefs against the claims of the catholic church.

The use of exorcisms to attack popery was combined with efforts to promote the 'reformation of manners', the attempt to impose new standards of religious and moral behaviour on the laity. The words and actions attributed to people gripped by evil spirits often read like a list of the sins most trenchantly denounced by the godly clergy. Thus Darrel gave the following account of the actions of William Sommers in 1598:

> This evening he acted many sins by signs and gestures, most lively representing and shadowing them out unto us, as namely: brawling, quarrelling, fighting, swearing, robbing by the high wayes, picking and cutting of purses, burglary, whoredome, pride both in men and women, hypocrisie, sluggishnesse in hearing the Word, drunkennesse, gluttony, also dancing with the toyes thereto belonging, the manner of anticke dances, the games of dicing and carding, the abuse of the viole, and other instruments.[80]

It is hard to ignore the propaganda contained in this extraordinary performance, though one can only guess at the impact it made on its audience and the readers of Darrel's account. A similar catalogue of misdemeanours was recorded in the speeches of a possessed boy in the Cheshire town of Northwich, whose exorcism was witnessed by the puritan divine, Thomas Pierson, in 1603. According to Jacqueline Eales, the boy's words 'constituted a bizarre parody of the specific spiritual values that Pierson and his colleagues were trying to inculcate in the town', and afforded them a dramatic opportunity to press home their case for a reformation of manners.[81]

Cases of possession also helped to cement the links between puritan clergy and sympathetic layfolk. Darrel's exorcisms in the 1590s were usually witnessed and assisted by like-minded protestants in the places he visited. Similarly, Pierson described a large gathering of zealous ministers and layfolk for the exorcism in Northwich. The dispossession took place over several days, and provided the occasion for a series of fasts and sermons. According to Stanley Gower, Richard Rothwel's confrontation with the devil in Nottingham was witnessed by a 'company' of fellow Christians. Subsequently, the man who had been possessed was the subject of prayers 'every Sabbath and lecture day in many places'.[82] A similar example of the mutual support of godly protestants occurred in 1634, when Anthony Lapthorne, the pastor of Tretire in Herefordshire, 'invited many foreigners of other parishes' to assist in the exorcism of members of his flock.[83] Such events helped to maintain the networks of godly 'professors' which constituted an informal church structure in many regions.

It was probably these factors, combined with the unusual propensity of godly protestants to succumb to the affliction, that caused zealous pastors to take the idea of possession seriously. Equally, the campaign by the church hierarchy to discredit and restrict the activity of godly exorcists can be viewed as part of a wider effort to rein in the excesses of 'over hot' ministers, which threatened the authority of the institutional church. With this in mind, it is hardly surprising that Samuel Harsnet, the most vociferous and determined of John Darrel's detractors in the 1590s, went on to become an aggressively anti-puritan Bishop of Norwich.[84] During the reign of Charles I, the performance of exorcisms was one of many areas of nonconforming behaviour that was dealt with severely by the ecclesiastical courts. Anthony Lapthorne, for one, was prosecuted in the High Commission for attempting to cast out demons, along with his refusal to make the sign of the cross in baptism and administer the eucharist 'according to the prescript form appointed in the Book of Common Prayer'.[85] Similarly, Richard Rothwel and Robert Balsom combined their work as exorcists with opposition to the ecclesiastical policies pursued by Archbishop Laud, and both were troubled by the courts during the 1630s. For both the supporters and opponents of exorcism, it appears that the practice was intimately connected with wider issues of religious affiliation within the Church of England, and attempts to suppress it were perceived as an attack on the godly ministry as a whole.

By accepting the reality of demonic possession, and taking the lead in its identification and treatment, zealous protestants ensured that traditional beliefs about the devil were combined with the message of the Reformation. Their appropriation of popular ideas about unclean spirits, along with the grossly physical view of the devil that this entailed, led to an unlikely but enduring fusion of reformed Christianity with much older practices and beliefs. This process made little sense in terms of theology: indeed, a more consistent application of protestant doctrine might have led godly men and women to adopt the sceptical opinions promoted by Samuel Harsnet. It appears, however, that the concept of possession appealed to the practical needs of many godly pastors and their flocks. A similar process of assimilation can be detected in protestant attitudes towards witchcraft, which are the subject of the following chapter.

7
WITCHCRAFT

In 1597 James Stuart, the King of Scotland and future James I of England, published a learned treatise on the subject of witchcraft. This contained a lengthy discussion of the relationship between witches and the devil, which included the king's interpretation of their secret assemblies, or 'sabbats':

> The devill, as God's ape, counterfeites in his servauntes this service & forme of adoration that God prescribed and made his servantes to practise. For as the servants of God publicklie . . . conveene for the serving of him, so makes he them in great numbers to convene (though publickly they dare not) for his service. As none conveenes to the adoration and worshipping of God, except they be marked with his seale, the sacrament of baptisme, so none serves Satan, and conveenes in the adoring of him, that are not marked with [his] marke . . . As the minister sent by God teacheth plainely at the time of their publick conventions how to serve him in spirit & truth, so that uncleane spirite, in his owne person, teacheth his disciples at the time of their conveening how to worke all kinde of mischiefe.[1]

This bizarre account is a perfect example of the tendency of sixteenth-century thinkers to see in witchcraft a mirror image of their own most cherished beliefs. According to James, Satan's followers performed rituals which were the exact reverse of Christian practices, down to the sermons which provided the centrepiece of worship in presbyterian Scotland. In this respect, his depiction of the sabbat was a collective version of the reversal of Christian behaviour described in cases of possession.[2] The king's text also highlights the contrast between witch beliefs in England and his homeland. Scotland, in common with much of mainland Europe, developed a theory of witchcraft as a devil-worshipping cult, which held nocturnal meetings to pay homage to its diabolical leader. English demonologists, in contrast, described nothing as elaborate as the sabbats depicted in James' treatise until the East Anglian witch panic of 1645. Before that, witch trials in England tended to centre on the practice of harmful magic, or 'malificium', rather than collective satanism.

The devil preaches to his followers, from *Newes From Scotland* (1572).

This distinction has encouraged historians to play down the diabolical aspects of English witchcraft. Since the belief that witches gathered together to worship the devil was fairly uncommon before the Civil War, there has been a tendency to assume that other Scottish and continental beliefs about the satanic nature of witchcraft were also absent in this period. The brilliant studies by Keith Thomas and Alan Macfarlane in the early 1970s established an image of English witchcraft centred on the fear of harmful magic in village communities, and largely untouched by continental notions like the demonic pact – or 'baptisme' as James called it – which formally bound the witch to the devil's service. When such ideas were recorded in trial records and pamphlets, as in the East Anglian cases of 1645–7, they have usually been explained by the alleged influence of 'continental' thinking on the witchfinder Matthew Hopkins and his associates. It is only recently that these assumptions have been challenged. As Jim Sharpe has pointed out, the records relating to the Hopkins trials 'constitute the largest single body of evidence concerning English witchcraft we possess, and it would be unhelpful to dismiss their superficially unusual features as untypical'.[3] In fact, some of the main themes which emerged in the East Anglian persecutions were found in popular accounts of English witchcraft throughout the sixteenth and seventeenth centuries, including the idea of the demonic pact and the devil's mark on the witch's body. To understand these ideas, however, we need to take into account the distinctly folkloric view of Satan which underpinned them.

THE DEVIL IN POPULAR WITCH BELIEFS

Jim Sharpe has suggested that 'the key to popular conceptions of the connection between the witch and the devil lay not so much in popular views of witchcraft as in the popular image of the devil'.[3] This view is confirmed by comparing the portrayal of Satan in witchcraft cases with his depiction in popular literature. When the devil or his minions were described in witchcraft depositions, their appearance and behaviour often recalled folk tales and ballads. For example, they commonly assumed the form of an animal, like the cat named 'Satan' who performed magic for Agnes Waterhouse in 1565, or the two black frogs who demanded the soul of Joan Cunny in 1589.[4] In later accounts, the devil took the guise of a black man or a handsome youth wearing striking clothes or possessing some notable physical characteristic. When he appeared in this form, he occasionally revealed his true nature by exposing a cloven hoof. These characteristics were combined neatly in the confession of Margaret Wyard, one of the women examined by Hopkins in 1645, who encountered Satan as 'a handsome yonge gentleman with yellow hayre and black cloaths', whom she observed to possess 'a cloven foote'. Typically, the fiend would deceive the witch with illusory promises of success or wealth. In 1645, for example, Anne Barker described how 'there came to her a little dun dog, and sayd to her, "if you cleave to me thou shalt want nothinge", and told her shee shold find mony under a stap in the hall garden, but she found none'.[5] This account resembled much older tales of the devil falsely promising to reveal buried treasure, and cheap publications like *A New Ballad Shewing the Great Misery Sustained by a Poore Man in Essex*, which was circulating in the region in the 1620s.[6] Similar parallels were apparent in cases of collective witchcraft. In 1621, for example, Edward Fairfax described a feast attended by witches and the devil at Timble Gill in the Yorkshire dales.[7] This scene resembled *A Strange Banquet*, an early seventeenth-century ballad depicting a satanic feast 'at the peak in Derbyshire'.[8]

In cases like this, it is often difficult to tell if statements about witchcraft were borrowed from folk tales about the devil or vice versa. Most probably, they both originated in widely held beliefs about the evil one, which were only partially influenced by protestant theology. These beliefs were also apparent in another common feature of English witchcraft. This was the tendency to associate the devil exclusively with unneighbourly or anti-social behaviour. For puritan demonologists like William Perkins and George Gifford, all magical practices involved an implicit pact with Satan. Moreover, such activities were just one aspect of his dominion over the minds of 'superstitious' people, who clung pathetically to the idolatrous belief that they could gain assistance in life through the use of charms, potions or magical words. In contrast, the great majority of those who gave evidence in witch trials appear to have distinguished between good and harmful magic, and only connected the devil with the latter. The depositions from one of the earliest witchcraft cases in England, handled by the Archdeacon's court in Essex in 1563, show that the accused was originally identified by a village magician, or 'cunning man', who diagnosed a man's lameness as a form of bewitchment.[9] The work of Thomas, Macfarlane and Sharpe has provided copious evidence that the most common defence against suspected witchcraft was counter-magic, designed to undo harmful spells or reflect the witch's magic back on the person responsible. In 1621, Edward Fairfax admitted that he was tempted to resort to such devices when his daughters fell victim to bewitchment. He observed that counter-magical practices like 'the sewing of certain words in set forms, the heating of iron tongs [and] the scratching of the witch' were practiced widely in his community, but resolved to leave such practices 'to them that put confidence in them, and to the devil who devised them'.[10]

Familiar Spirits and the Devil

The gulf between protestant theology and popular witch beliefs was illustrated further by the appearance of wicked spirits, or 'familiars', in a large number of English trials. The historical origin of these creatures is obscure, but their behaviour was remarkably consistent throughout the Elizabethan and early Stuart period. Usually taking the form of small animals – typically mice, cats or frogs – they performed tasks for their masters in return for small meals of blood. In the earliest accounts, like that provided by the Dorset cunning man John Walsh in 1566, this was offered as a single drop from the finger, which 'the spirit did take away on his paw'.[11] Later depositions had familiars sucking blood from 'teats' on their owner's body, usually located near the genitals. The importance of these creatures in English witchcraft is indicated by the efforts made to counteract their malign influence. As George Gifford noted in 1593, the practice of 'scratching' witches to draw blood from their faces was believed to rob their 'spirites' of power;

A witch feeds her familiar spirits, from *A Rehearsall Both Straung and True of Hainous and Horrible Actes* (1579).

and household protections like witch bottles and shoes buried in buildings were apparently designed to trap familiars.[12] The concept of the familiar's 'teat' was a curious variation on the continental idea of the devil's mark, which was used to identify suspected witches; and it was employed in a similar way in English cases, with midwives employed from the 1570s to examine the bodies of accused women for suspicious growths.[13] The presence of familiars in English witchcraft cannot, however, be attributed to the influence of continental demonology, since no equivalent creatures were described in European sources. Still less can it be traced to the work of those English theologians who wrote on the subject, since they maintained that the devil had no need to employ such bizarre agents. Instead, it appears that the belief was rooted in popular traditions which probably pre-dated the Reformation.[14]

The distinction between familars and the devil was often blurred in witchcraft depositions and printed accounts of trials. In some instances, creatures identified as 'wicked spirits' behaved in ways clearly reminiscent of Satan. In 1565, for example, the familiar spirit serving Agnes Waterhouse appeared to her daughter as 'a great dog' and demanded that 'thou shalt give me your body and soul'. Not only did the creature assume a form closely associated in folk belief with the devil, but it took the name 'Satan'. At Chelmsford in 1589, familiar spirits offered riches to their human accomplices in return for their

A witch with familiar spirit, from *A Rehearsall Both Straung and True of Hainous and Horrible Actes* (1579).

souls. Similar behaviour was reported from Lincoln in 1619, when Philippa Flower made the following confession:

> She . . . saith that she hath a spirit sucking on her in the form of a white rat, which keepeth her left breast and hath so done for three or four years; and concerning the agreement betwixt her spirit and herself, she confesseth and saith that when it came first unto her she gave her soul to it and it promised to do her good and cause Thomas Simpson to love her, if she would suffer it to suck her, which she agreed unto.

In an earlier confession from Windsor, Elizabeth Stile claimed to have kept a rat, 'being in very deed a wicked spirit', which she fed from blood drawn from the right side of her body. She admitted 'that she gave her right side to the devil' A pamphlet from 1612 conflated the continental idea of the devil's mark on the witch's body with the teat 'where the spirits suck'. More strikingly, Thomas Potts' account of the Pendle witches in the following year described the devil sucking blood from the bodies of his disciples, and sometimes transforming himself into an animal to do so.[15] In 1645 the confessions of the East Anglian witches examined by Matthew Hopkins and his associates tended to collapse the distinction between Satan and familiar spirits. When the two were distinguished, it was made clear that the devil was the master of the witches' 'imps'. Occasionally, the evil one even warned his human confederates to 'send them away' to prevent their discovery by searchers.[16]

It is tempting to attribute the ambiguous relationship between familiars and the devil to the influence of those educated men who involved themselves in witch trials and the writing of pamphlets. In some cases, learned notions of the devil might have been imposed on the evidence of ordinary people, who did not themselves perceive familiars in demonic terms. There is a suggestion of this in the 1612 pamphlet, *The Witches Of Northampton*, where references to the devil were made in interpretive passages composed by the narrator. The account of the three spirits possessed by Arthur Bill, for instance, noted that their master gave them 'three special names', but 'the devil himself sure was godfather of them all'. Elsewhere in the tract, words were ascribed to the devil which the suspects apparently attributed to familiars.[17] Similarly, it is reasonable to assume that Matthew Hopkins' preconceptions about the devil's role in witchcraft coloured the testimony of some of those accused in the East Anglian trials. But this process cannot fully explain the satanic dimension of many witches' familiars. In numerous cases, the encounter between the witch and the devil 'or wicked spirit' was embedded in a folkloric context which apparently owed little to the assumptions of the interrogators. As Lyndal Roper has suggested, the narratives of many confessions involved a collusion between the suspect and the questioner, with the accused drawing on their own experiences, beliefs and fantasies.[18] Moreover, the confusion between the devil and other kinds of spirits was by no means confined to popular culture. Protestant exorcists like John Darrel and Richard Rothwel used the words 'demon', 'spirit' and 'Satan' as if they were interchangeable, and frequently addressed individual demons as if they were the fiend himself. In Stanley Gower's account of Rothwel's dispossession of John Fox, for example, the invading spirit was first introduced as an individual demon but later addressed as the devil and 'father of lies'.[19]

In all probability, the distinction between Satan, demons and familiar spirits was much less important to the witnesses and accused in witch trials than they were to contemporary theologians or modern historians. The victims of witchcraft were more concerned with the harm caused by these creatures, and the means available to prevent it, than speculations about their origin or nature. Nonetheless, the similarities between these beings and popular representations of the devil suggest a connection between the two, though the boundaries were often vague. In *The Discoverie of Witchcraft*, Reginald Scot noted the tendency of 'common people' to attribute the power of witches to the devil, and George Gifford's *Dialogue Concerning Witches and Witchcraftes* (1593) implied that popular views on witches, familiar spirits and the devil were often intertwined. The tendency to conflate familiars with Satan was also apparent in entertainments based on witchcraft. The play *The Witch of Edmonton*, which was first performed in 1621, presented the devil as a black dog which performed harmful deeds against its mistress's enemies. Similarly, tales about Mother Shipton in the 1660s attributed to Satan the kind of behaviour normally associated with familiars. In *The Life and Death of Mother Shipton* (1667), for instance, the devil appeared to Shipton's mother and 'pluckt her by the groin, and there immediately grew a kind of tet, which he instantly suckt, telling her that must be his constant custom morning and evening'.[20]

This material suggests there was a broad continuum in popular belief between familiar spirits and the devil. This impression is confirmed by cases of demonic 'obsession' and possession. In the former instances, individuals were tormented by evil spirits, and in the latter they were physically invaded by demons. In both cases, the sufferings of the victim were usually attributed to witchcraft, and the attacking spirit itself was often believed to be a familiar. But once a case of possession was diagnosed, it was relatively easy for the spirit to become identified with the devil himself, especially if the services of an exorcist were engaged. It is now time to consider this process.

Witchcraft, Obsession and Possession

In 1593, a striking case of demonic obsession was recorded in Huntingtonshire. Lying in her bed at night, the wife of Sir Henry Cromwell of Ramsey was suddenly awoken and 'very strangely tormented by a cat (as she imagined) . . . which offered to pluck off all the skin and flesh from her arms and body'.[21] A few years later, a similar experience was described by Joan Jorden of Stradbroke in Suffolk, who was terrorised by an evil spirit which visited her repeatedly at night. On one occasion the creature, which also assumed the shape of a cat, 'kissed her three or four times, and slavered on her, and (lying on her breast), he pressed her so sore that she could not speak'. When it returned on other evenings, it 'held her hands that she could not stir, and restrained her voice that she could not answer'.[22] Similar visitations were endured by the patients of the Buckinghamshire physician, Richard Napier, in the 1620s and 1630s. In some instances, these expereinces were so prolonged and severe that his patients went for weeks without sleeping.[23] The torments of these men and women recalled the 'night terrors' endured by godly protestants, and were probably caused by the same sleep disorder – known as 'the hag' – which involves paralysis, lucid dreaming and sudden, intense surges of fear. But unlike the experiences described in Chapter Three, they were not perceived by their victims as trials of faith. Instead, they were understood as signs of witchcraft, and the creatures responsible were believed to be familiar spirits.

Such attacks were often linked to demonic possession. Lady Cromwell received her nocturnal tormenter on the evening she returned from Warboys to visit the possessed children of the Throckmorton family. Among other symptoms, the children claimed to be menaced by devilish apparitions in the form of animals. The spirit which assailed Joan Jorden at night later possessed her body, giving her such violent convulsions that it took 'six strong men' to hold her down.[24] The patients treated by Napier sometimes believed they were possessed, like the man in 1634 who felt an evil spirit enter his body as he lay in bed on Whitsun eve.[25] It was common in such cases for an individual witch to be accused of sending the 'imp'. In each of the possession cases involving John Darrel in the 1590s, his patients named a person who they believed was responsible for their sufferings. When Thomas Darling was visited by the alleged witch, Elizabeth Wright, in 1596, he screamed and suffered a violent seizure, which only subsided when she left the room. Likewise, the victims of Edmund Hartley in Lancashire fell down speechless when he came near them.[26] The connection between witchcraft and possession was so strong that fake demoniacs, who subsequently admitted their fraud, claimed that witches were responsible for their plight. Thus George Purie, 'the boy of Bilson' in Staffordshire, accused a woman of sending a spirit into his body. When he was brought to the assizes to confront her, he pretended to be affected in her presence with 'strange pranks', until his imposture was exposed by the Bishop of Lichfield.[27] In this, and other cases of feigned possession, it seems that the allegation of witchcraft was not intended primarily to accuse an innocent person, but to confirm the genuineness of the victim's alleged condition. The involvement of witches, it appears, was one of the widely recognised signs of the affliction.

The role of familiar spirits in possession sheds light on one of the more puzzling and unpleasant aspects of the phenomenon. This was the moving lumps on the bodies of victims, which were reported throughout the Elizabethan and early Stuart period. For many of those suffering from the condition, it appears that these bodies were perceived as 'wicked spirits' or imps inside them. The ability of familiars to enter human bodies was described crudely in the case from Stradbroke in 1599. Joan Jorden attested that the familiar spirit of Olive Barthram had killed one of her neighbours by getting inside him and tearing 'his heart in pieces'. When the creature subsequently possessed her own body, numerous witnesses claimed to observe a lump moving inside her. In this particular case, the imp was held responsible for a wide variety of intensely physical experiences, ranging from nocturnal visitations to bodily possession and the killing of a person 'from inside'. Similarly, it appears that Thomas Darling was tormented by a witch's familiar before the creature took possession of his body; and when he was finally exorcised, bystanders claimed that a small creature like a mouse scurried out of his mouth.[28] In 1634 Edward Bonavent, a servant from Reading, suffered shaking fits and the sensation that a mouse was running up and down inside his body. He accused one of his neighbours, Edith Walles, of afflicting him with the spirit.[29] A year later, Richard Napier noted that one of his patients, Jane Slade, 'feeles something stir in her body with a riseing up and downe, her face is much swelled and [she is] payned in her teeth, and feares that Joan Braie and her son Harry have bewitched her'.[30] That these swellings were believed to be the physical signs of familiar spirits inside their victims is apparently confirmed by the fact that other sufferers of bewitchment, who did not endure the same symptoms, tended to see familiar spirits outside their bodies. This was the case with the Throckmorton children in the 1590s and the daughters of Edward Fairfax in 1621.

The belief that familiars could take residence inside a human body was also confirmed by a number of witchcraft confessions. In 1593 Alice Samuel told Robert Throckmorton that her own imps had 'gotten into my belly'.[31] Elizabeth Clarke, the first woman accused of witchcraft in the Chelmsford trials of 1645, informed one of her examiners that her familiar could go 'into his throate, and then there would be a feast of toades' in his stomach. Another confession from the same proceedings affirmed that witches' imps could control a person's behaviour from within. After a servant from St Osyth had fallen into a 'shaking fit', in which he sang 'perfect tunes' and emitted the sounds of various animals, Joyce Boanes admitted that the boy was possessed by three familiar spirits. She claimed that her own 'imp made the servant to barke like a dog, the imp of Rose Hallybread inforced him to sing sundry tunes in the great extremity of paines, the imp of . . . Susan Cock compelled him to crow like a cock, and the imp of Margaret Landish made him groan in such an extraordinary manner'.[32]

In the majority of cases, the victims of familiar possession displayed other classic symptoms associated with demoniacs, including trances, fits, speaking in strange voices, and a revulsion from holy objects and prayers. It was easy to interpret these manifestations as the work of the devil, and the distinction between Satan and the familiar spirit could become decidedly blurred. The full range of symptoms was described in an incident from Hockham in Norfolk in 1600. In this instance, the affliction ended when the victim, Joan Harvey, scratched the alleged witch, and no dispossession was required. Thus the surviving account of her bewitchment offers a striking picture of the experience of spirit-possession without the intervention of an exorcist:

> In her fits, when she seemed dead and senseless, she spoke very strangely, in the name of an ill spirit, nothing but as an ill spirit, and complained of Mother Frauncis the witch, telling how many imps she had, and what were their names, and why she vexed this wench, and how many she vexed in the town, and what were their names; and speaking against their prayers, their sending for learned preachers, their giving of her physic; sometimes storming at God and good men, and sometimes blaspheming God, and saying God is a good man, I can do as much as he, I care not for Jesus, etc. Some things were uttered, unknown before to the maid, in a strange and snappish voice, and sometimes to the tune of the witch and in her phrases and terms. And [she said these things] when the maid's mouth was wide open and gaping, and her lips not stirring, nor her tongue, and sometimes when her tongue was seen doubled in her mouth, and pulled into her throat or pinned up to the roof of her mouth, she being as dead and senseless.[33]

For Joan and those who witnessed her ordeal, it appears that the experience of possession was centred on the influence of the witch and her familiar. It was not the devil, but one of these 'ill spirits' which spoke through her body, and she later took on the voice of the witch herself. But this did not mean that the creature possessing her had no satanic affiliations. It blasphemed against God and raged at prayers and preachers; and another passage described how the girl spat violently when she heard the name of Jesus. Such behaviour was typical of the fiend, and suggests that Joan and the witnesses believed the possessing spirit to be at least partly diabolical. Given this, it is easy to see how the devil himself might have emerged as the spirit responsible for her torments had one of the 'learned preachers' consulted on the case decided to conduct an exorcism. The willingness of people to conflate familiar spirits with the devil helps to explain how other cases of witch-related possession in the 1590s, such as the Throckmorton children, Thomas Darling, the Starkie family in Lancashire and William Sommers in Nottingham, were transformed into fully-fledged demonstrations of Satan's power.

The blurred distinction between familiar spirits and the devil allowed a distinctly un-protestant view of the evil one to emerge in many cases of witchcraft. The devil, or his minions, could take the form of small animals which were impeded by physical barriers; they entered and left the body through the mouth or other orifices, and moved inside their victims like parasites. All this was far removed from the lofty doctrines of William Perkins and other godly divines. This contrast becomes even more acute when one examines the most popular forms of protection against witches and familiar spirits.

Witch-bottles and Other Protections

The most impressive evidence of the widespread use of protections against evil spirits in early modern England is provided by archaeology. The discovery of objects, particularly shoes and bottles, concealed in the hearths and foundations of buildings sheds light on popular perceptions of the devil and familiar spirits, and the most appropriate means to combat them. The Concealed Shoes Index at Northampton Central Museum holds records of over 1,000 items from the British Isles, and a current survey of glass and earthenware bottles has identified 194 finds to date.[34] Given the vagaries of preservation and reporting, these figures probably represent only a small sample of the total number of objects hidden in this way. Large numbers of specially designed bottles, or 'bellarmines', were imported from Germany during the sixteenth and seventeenth centuries, and the market was apparently still buoyant in 1626, when the potters Thomas Rous and Abraham Cullen obtained a patent for making similar objects in this country.[35] These vessels were used principally for the sale of beer, but they were also one of the main artefacts concealed in houses for magical purposes.

What were these objects for? By their very nature, it is impossible to be certain of their original function, but the most plausible interpretation is that they served as deterrents to evil spirits which wished to invade the home. This view is supported by the location of the artefacts. Shoes were most commonly concealed in chimneys, which provided openings through which hostile entities might pass.[36] Just under half the surviving bellarmines were found in chimneys or under hearthstones, and another 10 per cent were found near the entrances of buildings. While these objects have also been recovered from wall cavities and gardens, it appears that their principal use was to defend thresholds.[37] The capacity of 'ill spirits' to come down chimneys was recorded in witchcraft depositions. In 1599, for instance, the familiar which menaced and possessed Joan Jorden first scuttled down the chimney in the form of a cat, and preceded its subsequent visits by banging and 'scraping on the walls'.[38] When his household was being tormented by familiar spirits in 1663, John Mompesson discharged his pistol at an object moving in the fireplace. Subsequently, he 'found

Illustration from *The Apprehension and Confession of Three Notorious Witches . . . at Chelmsforde* (1589).

several drops of blood on the hearth'.[39] The role of these objects as 'spirit traps' is also supported by the nature of the artefacts. According to tradition, the thirteenth-century divine John Scorn had conjured the devil into a boot, and this legend might have encouraged a belief that boots and shoes could capture evil spirits.[40] More detailed evidence is provided by the appearance and contents of bellarmines. These were normally adorned with a crude representation of a human face, or 'mask', and often contained organic material, particularly hair, urine and bones. Pieces of fabric cut into the shape of a heart were also found in four surviving bottles. Such features suggest that the vessels were intended as 'decoy' bodies, designed to deceive malevolent spirits into attacking them instead of their human targets. This interpretation is consistent with the other most common material found in the bottles: pins and nails, which were probably intended to harm the invading spirit. Again, this hypothesis is supported by documentary evidence. In 1574 the spirit possessing Alice Norrington, a servant from Westwell in Kent, informed her exorcists that it had previously been trapped in a bottle, and was released by its present owner to torment and possess her enemies.[41]

The use of bellarmines and shoes to trap evil spirits reinforces the impression that folkloric perceptions of the devil and his minions were widespread in early modern England, despite the efforts of the godly to promote alternative views. Presumably, the location and function of 'witch bottles' reflected the belief that demons were restrained by physical barriers. Such attitudes probably influenced beliefs about Satan, since the distinction between the devil and familiar spirits was unclear. The creature that possessed Alice Norrington, for example, announced that he was 'Satan' and claimed to have a servant called 'Little Devil'. But he also admitted that for twenty years he had been trapped in a bottle belonging to an old woman. The image of the devil in popular witch beliefs was based on profoundly non-protestant concepts: instead of a powerful, pervasive force for spiritual evil, he was a limited, essentially physical creature who could assume various guises but preferred to appear as a small animal. He busied himself mainly by harming the health and property of innocent Christians, who could defend themselves with magical objects like bottles and shoes.

One other aspect of witch-bottles is worth noting. This is their popular name, which changed during the sixteenth and seventeenth centuries. In the Elizabethan period they were known as 'alvas'; and from the middle of the seventeenth century they were commonly referred to as 'bellarmines'. The origin of these names cannot be ascertained with certainty, but it is striking that both appellations were linked to well-known catholic figures. The Duke of Alva played a role in the suppression of Dutch protestants in the 1560s, and acquired the status of a hate figure among their co-religionists in England. Similarly, Cardinal Bellarmine was a leading figure in the Counter-Reformation in the early seventeenth century. Given that witch bottles were designed for the unpleasant purpose of trapping demons, and often contained noxious substances like urine, it is reasonable to assume that the names they acquired reflected anti-popish sentiments. If this is correct, it provides a nice example of the fusion of anti-catholicism with distinctly non-protestant beliefs, and reflects the ability of traditional culture to absorb aspects of the Reformation while ignoring its central message. The second part of this chapter will argue that a similar process worked in reverse, since godly ministers who became involved in witchcraft cases were obliged to endorse folk beliefs surrounding the subject. Before this, however, it is necesary to consider the protestant theology of witchcraft in more detail.

WITCHCRAFT AND GODLY RELIGION

Perhaps the most consistent exponent of the protestant theory of witchcraft was William Perkins, who composed a treatise on the 'damned art' and devoted passages to the subject in many of his other works. For Perkins, the prevalance of witchcraft was a sign of Satan's dominion over 'earthly' people, who resorted instinctively to superstitious practices in order to fulfil their needs. Without realising it, the practitioners of all forms of magic made an 'implicit' compact with the devil, even if they intended to do no harm. Thus even so-called 'white witches', who used magical devices to heal or protect their neighbours, were in reality 'the devil's prophets'. This view was spelt out in *The Calling of the Ministry* (1605), which contrasted godly preachers to 'cunning' men and women:

Consider the difference between these two: the wizard and charmer has his fellowship with the devil, the preacher with God; the charmer has his calling from the devil, the preacher has his from God. The charmer's charm is the devil's watchword – when he charms, the devil does the feat; but the preacher's doctrine is God's watchword – when he truly applies it, God himself ratifies and confirms it. So we should fear to have anything to do with the devil in this way, [by] seeking guidance from those who are his slaves.[42]

As this passage suggests, Perkins' definition of witchcraft was much wider than anything found in folk traditions, and was integrated into a general theory of the nature of true religion. He viewed catholicism as little more than a highly organised form of witchcraft, since its claim to authority rested on the use of charms. Similar views were expressed by godly authors throughout the sixteenth century. In the 1550s, John Olde accused the Roman church of 'bewitching the people'; and the preface to a catechism in 1586 implied that the catholic shrine at Walsingham had been a centre of witchcraft, which 'enchaunted the mindes of kinges and princes with the baneful dregges of men's inventions'.[43] The view that all forms of superstition were tantamount to witchcraft was reflected in the casual use of the word by protestant writers in the seventeenth century. Thus John Reynolds lamented the power of 'the bewitching world, the alluring flesh and the inticing devill' in 1635, and the author of a book of meditations in 1639 decried 'the witcheries and vanities of this world'.[44]

That these opinions were not confined to the abstract world of theology is suggested by the remarkable notebook of Richard Newdigate, a puritan lawyer from Nuneaton. In 1631 he attented a sermon by Josiah Packwood, the pastor of Fillongley, in which the minister denounced members of his flock for seeking help from 'cunning men'. In the eyes of the pastor, such actions were nothing short of witchcraft. Newdigate made a careful record of the preacher's advice on how to reprove 'those that seeke to witches for remidies'. This included the most common arguments that such people used, together with the appropriate response:

Objection: Wee seeke not to the divell but to God for helpe.
Solution: God will not have the divell to be his agent. Should not a people [seek help] from the Lord?
Objection: Wee goe to those that are good men, and wee never heare hurt of them.
Answer: The divell is full of subtilty and simulation. His end is to inlarge his kingdome by curing diseases.

Newdigate went on to list the main arguments against the practice of 'healing' magic. These included the observation that all magicians 'deale with the divell and his instruments', and the assertion that diseases were 'God's signs', which could only be cured by His hand.[45] His notes indicate the gulf between godly perceptions of witchcraft and the views of the majority, and show the willingness of some puritan clergy and parishioners to challenge widely held beliefs. But it seems they were facing an uphill task. In the 1590s George Gifford had identified similar opinions among the 'common sort of Christians', and after forty years of preaching they showed few signs of going away.

The belief that Satan was responsible for all forms of superstition, from the 'white' magic practised in Packwood's parish to the abomination of the Roman mass, made it difficult for godly protestants to deal with the concept of witches' familiars. After all, if such creatures existed they were likely to distract people from the more ubiquitous manifestations of the devil's power. A minority of zealous protestants took the extreme view that familiar spirits were simply figments of the superstitious mind. To Reginald Scot, the activities of 'white spirits and black spirits, grey spirits and red spirits, devil toad and devil lamb, devil's cat and devil's dam' were quite inconsistent with 'the word of God and true philosophy'. He also poured scorn on the notion that devils could be 'made tame and kept in a box'.[46] For most puritans, however, the existence of wicked spirits was confirmed by the evidence of scripture and a wealth of contemporary reports. According to John Malin, another preacher recorded in Newdigate's notebook, there were whole 'orders of evill angells' at large in the world.[47] Writers like Perkins and Gifford acknowledged the existence of such beings, but rejected most of the beliefs surrounding them. In 1593, Gifford lambasted the idea that demons resided in lowly places like tree trunks, noting that this was barely compatable with the biblical image of the devil. 'Doe you thinke Satan lodgeth in a hollow tree?', he asked in the *Dialogue Concerning Witches and Witchcraftes*, 'Is hee become so lazy and idle? Hath he left off being a roaring lion?'[48] The notion that satanic power was constrained by physical barriers, or could be repelled by magical objects or words, was equally absurd. In *The Whole Armour of God* (1616), William Gouge condemned the perilous folly of 'conjurers, sorcerers and such like, who imagine the divell may be driven away by charmes'. On the contrary, such beliefs only confirmed his dominion over their minds.[49]

Given all this, it might appear that the gulf between the godly theory of witchcraft and the beliefs of ordinary people was completely unbridgeable. But that was not the case. In fact, a number of committed protestants came tacitly to endorse the ideas about witchcraft that were accepted by the ungodly majority, and it is probable that this process made it easier for witch trials to take place. It is now time to consider this remarkable synthesis.

Puritanism and Traditional Witch Beliefs

A consistent application of the protestant theory of witchcraft would have involved an assault on the practice of all forms of magic, as well as many other idolatrous and 'pagan' activities. As Stuart Clark has suggested, godly demonologists were determined to eradicate witchcraft in all its forms, not just the working of harmful magic.[50] Continental studies have shown that protestant witch persecutions were combined with much wider attempts to suppress popular 'superstition'.[51] In England, the statutes against witchcraft allowed magistrates to apply a similarly wide-ranging interpretation of the crime, though the death penalty was reserved for murder by magic and, from 1604, the conjuration of evil spirits. The activities covered by the offence were spelt out in the first Elizabethan statute of 1563:

> If any person or persons . . . take upon him or them, by witchcraft, enchantment, charm or sorcery, to tell or declare in what place any treasure of gold or silver should or might be found or had in the earth or other secret places, or where goods or things lost or stolen should be found or become, or shall use or practise any sorcery, enchantment, charm or witchcraft, to the intent to provoke any person to unlawful love . . . [they shall] suffer imprisonment for the space of one whole year.[52]

Occasionally, individuals were reported for 'witchcraft' of this kind. This was the fate of seven people from Berkswell near Coventry in 1636. After using magical techniques to 'find out the thief which had stolen a wastcoate of Elizabeth Lane', they were reported to the Bishop of Lichfield for making an 'implicit compact with the divell'.[53] Such prosecutions were rare, however. Only seven such cases were referred to the consistory court at Lichfield between 1614 and 1639.[54] Moreover, the practice of 'white' magic was normally dealt with by ecclesiastical tribunals, whose punishments were more limited than those available to the secular courts. The most serious cases of witchcraft, which were handled by the quarter sessions and assizes, were normally inspired by allegations of hurtful magic rather than 'innocent' practices like divination or the use of charms. This reflected the dependence of the courts on the co-operation of local people, who were usually only prepared to report witches when they felt threatened by malicious magic.

This situation placed puritan divines in a rather ambiguous position. For most of them, the attack on witchcraft was part of a much wider 'reformation of manners', by which they sought to reform popular behaviour and instil the principles of true religion into their often recalcitrant flocks. In some instances, godly ministers openly denounced their impious parishioners as servants of the devil. Thus Francis Abbot, the vicar of Poslingford in Suffolk, was reported to the High Commission in 1634 for telling a woman 'she had served the devil three-score years'. When he was accused of nonconformity by one of his churchwardens, he claimed that Satan was the man's 'black grandfather'.[55] Similarly, the suppression of idolatrous entertainments was sometimes linked explicitly with the struggle against Satan, as when Thomas Hall announced in 1662 that the only beneficiaries of May games were the devil and catholic 'locusts from hell'.[56] But it was difficult for godly pastors to involve themselves in witchcraft cases without appearing to endorse the view that only harmful magic was the work of Satan. Moreover, their active support for the prosecution of witches could bring them in contact with folkloric beliefs about the practice, which were sometimes as dangerous as the crime itself. But a section of the godly community was prepared to take these risks, as the benefits of witch persecution appeared to outweigh the problems it entailed. First, the rooting out of witches could offer an admirable demonstration of the power of the godly ministry. Thus John Darrel proclaimed in 1599 that the people of Nottingham became zealous hearers of the Word during his stay in their town, when he was responsible for the apprehension of thirteen alleged witches.[57] Second, witchcraft was intimately linked to demon-possession, and for reasons discussed in the previous chapter, this phenomenon was a subject of special interest to many puritan divines.

This is not to say, of course, that protestant zeal was one of the major causes of English witch trials. As Alan Macfarlane has observed, the prosecution of witches did not depend on godly ministers, and trials could proceed without the 'presence of a band of exorcists or a series of sensational cases of possession'.[58] But when puritan churchmen did become involved in these matters, they could have a dramatic effect on their own ministry. The potential usefulness of witchcraft to preachers was demonstrated strikingly in the case of Dr Dorington, the Huntingtonshire minister who participated in the prosecution of Alice Samuel in 1593. Following her admission that she had given her soul to the devil, and sent imps to torment members of the Throckmorton family, he delivered a Christmas Eve sermon in the presence of the accused woman. As he 'declared in the open assembly all the matter of [her] late confession', Samuel 'did nothing but weep and lament, and many times was so very loud with sundry passions that she caused all the church to look on her'. It is not hard to imagine how this spectacle confirmed the pastor's authority, and amplified the message of his sermon on the need for true repentance before God.[59] The powerful effect of such events was not lost on the enemies of John Darrel, who complained that he capitalised on the lurid appeal of witchcraft and possession. According to Samuel Harsnet in 1599, the exorcist's influence meant that the pulpits of Nottingham 'rang of nothing but divels and witches'.[60]

In return for these opportunities, pastors and their lay supporters were sometimes obliged to endorse folkloric ideas about the devil. Dr Dorington initially objected to the 'superstitious' practice of scratching witches to remove the power of their evil spirits, but he eventually agreed to attend the scratching of Alice Samuel's daughter, Agnes, by one of her alleged victims. He even addressed a sermon to the unfortunate girl after her ordeal, in which he declared that God would not allow her to be visited with such punishments if she did not have at least 'some knowledge of the wicked practices to which her mother had confessed'.[61] A few years later, the dispossession of Thomas Darling was preceded by similar attempts at counter magic. Despite his puritan sympathies, Darling scratched the woman he accused of bewitching him. She was also examined by a cunning man. In 1597, John Darrel endorsed the practice of testing alleged witches by asking them to recite the Lord's Prayer. It was widely believed that they were unable to utter the line 'Forgive us our trespasses', though this was hardly consistent with the protestant rejection of the magical power of words.[62] In the company of other godly ministers, Darrel tested the 'wise man' Edmund Hartley in this way to affirm that he had sent demons into the children and servants of the Starkie household of Cleworth in Lancashire.[63] The pastor also tolerated popular ideas about possession by witches' familiars. His pamphlet account of the case of William Sommers, which is reprinted in the appendix, implied that the youth ingested the spirit on a piece of bread, which he was forced to eat by a witch; it also suggested that the entity was ejected from his mouth at the climax of his exorcism.[64] In another text, he claimed that the swelling on Sommers' body moved backwards and forwards in response to people around him. It even played tricks on 'some popish persons' by pretenting to be afraid of a cross, and allowing them to chase it with that object 'from head to foote'.[65] As he came under mounting pressure from the church hierarchy to defend his activities, the exorcist was increasingly obliged to rely on such bizarre pieces of physical evidence. In the process, he also appeared to authenticate much of the folklore surrounding demonic possession and witchcraft.

The description

Great griefe affailes the Lecherous minde : of fuch as doth the youth alure:
More worfe then beaftes I do thẽ finde : fuch youth to lechery to procure.

The fignification.

THe Goate fignifieth Lechery : the woman Whoredome:
fhe which leadeth the Goate by the beard is *meretrix*, the
baude : and the deuill *Nicticorax*, a blinde guide or de-
ceauer.

Lechery

9. The devil leads the way to sin, from Bateman's *Christall Glasse* (1569).

10a. The pope's reward in hell, from the seventeenth-century ballad *The Great Assize*.

10b. The fiend encourages William Purcas to murder. From the ballad *The Wofull Lamentation*.

ANTHONY PAINT[ER]

THE

Blaspheming Caryar.

Who sunke into the ground up to the neck, and there Stood two day[s]
two nights, and not to bee drawne out by the strength of Ho[rse]
or digged out by the help of man: and there dyed the
3. of Nouember, 1613.

Also the punishment of *Nicholas Meſle* a most wicked blasphemer,

Reade and tremble.

Publiſhed by Authoritie.

At London printed for *Iohn Trundle* : and are to be sold at
Chriſt Church Gate. 1614.

11. The devil claims a blasphemer, from *Anthony Painter* (1614).

STRANGE

Newes from *Antwarpe*, which happened the 12. of Auguſt laſt paſt. 1612.

FIRST PRINTED In DVTCH

at Bergen ap Zoame by Ioris Staell and
now tranſlated into Engliſh by I. F.

¶ At London printed by Ralph Blower. 1612.

12. Satan attacks a catholic church in *Strange Newes from Antwerpe* (1612).
(*Opposite top*) 13a. The pope as Antichrist from a 1642 pamphlet.
(*Opposite bottom*) 13b. Archbishop William Laud as Antichrist, from a 1642 pamphlet.

Of Pride.

When daintie dames hath whole delight : with proude attyre them selues to ray.
Pirafmos ſhineth in the ſight : of glittering glaſſe ſuch fooles to fray.

¶ The ſignification.

*T*He woman ſignifieth pride : the glaſſe in her hand flattery or deceate : the deuill behinde her temptation : the
death head which ſhe ſetteth her foote on, ſignifieth forgetfulnes of the life to come, wherby commeth deſtruction.

H.iij.   Take

14. Satan exploits the female sin of pride, from Stephen Bateman, *A Christall Glasse of Christian Reformation* (1569).

15. Familiar spirits depicted in the illustration from Matthew Hopkins, *Discovery of Witches* (1647).

A

Timely Warning

To Rash and Disobedient

CHILDREN.

Being a strange and wonderful RELATION of a young Gentleman in the Parish of *Stepheny* in the Suburbs of *London*, that sold himself to the Devil for 12 Years to have the Power of being revenged on his Father and Mother, and how his Time being expired, he lay in a sad and deplorable Condition to the Amazement of all Spectators.

EDINBURGH: PRINTED ANNO 1721.

16. An eighteenth-century warning of the dangers of Satan.

The strange alliance between puritanism and traditional witch beliefs did not end with the career of John Darrel. Several of the clergy involved in the dispossession of Thomas Darling and the Starkie children, like Arthur Hildersham, John Brinsley and Richard Bernard, went on to become prominent figures in the Jacobean church. Around 1612, Bernard was involved in another spectacular exorcism in Nottingham, though this case was not linked explicitly to witchcraft.[66] In the same year, a relative of the Starkies, Roger Nowell, initiated a series of witch prosecutions in the north of England. The depiction of the devil in these cases owed a great deal to folklore, despite the strong tradition of godly religion in Nowell's family. According to the confession of Elizabeth Southernes, one of the ten witches hanged at Pendle in Lancashire, she was walking in a forest when she met 'a spirit or devil in the shape of a boy, the one half of his coat black and the other half brown, who bade . . . her that if she would give him her soul, she should have anything that she would request'. She offered her soul to the boy for the space of six years. When this time had elapsed, the spirit returned 'in the likeness of a brown dog', which sucked blood from her left arm. Subsequently, it taught her magical techniques to harm her neighbours, and threatened her with physical violence when she refused to obey its commands.[67]

Further evidence of the willingness of godly protestants to accommodate folkloric beliefs about witches was provided by the Fairfax family of Fuyston in Yorkshire. When Sir Edward's daughter, Helen, believed herself to be bewitched by a group of local women in 1621, he rejected as superstitious the magical remedies recommended by his friends. Nonetheless, he allowed one of the accused to be tested with the Lord's Prayer, and affirmed that she was unable to recite the crucial line. He also defended the widespread belief, rejected by the great majority of protestant demonologists, that witches could transform themselves into animals. 'The changing of witches into hares, cats, and the like shapes, is so common', he argued, that only 'the stupidly incredulous' could deny it. Helen Fairfax herself seems to have combined traditional beliefs about the devil with insights from protestant doctrine. When the fiend appeared to her in a vision, he assumed a guise familar from folk tales and ballads: 'she saw a black dog by her bedside, and after a little sleep, she had an apparition of one like a young gentleman, very brave, and [with] a hat with a gold band'. Throughout her ordeal, which involved repeated appearances by the devil and an array of familiar spirits, she maintained that Satan was powerless against a person with true faith, and could not act without the permission of God. As she announced to an apparition of one of the witches responsible for her torments, 'Our God is the God of heaven, even Jesus Christ our saviour, whom we serve, and your god is the devil of hell, and he can do nothing but what our God doth suffer him.'[68]

In each of these cases, it seems that godly protestants tried sincerely to reconcile their religious beliefs with traditional ideas about witchcraft. Darrel, for instance, denied that the activity of witches and the devil contradicted the supreme power of God, since the Lord employed Satan as a tool for his own purposes. Witchcraft was 'the work of God by the ministry of the devill'.[69] Edward Fairfax agonised over the appropriate response to his daughter's affliction, and only accepted those popular ideas about witches that he believed to be supported by strong evidence. Nonetheless, it is clear that such men were prepared to accept beliefs and practices which did not originate in protestant theology, and were understood in decidedly non-protestant ways by most of the population. This point is important, since cases of witchcraft and possession attracted an audience beyond the normal constituency of godly 'professors'. Large crowds gathered to witness the dispossession of Thomas Darling and William Sommers, and the pamphlet account of the Throckmorton case claimed that 'five hundred men' visited the afflicted girls during the trial of Alice Samuel.[70] There is no reason to assume that these people understood the events they witnessed in the same way as the godly protestants who endorsed them. By accepting the existence of witches' familiars and the physical reality of Satan, and tacitly endorsing the view that witchcraft involved an explicit pact with Satan rather than the 'implicit compact' associated with the practice of all forms of magic, godly protestants forged an alliance with traditional beliefs about the devil. The full implications of this alliance were realised in the 1640s and 1650s.

The 1645 Witch-Hunt

During the winter of 1644–5, a minor gentleman from Essex named Matthew Hopkins became alarmed at the activity of a group of witches in his home town of Manningtree. According to his own account, published two years later, a gathering of 'that horrible sect of witches' was convening at night in an area beside his house. He heard them conversing with their imps and offering 'solemne sacrifices to the devill'. On one occasion the witches mentioned the name of Elizabeth Clarke, an elderly, one-legged widow, whom Hopkins duly reported to the authorities. Clarke was 'thereupon apprehended and searched by women who had for many yeares knowne the devill's marks, and found to have three teats about her, which honest women have not'.[71] Subsequently, she was subjected to the process of 'watching', whereby she was kept awake at night in the hope that her familiars would visit her. In March 1645 Clarke confessed to the allegations, and similar proceedings began against her supposed associates. Following a string of similar confessions, thirty-six witches were eventually tried at the Essex assizes in July. By this time the accusations had crossed the border into Suffolk, where at least 117 alleged witches were examined or tried before the end of the year. Hopkins and his associate, John Stearne, played an active role in most of these accusations, which spilled over into Huntingdonshire, Cambridgeshire, Northamptonshire, Bedfordshire and Norfolk in 1646. In total, nearly 250 witches were investigated in the eastern counties between 1645 and 1647, and approximately 100 were hanged.

The East Anglian trials were by far the most serious outbreak of witch-hunting in English history, and bear comparison with the mass persecutions in Scotland and continental Europe. Along with the other factors involved in this extraordinary event, the role of protestant zealotry has been repeatedly examined by historians. According to Alan Macfarlane, puritanism played very little part in the accusations. He points out that godly protestants were divided over the merits of Hopkins' actions, and the witchfinder himself 'cannot be shown to have been a puritan, or particularly interested in religion at all'.[72] This view has been echoed by William Lamont, who cautions against the 'myth' that the trials were produced by 'a simple application of literalist-minded puritan doctrine'.[73] Jim Sharpe has observed that the Hopkins prosecutions were not followed by a sustained attempt to eradicate witchcraft in England, despite the political ascendency of puritanism in the decade that followed. This tendency to play down the role of godly religion in the East Anglian trials is part of the present consensus that puritanism was not a major cause of the witch-hunt. That interpretation will not be challenged here. There is little evidence that puritanism *per se* was responsible for the dreadful events of 1645–7. There is, however, good reason to assume that many of Hopkins' supporters were members of the godly community, who came to accept folkloric ideas about witchcraft which had little to do with godly religion. In other words, the Hopkins trials were a striking example of the assimilation by godly protestants of popular ideas about the devil.

The religious opinions of Matthew Hopkins are notoriously hard to pin down. He made few recorded comments on the religious controversies of the Civil War period, though the views he did express were consistent with the puritan cause. Around 1645, for instance, he observed that the devil used the Book of Common Prayer to consecrate his marriage to witches.[74] But despite this hint of puritan zeal, the pamphlet he published to defend his activities in 1647 made no reference to godly religion. The views of Hopkins' associates are easier to discern. His principle collaborator, John Stearne, appears to have been an ardent proponent of godly reform. In a treatise of 1648, he described the campaign against witches as a form of spiritual combat akin to the struggle with popery. He equated the role of the witchfinder to a godly soldier, going 'well armed against these rulers of darknesse, devills and evil spirits, furnished with the heavenly furniture and spirituall weapons of which the apostle speaketh . . . and being thus qualified and armed to trust in God only, who will keep thee under the shadow of his wings'.[75] When Hopkins and Stearne visited Bury St Edmonds in 1645, a commission was appointed for the trial of witches. Among its members was Samuel Fairclough, a puritan pastor who had been prosecuted for nonconformity by Darrel's old adversary, Samuel Harsnet, during the 1620s.[76] Another commisioner was the godly divine, Edmund Calumy. Calumy's role in the prosecutions was later applauded by Richard Baxter, the famous puritan preacher and polemicist. Baxter himself had no doubt that the 'sad confessions' of the witches were genuine, having spoken 'with many understanding, pious and credible persons that lived in the county, and some that went to them in the prisons'.[77] The involvement of such people does not mean that Hopkins enjoyed the unanimous backing of the godly community: indeed, the witchfinder's principal opponent was the puritan pastor, John Gaule. But the activity of Stearne, Fairclough and Calumy in 1645 does show that he commanded support among a section of the godly.

The endorsement of these men is striking given the nature of the allegations in 1645. They were based on an image of the devil drawn largely from folklore, and quite unrelated to the protestant conception of Satan. Most of the confessions maintained the distinction between the fiend and familiar spirits, but their description of the 'imps' made them appear very similar to the devil. Anne Usher encountered a familiar in the guise of a polecat, which skipped onto her lap and 'said if she would deny Christ [and] God he wold bring her wittles'. Conversely, the admissions of other witches had the devil behaving like a familiar spirit. According to Elizabeth Greene, he appeared as a man at her bedside 'and nipped her by the neck', then drew 'three drops of blood of her arme'. He paid a similar visit on Elizabeth Hobart, who confessed that he came 'like a black boy and drew blood against her will at her back'.[78] Some of the confessions from Chelmsford in April 1645 collapsed the distinction completely. This was exemplified by the statement of Helen Clark:

This informant confesseth that about six weeks since, the devill appeared to her in her house, in the likenesse of a white dog, and that she calleth that familiar Elimanzer; and that this examinant hath often fed him with milk-pottage; and that the said familiar spake to this examinant audibly, and bade her deny Christ, and shee should never want, which she did then assent unto.

Another of the accused, Rebecca West, described the appearance of Satan at a gathering of witches:

Forthwith the devill appeared to them in the shape of a dogge; afterwards in the shape of two kitlyns, then in the shape of two dogges; and the said familiars did doe homage to . . . Elizabeth Clarke, and skipped up into her lap, and kissed her, and then kissed all that were in the roome . . . Rebecca told this informant that shee promised to keepe all their secrets, and moreover, they all told her that shee must never confesse any thing, although the rope were about her necke and shee ready to be hanged: and that after she had consented to all these things, the devill came into her lap, and kissed her, and promised to doe for her what she could desire.[79]

The merging of Satan with familiar spirits in these confessions faced Hopkins and his supporters with some obvious problems. Was it credible for the 'prince of this world' to appear as a white dog and feed on milk-pottage? Did he really take the form of a small animal to suck blood from his human confederates? These difficulties were acknowledged by Hopkins in *The Discovery of Witches* (1647), which identified queries 'which have been and are likely to be objected' to his activities. One query stated the problem succinctly: 'How can it possibly be that the devill, being a spirit, and wanting no nutriment or sustenation, should desire to suck any blood? And indeed, as he is a spirit, he cannot draw any such excrescences [as teats on witches' bodies], having neither flesh nor bone.' Hopkins' response affirmed his own belief that Satan was present in the bodies of familiar spirits. He argued that the devil 'doth really enter into the body [of a] reall, corporeall, substantial creature, and forceth that creature (he working in it) to his desired ends, and useth the organs of that body to speake withall, [and] to make his compact up with the witches, be the creature [a] cat, rat or mouse'.[80]

As well as conflating Satan with familiar spirits, the Hopkins trials endorsed a plethora of folk beliefs about witchcraft. The confession of Ellen Driver, for instance, was a bizarre combination of folklore and personal fantasy. She claimed that 'the devill appeared to her like a man, and that she was married to him in one . . . parish, and that he lived with her three years, and that she had two children by him in that time, which were changelings'. One night 'in bed with him, she felt of his feet and they were cloven'.[81] Hopkins's godly assistant, John Stearne, confirmed the traditional belief that witches could transform themselves into animals. He told the tale of a witch who received an injury while she was in the shape of a dog, then displayed the same wound when restored to her human body.[82] The prosecutions also appeared to endorse the practice of counter magic against witchcraft, which was mentioned in a number of the Chelmsford depositions in 1645. The evidence from Hopkins against the original suspect, Elizabeth Clarke, was supported by testimony from another Manningtree resident, John Rivet. After his wife had been 'taken sicke and lame, with such violent fits that . . . [he] conceived her sicknesse was something more than naturall', Rivet went to 'a cunning woman, the wife of one Hovye at Hadleigh in Suffolke', who told him that Clarke had bewitched her. Another witness in the proceedings scratched an alleged witch in order to relieve her stomach pains, which she believed the suspect had caused. She claimed that her 'extraordinary pains left her' as soon as she made the accused woman bleed.[83]

By tacitly accepting such beliefs, Hopkins and his supporters further compromised the puritan view of the devil, and the godly position that all magic constituted a form of witchcraft. At the same time, another aspect of the 1645 trials tended to undermine the protestant theology of Satan. This was the view, promoted energetically by Hopkins and Stearne, that

The devil and witches, from Joseph Glanvill's *Saducismus Triumphatus* (1689).

witchcraft was a collective enterprise. The belief that witches joined together to practice magic and pay homage to the devil had surfaced in the Lancashire trials of 1612, and was mentioned in Thomas Fairfax's account of his family's experience of witchcraft in 1621, but it was generally absent from English prosecutions before the Civil War.[84] By publicising the idea of a 'horrible sect of witches', the Hopkins trials endorsed the widespread view that the menace of witchcraft was confined to the practice of harmful magic, and strongly implied that this practice was restricted to a diabolical cult. The source of Hopkins' idea of a witch cult remains unclear, though Jim Sharpe has recently suggested that it had some roots in popular culture.[85] It seems certain, however, that many other aspects of the 1645 trials originated in folk religion and 'superstition'. This was the main reason why some godly protestants, like Thomas Ady and John Gaule, were opposed to Hopkins' proceedings. The objections of such men were consistent with the protestant theory of witchcraft developed by Perkins and Gifford in the sixteenth century. That these objections did not prevail with Hopkins' godly associates in 1645 is a measure of the willingness of some protestants to reconcile their beliefs with traditional ideas about the devil.

Dr Lamb's Darling

The Hopkins trials were part of a wider tendency for protestant doctrine and traditional beliefs to become entwined in the 1640s and 1650s. Following the outbreak of the Civil War, this process was encouraged by the propaganda needs of the parliamentarian party, which needed to present puritan ideas to a wide audience of potential supporters, and the collapse of censorship, which promoted an unprecedented outpouring and cross-fertilisation of ideas. In 1653, the integration of protestantism and folk beliefs about the devil reached its zenith in an extraordinary witchcraft pamphlet, *Doctor Lamb's Darling, or Strange and Terrible News From Salisbury*. This tract – which took its name from the infamous Dr Lamb, who was accused of sorcery and rape in 1628 – told the story of a serving maid called Anne Stiles.[86] Following the disappearance of a plate from her mistress's house, Stiles was sent to the witch, Anne Bodenham, who was famed for her ability to recover missing objects. Upon her arrival, the witch 'made a circle, and called [upon] Beelzebub, Tormentor, Lucifer, and Satan [to] appear; then appeared two spirits in the likeness of great boys, with long shagged black hair'. Bodenham then persuaded the terrified maid to write her name in blood 'in the devil's book'.

After making this compact, the tale's heroine was afflicted for days with dreadful visions and bouts of sickness. She eventually succumbed to possession by the devil, who entered her physically in the manner of a familiar spirit: 'the devil came in a terrible shape to me, entered within me, and there he lies swelling in my body, gnawing at my heart'. Falling into a deep trance, Stiles was assailed by further visions of the fiend, who watched her 'with glittering eyes' and promised to drag her down to hell. The climax of her ordeal came when the evil one appeared at her bedside 'in the likeness of a great black man', and engaged her in a terrible combat for her soul:

> [He] told her she must go with him, he was come for her soul, she had given it to him. But the maid answered that her soul was none of her own to give. It belonged to her lord and saviour, Jesus Christ, who had purchased it with his own precious blood; and although he [Satan] had got her blood, yet he should never have her soul. Whereupon, after tumbling and throwing the maid about, the devil vanished in a flame of fire.

The maid's triumph was achieved through her saving faith in Christ, but her encounter with the fiend was presented in starkly physical terms, far removed from the 'spiritual combats' fought by godly protestants like Margaret Hoby and John Bunyan. The devil himself was an amalgam of traditional images of Satan and the 'imps' described in contemporary witchcraft tracts. The witch who caused the woman's ordeal was presented as a 'cunning woman', from whom people sought advice about illnesses and stolen goods, but she was also a devil-worshipper. She also retained many of the qualities attributed to witches in folklore. The pamphlet noted, for example, her ability to transform herself into a wondrous variety of animal forms.[87]

It would be hard to imagine a more extraordinary concoction of protestant sentiments and folk beliefs than the story of *Dr Lamb's Darling*. But its mixture of traditional ideas and godly religion was, perhaps, typical of popular perceptions of Satan by the middle of the seventeenth century. It could be argued that such publications demonstrate the failure of the Reformation to transform the world-view of ordinary people, and lend support to the pessimistic accounts of godly contemporaries regarding 'the generall ignorance in all parishes and congregations'.[88] But this would probably be too harsh. The Reformation introduced a radical concept of the devil, which made him the master of all men and women who were not 'delivered by Christ out of Satan'. As its proponents acknowledged, this was a difficult and counter-intuitive doctrine, which was extremely hard to teach; and even godly protestants were sometimes forced to compromise with older, less demanding ideas about the devil's role in the world. The protestant vision was accepted in its entirety by a zealous few, but was tempered with traditional beliefs by the rest of the population.

8
CONCLUSION

THE DEVIL IN WAR AND PEACE

In one of the most lurid and unforgettable images of the English Civil War, the title page of the royalist pamphlet *The Devil Turn'd Roundhead* (1642) depicted Satan giving birth to a 'crop-headed' supporter of the king's rebellious parliament. In the accompanying text, the fiend assumed the guise of a fanatical puritan who professed to 'hate all good manners, all orders, orthodoxe divinitie, rule and government in the commonwealth and church'.[1] This viciously effective little tract was quickly answered by a parliamentarian rejoinder. *A Short, Compendious and True Description of the Round-heads and the Long-heads* (1642) exposed the king's supporters as 'the seed and spawn of the devil', distinguished by their 'grosse and palpable ignorance and blindnesse in spirituall and heavenly things', their addiction to prostitution, and their 'hatred against the appearance of any goodnesse'.[2] The invocation of Satan in these works was typical of the propaganda created by both sides during the war. Since the high profile of the devil in early modern England was caused largely by the religious conflicts which dominated the period, it was hardly surpising that the experience of civil war encouraged an outpouring of new writings about the fiend. At the level of high politics, godly preachers urged the parliament to redouble its efforts against the satanic enemy, who was readily identified with the opponents of a 'thorough reformation' of the English church. As Robert Baillie informed the House of Commons in February 1643, 'the great and chief leader of all who oppose the reformers of a church or state is the devil'.[3] In a less elevated context, each side in the conflict routinely demonised the other in cheaply produced newsbooks, pamphlets and ballads.

While it is impossible to measure the precise effects of the civil war on conceptions of the devil, it is likely that the conflict had two major consequences. First, it appears to have intensified anxieties about Satan, and to have extended these anxieties beyond the community of devout protestants. Popular literature of the period abounded with tales of the devil: he manifested himself to soldiers on both sides of the war, wreaked revenge on sinful innkeepers who stole the property of their guests, and

161

stole away unfaithful maidens who betrayed their lovers. On the parliamentarian side, it was rumoured that the royalist commander, Prince Rupert, had entered a pact with the fiend, and his favourite dog was a demonic familiar. These rumours were exploited in ballads like the *Dialogue Betweene the Devil & Prince Rupert* (1645). It is possible that this atmosphere contributed to the witchcraft panic in the eastern counties in the same year. In a small number of cases, witch beliefs were linked explictly to the war, such as the two women from Chelmsford who confessed to giving an imp to a young man who was 'resolved to goe to the king's party with it'.[4] More generally, it appears that the conflict encouraged a public awareness of the devil's activity in the world, which was conducive to the persecution of his alleged confederates.

The second consequence of the war was to accelerate the process of integration between protestant theories of Satan and traditional beliefs. The propaganda needs of both sides encouraged them to exploit popular ideas about the devil, despite the potential contradictions this involved. Thus parliamentarian tracts depicted the fiend as an avenging figure who punished the transgressions of royalist troops, often in a crudely physical fashion. In publications like *A Wonderfull and Strange Miracle, or God's Just Vengeance Against the Cavaliers* (1642), the blasphemy and drunkeness of the king's soldiers singled them out as targets for the devil's wrath. Such tracts reinforced the conventional wisdom that only the outwardly wicked were punished by the fiend. Later attacks on sectarian groups like Baptists and Quakers integrated folkloric tales about Satan with the familiar protestant theme that he was the 'father of lies'. In *A Sad Caveat to all Quakers* (1657), a Quaker apprentice from Worcester was beguiled by the evil one, who appeared to him in the guise of Jesus:

> It seems that the prince of darkness had appeared to him in the shape of some godly personage, and this credulous young man was apt to believe that it was Christ . . . [He said] that Christ had taken him by the hand, and that he had apointed him to come to him again, and that he must go unto him.

The unfortunate youth vanished soon afterwards, and his body was found in the river. According to the pamphlet, the spiritual message of this tragedy was pressed home by one of the town's godly pastors, who preached on the temptations of Satan 'and how neere of kinne is spiritual pride to hell'.[5] Such tales reinforced the idea that the devil was the animating 'spirit of falsehood' behind separatist groups in the 1650s, a theme developed at length in the writings of godly protestants like Jane Turner and Richard Baxter.[6]

Among royalist sympathisers, the assimilation of popular beliefs about Satan was evident in tales that the leaders of the republic established in 1649 were tormented by demons for their crimes against the king. In some versions, the devil appeared almost as a supernatural ally of earthly supporters of the monarchy. For instance, *The Just Devil of Woodstock* (1660) chronicled the 'apparitions, the frights and punishments' inflicted by a vengeful fiend on the despoilers of royal estates. It claimed that the surveyors of Woodstock park were disturbed by 'dreadful noises' and apparitions, which showed that 'the devil himself dislikes their doings'. The tract also announced that the Lord Protector was so terrified by demonic visitations that he kept 'nightly guards in and about his bed-chamber, and yet so oft [had] to change his lodgings'.[7] Such bizarre reports echoed earlier broadsheet ballads and protestant texts, such as *Strange Newes From Antwerpe* (1612), which presented Satan as a just destroyer of the enemies of true religion and good government.

Satan's Decline

If the tumultuous years between 1642 and 1660 marked the zenith of anxieties about Satan, and witnessed an unprecedented slew of publicity concerning his earthly activities, the period after the Restoration marked the beginning of his slow decline in some areas of public life. As has often been noted, belief in witchcraft diminished among intellectuals in the last quarter of the seventeenth century. This was accompanied by an increased scepticism about the physical manifestations of Satan's power, which provoked clerical authors like Joseph Glanvill and Richard Baxter to compile lengthy empirical treatises on the reality of the fiend, together with other entities belonging to the invisible 'world of spirits'. While Baxter regarded physical 'proofs' of Satan's existence as less compelling than theological arguments, he hoped they would leave sceptics 'that readeth them either convinced or utterly without excuse'.[8] Despite such efforts, however, educated opinion was increasingly divided on the question of the devil's power in the world. In 1677 the physicist Robert Boyle lamented that supernatural agencies of all kinds were derided by 'too many that would pass for wits'. A few years later, Henry Hallywell noted that belief in the devil was an invitation to mockery.[9] This movement in opinion was part of a much wider trend in intellectual circles, influenced by developments in science, the establishment of new standards of empirical evidence, and a general distaste for the perceived excesses of religious 'enthusiasm'. It is beyond the scope of this work to discuss these developments in detail, but it is reasonable to assume that each of them contributed to scepticism about the pervasive influence of Satan.

The arguments developed in this book also suggest that the reduction of religious conflict in the later seventeenth century might have played an important role in promoting new thinking. Under Elizabeth and the early Stuarts, it was the perception of devout protestants that they were a threatened minority – surrounded by hostile 'worldlings' at home and military enemies abroad – that encouraged them to emphasise the devil's great power. By the last quarter of the century, confessional warfare had subsided in Europe and conflict within the established church was rather less intense. As Jim Sharpe has noted, it would be misleading to state that religious intolerance declined sharply in the period after the Restoration. Nonetheless, he argues that a changed 'mental environment' did emerge, in which 'consensus was valued, where the dangers of religious heterodoxy had been demonstrated by recent experience, and where theological debate interacted constantly with the strain of maintaining a new political equilibrium'.[10] This new environment did not necessarily entail a decline in protestant commitment. Rather, it encouraged some thinkers to develop the potential that had always existed within protestant doctrines to diminish the role of Satan by emphasising the supreme power of God. In the early seventeenth century a minority of puritan divines had argued that Christians should not dwell excessively on the devil's power. As Richard Greenham advised a devout lady in 1618, such speculations were pointless 'since all is done and governed by divine providence for your good'.[11] But in an atmosphere of religious conflict and political instability, there was perhaps little incentive to promote such a relaxed approach. Arguably, such attitudes were more likely to flourish in the more settled circumstances of the late seventeenth century.

The emergence of less pessimistic ideas about the devil did not mean that the protestant theology of Satan faded away. Recent research has tended to emphasise the diversity of opinion within the late Stuart church, and suggests that the legacy of William Perkins remained vital among a section of the clergy.[12] Even Archbishop John Tillotson, a celebrated proponent of the pragmatic view that religion should 'tend to the public welfare of mankind and the peace and happiness of human societies', appears to have endorsed a Calvinist interpretation of the demonic predisposition of human nature: he affirmed that 'the lusts and passions of men do sully and darken their minds, even by a natural influence', and 'the foundation of hell is laid in the evil disposition of men's minds'.[13] Equally, popular traditions about the devil continued to develop and flourish, often garnished with anti-catholic sentiments. There is every reason to assume that the assimilation of popular beliefs and protestant doctrines continued after the period covered by this book, since the basic factors which caused this to happen remained in place.

First, the godly view of the devil was counter-intuitive and extremely demanding. It required individuals to accept that their natural inclinations were completely ensnared by Satan, and asked them to enter a lifelong combat against him. This idea was hard to communicate in popular media such as pictures, stories and songs. Second, pastors on the evangelical wing of the church were frequently tempted to exploit traditional beliefs about the devil, either to enhance their reputations by casting out demons or to promote their own religious agenda. This sometimes led them to compromise on theological issues, and to communicate a partially reformed view of Satan to the population at large. It appears that a similar dynamic continued to operate in the eighteenth and nineteenth centuries. With this in mind, the final section will offer a brief glimpse at the later career of the protestant devil.

AFTER THE REFORMATION

Writing in the 1680s, John Aubrey lamented the willingness of 'vulgar' people to believe in tales of fairies, apparitions and demons. These stories, he asserted, were commonly passed down from 'old women' to their children, 'who can hardly be of any other opinion, so powerful a thing is custom joyn'd with ignorance'.[14] Aubrey's insistence on the tenacity of such beliefs was echoed by other antiquarians in the early eighteenth century. In 1725 Henry Bourne, a curate from Newcastle, noted that many folk 'in country places' claimed to have seen fairies and spirits, 'and some have even seen the devil himself, with a cloven foot'.[15] The work of historians such as Owen Davies and James Obelkivich suggests that folkloric ideas about Satan remained firmly entrenched in much of the country throughout the eighteenth and nineteenth centuries. These ideas stressed the existence of Satan as a physical being rather than an abstract, spiritual force. An account from the late eighteenth century, for example, recorded the appearance of the fiend at a farmhouse in north Yorkshire. Assuming the unlikely disguise of a 'pig all a-fire', he proceeded to smash china on the kitchen floor.[16] More commonly, the evil one appeared as a well-dressed man. It was in this form, according to the nineteenth-century folklorist John Penny, that he appeared to a Lincolnshire man as he walked home penniless from a night's drinking. When he stooped to pick up a half crown from the road, he was approached by a stranger who offered him riches if he agreed to be his servant. The devil fled when the man replied that he was a servant of God. In other cases, clergymen dressed in black were mistaken by villagers for the evil one, coming to drag them to hell. As Obelkivich notes, such beliefs owed very little to official religious teachings. In contrast to academic theology, the devil 'in popular religion was a person, not a principle; he was a familiar, with nicknames, whom one met face to face'.[17]

As in the seventeenth century, it was evangelical clergy who proved most willing to endorse folkloric beliefs about the devil. From the 1740s onwards, Methodist pastors in particular were prepared to condone popular ideas about witchcraft, possession and exorcism, despite scepticism and disapproval from the church hierarchy. In part, this reflected John Wesley's well-publicised belief in the reality of witchcraft. Throughout his career, Wesley took a keen interest in cases of alleged possession and maintained a detailed correspondence on the subject.[18] The willingness of Methodist pastors to act as exorcists also reflected their need to establish their credentials as true servants of Christ. This need was especially strong because of the movement's semi-independent relationship with the Church of England, and its reliance on a powerful preaching ministry. One of the most dramatic Methodist exorcisms took place in Bristol in 1788. The demoniac, George Lucas, claimed to be possessed by seven demons, and believed that only the faithful prayers of seven ministers could drive them out. After an unsuccessful plea to the local Anglican clergy, the dispossession was performed by Joseph Easterbrooke, the vicar of Temple, together with six Wesleyan pastors. While the devil in George Lucas 'bid them defiance, cursing and vowing dreadful vengeance on all present', the company valiantly prayed, sang hymns, and commanded him to quit the man's body. Their efforts eventually overcame the fiend, who left his victim with a terrible howl.[19] While this case attracted considerable publicity, Wesley's journal and the 'spiritual experiences' published in his *Arminian* magazine suggest that similar cases occurred periodically throughout the eighteenth century, and were particularly associated with the Methodist ministry. Such incidents were siezed on by the movement's enemies in the established church, who cited them as evidence of its irrationality and dangerous 'enthusiasm'.

Like John Darrel and the godly supporters of Matthew Hopkins before them, some Methodist preachers were prepared to tolerate popular ideas about Satan when they suited their own purposes. In an early example from Bristol in 1739, a thunderstorm during a Methodist meeting provoked some people to rush around crying 'The devil will have me'. One yelled out that the 'fearful thunder is raised by the devil; in this storm he will bear me to hell'. According to John Cennick, the Wesleyan preacher who witnessed this tempest, the devil's wrath was provoked by the working of the Holy Spirit in the congregation. Cennick himself appears to have believed that the storms were raised by the evil one.[20] The willingness of Methodist clergy to endorse such ideas was particularly marked in rural areas. During the 1820s, Primitive Methodist preachers in Cheshire and Lincolnshire were convinced of the power of witches, and accepted that the process of religious conversion could involve physical encounters with Satan. As R.W. Ambler has noted, 'God and Christ were remote or talismanic figures' to many Lincolnshire Methodists, but Satan was a 'very real' presence in the world. In their struggle to save individual souls, local preachers often 'met and overcame what they saw as personal manifestations of the devil, using language and imagery which were meaningful for their converts'. These experiences were assimilated readily into accounts of local 'revivals', like the one recorded at the Holbeach branch of the Primitive Methodists in 1851:

> The consciences of the guilty have been grappled with; a free, full and present salvation has been urged; and though we have had some dreadful conflicts with the powers of darkness, the hosts of Israel have been more than victorious. Satan's right to the souls of those whom he has long held as his slaves has been courageously disputed by the servants of the living God; and the grand adversary has, in many cases, been defeated. Jesus has come to our help; the prey has been taken from the mighty; and upwards of sixty souls have professed to obtain the blessing of sin forgiven, and united with the church of Christ.[21]

In this instance, it appears that the protestant theology of Satan was imposed loosely on folk traditions, while evangelical clergy continued to endorse older beliefs about witchcraft, evil spirits and the devil.

Despite its formal split with the established church in the 1790s, and its subsequent division into a constellation of smaller denominations, the Methodist movement remained within the mainstream of English protestantism. Outside the orbit of conventional protestant theology, other groups developed their own, more idiosyncratic views about the devil. A spectacular example was provided by the Southcottian movement of the early nineteenth century, founded by the west country prophetess Joanna Southcott. Throughout her career as a religious leader, Southcott fought a series of ferocious battles with the evil one. In *A Dispute Between the Woman and the Powers of Darkness* (1802), she recorded a week-long combat with the enemy, whom she eventually overcame through the power of the Holy Ghost. Like Methodist exorcists, she presented her victory as a vindication of her faith; but she went on to proclaim that she enjoyed a special status as the mouthpiece of the Lord. Her work also incorporated traditional ideas about women and the devil, and echoed seventeenth-century chapbooks about the power of the female tongue to lash the fiend. At the end of their struggle, Satan proclaimed that 'God hath done something to chuse a bitch of a woman that will down-argue the devil, and scarce give him room to speak . . . It is better to dispute with a thousand men than with one woman.' In a further strange twist, he offered to surrender his earthly kingdom if he was defeated in a 'fair election'. This proposal neatly complemented the Southcottian practice of 'sealing', whereby the movement's supporters signed a petition demanding the defeat of Satan and the beginning of Christ's kingdom on earth.[22]

Joanna Southcott's exotic mixture of protestant theology, personal inspiration and folk beliefs about the devil was mirrored by another early nineteenth-century figure, the 'infidel' London preacher Robert Wedderburn. Like Soutcott, Wedderburn espoused a millenarian version of evangelical Christianity, but he combined this with radical anti-clericalism and an agenda for political reform. His writings also included elements of religious scepticism, though Iain McCalman has argued that he remained 'a radical Christian with millenarian leanings' throughout his career, while many of his followers 'believed in a mixture of folk magic and Christian supernaturalism'.[23] In 1828 Wedderburn produced a remarkable, semi-satirical tract expounding 'the holy liturgy, or divine service, upon the principles of pure Christian diabolism'. This presented Satan, or 'the God of this world', as a powerful but flawed divinity, deserving both the fear and respect of ordinary mortals. Despite his malevolent qualities, he would one day be converted to goodness, and this conversion was 'the necessary preliminary to the consumation of all earthly things'.[24] It appears that to Wedderburn the devil was a more immediate figure than the remote, omnipotent God of conventional protestant theology, and this view probably reflected the beliefs of the plebian radicals who attended his meetings.

The careers of Southcott and Wedderburn suggest that ordinary men and women were capable of appropriating the message of evangelical Christianity in creative and unpredictable ways. They also indicate the continuing potential for protestant teachings to become entwined with folk traditions. Both the prophetess and the London preacher came from lowly social backgrounds, and they both gathered a following among the poorest sections of English society. Both were initially attracted to Methodism, and incorporated some of its teachings in their idiosyncratic world-views. The combination of the evangelical movement, with its willingness to co-opt folklore to the cause of godly religion, and the readiness of ordinary people to select and reject elements of protestantism according to their own tastes, meant that popular conceptions of the devil were constantly mixed together with the protestant image of the evil one. This process had already begun in the sixteenth century, and was one of the many ambiguous legacies of the English Reformation.

APPENDIX

SELECTED SOURCES

With the exception of Jesus, the devil was probably the most popular biblical figure in early modern English literature. This makes it virtually impossible to present a completely representative sample of contemporary writing about the fiend. The following texts have been chosen because they illustrate some of the major themes developed in this book. In particular, they show the failure of the Reformation to impose a thoroughly reformed view of Satan on the 'common sort' of Christians, despite the anti-catholic sentiments expressed in texts like *God's Judgment Upon Hereticks* (1729). They also indicate the willingness of godly protestants to accept traditional ideas about the devil, especially in cases of witchcraft and demonic possession.

THE DEVIL AND THE SCOLD

This comic ballad, first printed around 1625, contains many elements that were common in pre-Reformation depictions of the devil. The fiend appears as a physical creature with bodily weaknesses, and the whole story is presented as a jocular entertainment. As was common in such tales, Satan is defeated by a determined woman, but her behaviour is linked to a typically female vice: in this case, the practice of 'scolding', or abusing her husband with insults and disobedient behaviour. The depiction of the fiend in the form of an animal was common in the seventeenth century. The image of a woman riding a devil-horse also echoed contemporary witchcraft pamplets, which described witches travelling in this way. Thomas Potts' *The Arraignement and Triall of Jennet Preston* (1612) and *The Wonderfull Discoverie of Witches in the Countie of Lancaster* (1613) described a familiar spirit 'like unto a white foale, with a blacke spot on the forehead'. After a gathering of witches at Malkin Tower in Lancashire, the witches departed 'on horseback like unto foals, some of one colour, some of another'.[1]

A Pleasant New Ballad you Here may Behold,
How the Devill, Though Subtle, was Gulled by a Scold (*c*. 1625)[2]

A woman well in years
Liv'd with a husband kinde,
Who had a great desire
To live content in minde.
But t'was a thing unpossible
To compass his desire,
For night and day with scolding
She did her husband tire . . .

Had he bid her goe homely,
Why then she would goe brave.
Had he cal'd her good wife,
She cal'd him rogue and slave.
Bade he, wife goe to church,
And take the finest pew,
She'd goe unto an alehouse,
And drinke, lye downe and spew.

The devill being merry,
With laughing at this mirth,
Would needs from hell come trotting
To fetch her from the earth.
And coming like a horse,
To tell this man his minde,
Saying, 'Sit her but astride my back,
I'll hurry her through the winde.'

'Kinde devill', quoth the man,
If thou a little will wait,
I'le bid her doe that thing,
Shall make her backe thee straight . . .

Content the devil cry'd,
Then to his wife goes he,
'Good wife, goe leade that horse,
So black and fair you see.'
'Goe leade, sir knave?', quoth she,
'And wherefore not goe ride?'
She took the devill by the reines,
And up she goes astride.

The devill neighed lowd,
And threw his heeles i'th ayre,
'Kick in the devill's name', quoth she,
'A shrew doth never fear.'
Away to hell he went,
With this most wicked scold,
But she did curbe him with the bit,
And would not loose her hold . . .

The devill shewed her all
The paines within that place,
And told her that they were
Ordain'd for scolds so base . . .

Then did she draw her knife,
And give his eare a slit.
The devill never felt
The like from mortall yet.
So fearing further danger,
He to his heeles did take,
And faster than he came,
He post haste home did make.

'Here take her', quoth the devill,
'To keep her here be bold,
For hell will not be troubled
With such an earthly scold.'

JUDGEMENT TALES

These simple, unpleasant stories indicate how hard it was to communicate the protestant message that all people were 'slaves of Satan' unless they were saved by Christ. It was much easier to depict the devil punishing individuals who were guilty of particular crimes. In the first tale, published shortly after the outbreak of the Civil War, a woman is carried away by demons after breaking a pledge to her 'sweetheart'. This theme recurred in contemporary stories like *A Good Warning for all Maidens* and *A Most Straunge and True Discoverie of the Wonderfull Judgement of God* (1600), which depicted satanic retribution on 'inconstant' women. In this instance, the text implies that the woman's fate is ultimately sanctioned by God, but it still conveys the message that only outwardly bad people will be punished in this way. The second tale, published in 1729, shows the persistence of this outlook. It tells the story of one Mr Woolstain, who was 'carried away by the devil from the house of Mr Stout, a barber in Abchurch Lane, on Wednesday the 9th day of April, 1729'. The story illustrates the persistence of grossly physical depictions of the devil, who left his victim 'on a dunghill near Shoreditch, with his bowels fallen out', and the view that only obvious malefactors attracted Satan's attention. As the victim was a notorious papist, the story also demonstrates the fusion of anti-popery with traditional ideas about the devil.

Strange and Miraculous Newes From Coventry (1642)[3]

In Coventry, within twelve miles of Warwicke, one Richard Boad, being in league with a maid, a mercer's daughter dwelling by the crosse, her name Anne Kirke, a contract [was] passed between them. He being in this troublesome time bent to the warres, came to her to take her leave, and to remember her former vowes and promises. She vowed and protested she would never marry any man but him if he survived this battaile . . . This she on her knees did sweare in private to him only, and desired him to take that for a reall satisfaction and called God to witness: That if she ever made a promise to any other in his absence, or thought of marriage, unlesse with him, that the same day she was married that the devil might fetch her, and have no pitty nor compassion but take her away, when she proved false in thought or deed.

They thus parted with many protestations and weeping teares, he to fight for the king and parliament, she to remaine at Coventry, his trusty and true joy, and all his delight. The battle at Keynton being done, and he not hurt, he got leave of his captaine on a Sunday morning, being then at Warwicke, to ride to Coventry to see this false perjured mayd. When he thither came, inquiring at the end of the city of this maid, his only joy and most delight, answer was made, 'She was this day married' . . .

The young soldier, being grieved, lay downe on a bed, and sent one to know when they were at their dancing . . . The time being come, thither he went, unknowne to any, the chamber being full with musicke and virgins danceing to the joy of the nuptuals. The bride passing by, he tooke her by the hand and said, 'Oh thou falce faire one, hast thou broke thy vowe?' She then replyed, 'A rash vowe is either broke or kept. Where is your witnesse?'

Just at that instant, two gentlemen being alighted at the doore, all in blacke, came up into the room. And [they] desired, being there wedding mirth and dancing, that one of them might have a dance with the bride. She gladly entertained it in the dance. The other [gentleman] standing by, fell in at last, [and] they tooke her up and away they carried her. They in the roome ran after; but no newes could they heare of the falce perjured bride. They ran into the fields, there being still a noyse in the ayre. At last, the two gentlemen in blacke came to them, with the brides garments, and said, 'Take these againe, we have power over her, but no power over her cloathes.' Then her sweetheart the soldier related to them the whole passage of her perjury.

God's Judgment Upon Hereticks (1729)[4]

For Wollstain now, that papist dog,
His sins full ripe were grown,
For not believing God or devil,
And worshipping of stone . . .

For lo! A form of monstrous size,
Black face and hideous mein,
With horrid shape, and glaring eyes,
The like was never seen.

'Thou wicked wretch', the devil said,
That thought'st my name a bubble;
Blazing to hell I'll carry thee,
And save the priests the trouble . . .

Next morn near Shoreditch, in a jakes,
His head quite turned behind,
His eyes sunk in, his tongue swell'd out,
Just so they did him find.

A GODLY EXORCISM

This arresting account was composed by Stanley Gower and published in 1651. As well as providing a colourful narrative of a protestant exorcism, it shows the relationship between demonic possession and the wider struggle between puritans and the devil. The first part of the extract describes how Richard Rothwel, the exorcist, suffered a possession-like experience himself, which he later related to the affliction of the demoniac, John Fox. During the exorcism itself, which took place around 1612, the dialogue between Rothwel and the devil dramatised the struggle between all godly protestants and the evil one. Subsequently, Fox kept a record of the temptations he continued to receive from Satan, and invited godly ministers to help him overcome them. Gower's story also includes some folkloric elements, which illustrate the fusion between protestantism and traditional beliefs about the devil. The fiend's attempt to prevent Rothwel from crossing a bridge, for example, resembles similar incidents described in contemporary witch trials; and his attempts to 'make a foole' of the exorcist recalls much older traditions of the devil as a trickster.

Stanley Gower, *The Life of Master Richard Rothwel* (1651)[5]

Two things (amongst many others) I think worthy [of] inserting into his life. The one is a strange sicknesse and recovery he had once at Bernards-Castle. His sicknesse was a vertigo capitis. He would have fourty fits at least in an houre, and every one of them accompanied with mischievous temptations, which when the fit was over, he dictated, and I writ down. These held him about three weeks, in which time he had the advice of learned physitians from London, Yorke, Newcastle, Durham, and other places. They all jumped in their judgements, imputing it to [too] much study, fasting, and inward trouble of spirit; their prescriptoins wrought kindly, but removed not his disease.

He desired divers Christians to pray for him on a day prefixed, and promised to joyne with them as well as he could, with some others that should be with him, assuring them that he was confident that disease would not be removed but by prayer and fasting. The morning of that day, he had a fit [which] continued foure houres together upon him, and the devil set upon him all that while, with most dreadful temptations, telling him he would make him the scorn of religion, and every man should reproach it for his sake, that had before by his means looked towards it, [and] that he should never preach more, but should blaspheme the name of God . . . The devil told him if he did fast and pray that day, he would torment and hinder him. We met at the time appointed, and Master Rothwell would needs have me to perform the duty, which through God's goodnesse I did, and the devil was not permitted to hinder or interrupt him or us, and God heard our prayers, so that he had never a fit after that . . .

The other is a relation which I had from himself, and from divers others to whom the story was known, that are yet alive . . . There was one John Fox living about Nottingham, who had no more learning then enabled him to write and read. This man was possessed with a devil, who would violently throw him down, and take away the use of every member of his body, which was turned as black as pitch in those fits, and then speak with an audible voice in him, which seemed somtimes to be heard out of his belly, sometimes out of his throat, and somtimes out of his mouth, his lips not moving. He lay thus, if I mistake not, [for] some yeares. Many prayers were put up to God for him, and great resort, especialy of godly ministers, [was made] to him, amongt the rest Master Bernard of Batcomb . . . and Master Langley of Truswel, betwixt whom and John Fox, I have seene divers passages in writing, he relating by pen his temptations, and they giving answers when he was stricken dumb.

As Master Rothwel was riding to see him, the devil told all that were in the house, 'Yonder comes Rothwel: but I will make a foole of him before he goes.' The people looked forth, and saw him coming, about a quarter of a mile from the house. As soon as he entred the roome, the devil said, 'Now Rothwel is come' . . . After a while, he further said:

Devil: *Say nothing [to] me of this man, for I tell thee he is damned*, and he added thereto, many fearfull blasphemies.

Rothwel: Thou are a lyar and the father of lies, nor art thou so well acquainted with the mind of God concerning this man, which makes thee thus to torment him, therefore I beleeve thee not, I beleeve he shall be saved by Jesus Christ.

Devil: *He is a murderer, and thou knowest no murderer must com into heaven.*

Rothwel: Thou liest again, for David murdered, and is in heaven; and the Jews with wicked hands cruicified the Lord of glory, yet both Christ prayed for them, and Peter exhorts them to repentance, that their sins may be blotted out.

Devil: *But this man hath not, cannot, shall not repent.*

Rothwel: If he had not, thou wouldst not have told him so, but if he have not, I beleeve God will give him repentance, and thou shalt not be able to hinder it.

Devil: *Thou art a murderer thyself, and yet talkest thus?*

Rothwel: Thou liest again. I have fought the Lord's battels against his known enemies, the idolatrous and bloody papists in Ireland, rebels to the queen my soveraign, by whose authority I bore armes against them, [but] otherwise I have killed no man.

Devil: (Swore and blasphemed) *Thou didst murder one this day as thou camest hither, and there is one behind thee will justifie it.*

Rothwel looked over his shoulder, and with that the devil set up a hideous laughter, that nothing could be heard for a great while, and then said:

Devil: *Look you now, did not I tell you I would make Rothwel a fool? And yet it is true, thou didst murder one this day. For as thou camest over the Bridge* (which he named), *there I would have killed thee, and there thy horse trod upon a flie and killed it.*

Master Rothwel's horse you must know stumbled there. It seems the devil had power to cause it, but without hurt either to Master Rothwel or his horse.

Rothwel: Thou hast oft beguiled me, I hope God will in time give me wisedome to discern, and power to withstand all thy delusions; and he it is that hath delivered me out of thy hands, and will I doubt not also deliver this poor man.

The devil blasphemed fearfully, quoted many Scriptures out of the Old and New Testament, both in Hebrew and in Greek, cavilled and played and critick, and backed his allegations with sayings out of the Fathers and Poets in their own language, which he readily quoted, so that the company trembled to heare such things from one that understood no learning, and that moved neither tongue nor lip. Master Rothwel was mightily enabled by God to detect the devils sophistry.

Devil: *What stand I talking with thee? All men know thou art Bold Rothwel, and fearest nobody, nor carest for words. Therefore I will talke to thee no more.* (That name he carried to his grave: they would say, 'that is he the devil called Bold Rothwel'.)

Rothwel, turning to the people, said, 'Good people, you see the goodnesse of our God, and his great power. Though the devil made a foole of me now, through my weaknesse, God hath made the devil dumb now. Do you see how he lyeth? Therefore let us go to prayer, that God who hath made him dumb, will (I doubt not) drive him out of this poor man' . . . They did so. Mr Rothwel kneeled by the bed on which the poore man lay. The devil for a quarter of an hour together, or more, made a horrid noise. Neverthelesse, Master Rothwel's voyce was lowder then the devil's . . . At length, the devil lay silent in the man, and after that departed from him. The man fetcht divers deep sighs, insomuch as they thought he had been expiring, but his colour returned to him, and the use of all his members, senses, and understanding; and at the next petition [in the prayer], he said, 'Amen', and continued to repeat his 'Amen' to every petition. Prayer was now turned into thanksgiving, and so concluded.

After prayer, John Fox said, 'Good Master Rothwel, leave me not. I shall not live long, for the devil tels me he will choak me with the first bit of meat that I eat.' Master Rothwel answered, 'Wilt thou beleeve the devil that seeks thy destruction, before thou wilt trust in God through Jesus Christ, that seeks thy salvation? Hath not God by his almighty power dispossessed him? Had he had his will, thou had'st been in hell before now. But he is a liar, and as he is not able to hinder thy soul's life, so neither shall he be able to destroy the life of thy body.' Wherefore get me something ready, saith he, for him, and I will see him eat before I go, and will crave a blessing upon it. When it was brought, 'Eat', saith Master Rothwell, 'and fear not the devil', shewing him that he might do it in faith of that ordinance by which God appoints meat for means to preserve life . . . With much ado, and in great trembling at last, the man took, and ate it. 'Looke', saies Master Rothwel, 'you all see the devil is a liar. The first bit hath not choaked him, nor shall the rest.'

Master Rothwel left him, after which he was sticken dumb for three years together. I had a book written with his own hand, of the temptations the devil haunted him with afterwards, and the answers divers godly and reverend ministers gave to those temptations; but the cavaliers got them and all, my book and writings. Thus the poore man remained tempted, but no longer possessed. At length, by prayer also (which was instantly put up to God for him, every Sabbath and lecture day, in many places), the Lord opened his mouth, and restored his speech to him, one using this petition, 'Lord open thou his mouth that his lips may shew forth thy praise.' He answered in the Congregation, 'Amen', and so continued to speak, and spake graciously to his dying day.

THE DEMON OF TEDWORTH

This text describes an infamous case of demonic 'obsession' suffered by the Mompesson family of Tedworth in Wiltshire. In March 1661, John Mompesson reported 'an idle drummer' to the constable of a neighbouring town. Subsequently, his family was tormented by strange knocking sounds and spectral visitations, which were attributed to witchcraft. The drummer was tried at Salisbury assizes in 1663 and sentenced to transportation. The details of the case, which were later written up by Joseph Glanvill, provide a bizarre illustration of the conflation of the devil with a witch's 'familiar'. The creature assailing the Mompessons closely resembled the 'imps' described in Chapter Seven: it came down the chimney, visited its victims at night in the form of a small animal, and attacked the

The demon of Tedworth, from Joseph Glanvill's *Saducismus Triumphatus* (1689).

bodies of children. At the same time, it was explicitly identified as Satan, and likened to the 'unclean spirits' described in the New Testament.[6] The creature's behaviour, and the repeated attempts by its victims to destroy it with weapons like pistols and swords, indicate the continuing belief that demons were vulnerable to physical attack. The noctural apparitions also recall the symptoms of sleep disorders like 'the hag'.

Joseph Glanvill, *Saducismus Triumphatus* (1689)[7]

During the time of the knocking, when many were present, a gentleman of the company said, 'Satan, if the drummer set thee to work, give three knocks and no more', which it did very distinctly and stopt. Then the gentleman knockt, to see if it would answer him as it was wont, but it did not. For further trial, he bid it for confirmation, if it were the drummer, to give five knocks and no more that night, which it did, and left the house quiet all the night after. This was done in the presence of Sir Thomas Chamberlain of Oxfordshire, and divers others.

On Saturday morning, an hour before day, Jan 10 [1663], a drum was heard beat upon the outsides of Mr Mompesson's chamber, from whence it went to the other end of the house, where some gentlemen strangers lay, playing at their door and without, four or several tunes, and so went off into the air . . . One morning, Mr Mompesson, rising early to go [on] a journey, heard a great noise below, where the children lay, and running down with a pistol in his hand, he heard a voice, crying 'A witch, A witch', as they had also heard it once before. Upon his entrance, all was quiet.

Having one night played some little tricks at Mr Mompesson's bedsfeet, it went into another bed, where one of his daughters lay. There it passed from side to side, lifting her up as it passed under. At that time there were three kinds of noises in the bed. They endeavoured to thrust at it with a sword, but it still shifted and carefully avoided the thrust, still getting under the children when they offered at it. The night after, it came panting like a dog out of breath. Upon which, one took a bedstaff to knock, which was caught out of her hand, and thrown away, and company coming up, the room was presently filled with a bloomy smell, and was very hot, though without fire, in a very sharp and severe winter. It continued in the bed panting and scratching an hour and a half, and then went into the next chamber, where it knockt a little, and seemed to rattle a chain. Thus it did for two or three nights together.

After this, the old gentlewoman's Bible was found in the ashes, the paper being downwards. Mr Mompesson took it up, and observed that it lay open at the third chapter of St Mark, where there is mention of the unclean spirits falling down before our saviour, and of his giving power to the twelve [disciples] to cast out devils, and of the scribes' opinion that he cast them out through Beelzebub. The next night they strewed ashes over the chamber, to see what impressions it would leave. In the morning they found in one place the resemblance of a great claw . . .

There came one morning a light into the children's chamber, and a voice crying, 'A witch, A witch', for at least a hundred times together. Mr Mompesson at another time (being in the day), seeing some wood move that was in the chimney of a room where he was, as of itself, discharged a pistol into it, after which they found several drops of blood on the hearth, and in divers places of the stairs.

For two or three nights after the discharge of the pistol, there was calm in the house, but then it came again, applying itself to a little child newly taken from nurse, which it so persecuted that it would not let the poor infant rest for two nights together, nor suffer a candle in the room, but carry them away lighted up the chimney, or throw

them under the bed. It so scared this child by leaping upon it, that for some hours it could not be recovered out of the fright. So that they were forced again to remove the children out of the house. The next night after which, something about midnight came up the stairs, and knockt at Mr Mompesson's door, but he lying still, it went up another pair of stairs to his man's chamber, to whom it appeared standing at his bed's foot. The exact shape and proportion he could not discover, but he saith he saw a great body with two red and glaring eyes, which for some time were fixed steadily upon him, and at length disappeared.

Another night, strangers being present, it purr'd in the children's bed like a cat, at which time also the cloaths and children were lifted up from the bed, and six men could not keep them down. Hereupon they removed the children, intending to have ript up the bed. But they were no sooner laid in another, but the second bed was more troubled than the first. It continued thus four hours, and so beat the children's leggs against the bed-posts, that they were forced to arise, and sit up all night. After this it would empty chamber-pots into their beds, and strew them with ashes, though they were never so carefully watcht. It put a long piked iron into Mr Mompesson's bed, and into his mother's a naked knife upright . . .

About the beginning of April 1663, a gentleman that lay in the house, had all his money turned black in his pockets. And Mr Mompesson, coming one morning into his stable, found the horse he was wont to ride, on the ground, having one of his hinder leggs in his mouth, and so fastened there that it was difficult for several men to get it out with a leaver. After this, there were some other remarkable things, but my account goes no further. Only Mr Mompesson writ me word, that afterwards the house was several nights beset with seven or eight [apparitions] in the shape of men, who, as soon as a gun was discharged, would shuffle away together into an arbour.

WITCHCRAFT AND POSSESSION

John Darrel's account of the possession and exorcism of William Sommers in 1598 provides a perfect illustration of the intertwining of witchcraft, godly religion and traditional beliefs concerning the devil. Sommers claimed that his affliction was caused by witchcraft, and described his encounters with the 'old woman' who introduced the spirit into his body. His symptoms included the moveable swellings which were often associated with possession by familair spirits. These manifestations were also understood by Sommers and those around him as signs of the devil. The dispossession itself was a demonstration of the power of the puritan ministry. It was attended by three godly pastors as well as the exorcist himself, and apparently attracted a large crowd of spectators. The controversy surrounding the case resulted in the publication of alternative versions of the events described below, which shed some light on the demoniac's extraordinary symptoms. In 1599, for example, Samuel Harsnet challenged Darrel's assertion that the possessed man turned his head so that it faced backwards. Instead, he cited a witness who claimed that Sommers had 'turned his face a good way towards his shoulder', but no further. The same witness observed that the effects of poor lighting made the demoniac's behaviour appear more remarkable than it really was.[8] Despite such objections, Darrel and his associates maintained the genuineness of Sommers' affliction, and in the process they endorsed many folkloric ideas about witchcraft and the devil.

John Darrel, *The True Relation of the Grievous Handling of William Sommers of Nottingham, Being Possessed With a Devill* (1641)[9]

William Sommers of Nottingham, sonne in law to Robert Cowper of the said towne, and by grade of life a musician, about eight or nine yeares past, as he journed from Bellyn in the County of Wigorne (where hee then dwelt with one Mr Anthony Brackenbery) to Bromsgove, a market towne in that shire, accompanyed with an old woman dwelling in the said Bellyn, found an hat with a copper band. The woman requiring the same, he gave her the hat, though unwillingly, but the band he utterly refused to give, supposing it to bee of gold. Whereupon she threatning him, said that it had beene good for him to have given it her. After this, in the night he saw a strange light in the chamber where he lay, which cast him into a great feare, and thus hee continued frighted for a time. Shortly after, Mr Brackenbery, his master, removed to Holme, neare to Newark upon Trent in the County of Nottingham. Being there sent about his master's businesse unto Newark, in the way as he went thither, he was suddenly thowne into a ditch, some eight yards distant from the high way there in his journey, but by that he had gone a very little way further, he was taken again and cast into a thorne bush about sixty yeards distant from the high way. But how he came into it or the ditch hee knew not . . .

In his going thither [to Walton in Derbyshire], there met him in Blackwel Moors at a deepe coale-pit hard by the high way side, an old woman (as he thought) who asked him where he dwelt, and whither he was going, without any more words. Above two mile and halfe further (he having gone forward [at a] journying pace without stay), she met him againe, and passed by him without any words. The next day, he returning from Walton homewards, she met him at the aforesaid pit, and asked him how he did, saying further, 'I must have a penny from thee.' He answered that he had no money. 'Thou hast', quoth she, 'Mary Milwood gave thee a pence, I will have a penny of it or I will throw thee into this pit, and break thy necke' . . . He gave her three pence which indeed had bin given him by the said Mary. After this she put her hand to a bag she had about her, and taking thence a peece of bread with butter spred on it, bad him eate it. He refusing, shee threatned him againe to throw him into the pit and breake his necke if he would not eate it. Whereupon (greatly against his will, and for feare), he did eat it, and in the eating it seemed as sweet as any honey . . . Then a cat (as the boy thought) leapt up into her bosome, the which she imbraced, and with her armes claspt it unto her, and thus they parted each from other.

The said Sommers, being at Nottingham in the house of his [new] master, Thomas Porter, did use such strange and idle kinde of gestures, in laughing, dauncing, and such like light behaviour, that he was suspected to be mad. Sundry time he refused all kinde of meat for a long space together, in so much as hee did seeme thereby to pine away. Sometimes he shaked as if hee had had an ague. There was heard a strange noise or flapping from within his body. He was often seen to gather himselfe on a round heape under his bed clothes, and being so gathered to bounce up a good height from the bed; also, to beat his head and other parts of his body against the ground and bedstead, in such earnest manner, and so violently, than the beholders did feare that thereby he would have spoyled himselfe, if they had not by strong hand restrained him, and yet thereby received he no hurt at all. In most of his fits he did swell in his body, and in some of them did so greatly exceed therein, as hee seemed to be twice so big as his matiriall body. Oft also was he seene to have a certaine variable swelling or lump to a great bignesse, swiftly running up and downe betweene the flesh and skinne, through all the parts of his body, and many times when that swelling was [seen], these or the like words were heard out of his mouth: 'I will goe out at his eyes, or eares, or toes', at which speeches the said swelling, evidently appearing in such parts, did immediately remove and vanish away. This swelling did not onely run from eye to eye, from cheeke to cheeke, and up and downe along still in the body, but besides being now in the one leg, presently it would be in the other, and so of the armes in like manners . . .

In sundry of his fits, he did utter so strange and fearfull schrieking as cannot bee uttered by man's power, and was of such strength as sometimes four or five men, though they had much advantage against him by binding of him to a chaire, yet could they not rule him. And in shewing that strength he was not perceived to pant or blow, no more then if he had not strained nor strugled at all. Sometimes he cryed exteamly, so as teares came from him in great abundance. Presently after, he would laugh aloud and shrill, his mouth being shut closed. And being demanded concerning those accidents, he protested he knew of no such matter, neither felt he any paine. Moreover, he was often times cast into the fire, some bare part of his body also lying in the fire, and yet was not burned; and sometimes [he was] cast violently against the ground, and against the wall or posts of the house, without any hurt of his body, and in many wayes seeke to destroy himselfe, by reason where of they were driven to take away his knife, girdle, garters, etc . . . His speeches were usually vaine, delivered in very scoffing manner, and many times filthy and uncleane, very unfit once to be named, or blasphemous, swearing most fearfully, using one bloody oath after another, [and] sometimes saying, 'I am God', and sometimes, 'There is no God.'

Being moved to say the Lords Prayer, when he came to these words, Lead us not into temptation, hee would say, Lead us into temptation. Divers fond speeches did he use to interrupt them that prayed for him. Many strange speeces also were uttered by him, not in his owne name, but as spoken by an evil spirit possessing him . . . [He said] that his name was Lucye, that he was king, that he was prince of darknesse. 'You thinke I have no power of him, yet I can use his tongue, his teeth, lippes, hands, legges, his body and all parts of him.' And as the spirit named each part, hee used it . . .

One John Sherwood, charging him to tell who sent him thither, he answered, 'A woman'. He charged him againe to tell where she dwelt. He answered, 'In Worcestershire'. Whether is she living or dead? 'Dead', said hee. Wherefore did she send thee? 'For a hat and hatband'. Then the boy, when the fit was done, was questioned concerning these things, whereunto he returned for answer that which is set downe in the begining of this story, which he had concealed untill that time. Hereunto I might adde certaine direct answers he made in Latine to those speeches which in Latine were used unto him. A little Greek he also spoke, being ignorant in those languages, altogether in the one, and understanding little or nothing in the other.

In going thus with the boy, I was importuned on his behalfe, first by two letters, after by another from the mayor, and thereupon I went unto him . . . Towards that evening [when] I came, he seemed to be sicke, and his sicknesse greatly to increase upon him, so as they feared he would have dyed, or had been dead. For he lay an houre with his face and hands blacke, cold as ice, not breath being perceived to come from him . . . I did assure him that he was possessed, and had in that body of his a divell, and did so frame the words of my mouth, as might best serve to prepare and stir him up to a spirituall fight against Satan, or resistance of him in faith. This evening he acted many sins by signes and gestures, most lively representing and shadowing them out unto us, namely: brawling, quarrelling, fighting, swearing, robbing by the high wayes, picking and cutting of purses, burglary, whoredome, pride both in men and women, hypocisie, slugishnesse in hearing the Word, drunkennesse, gluttony, also dancing with the toyes thereto belonging, the manner of anticke dances, the games of dicing and carding, the abuse of the viole, with other instruments. At the end of sundry of these he laughed exceedingly, divers times clapping his heands on his thighes for joy. And at the end of some of them, as killing and stealing, he shewed how he brought them to the gallowes, making a signe thereof. During this time, which continued about an houre, as hee was altogether silent, so was hee most active, though his eyes were closed . . . In a word, these things were in such lively and orient colours painted out (as I may say) unto us that were present, being to the number of some sixty, that I for my owne part, (and I am perswaded the rest of the beholders are of my minde) doe verily thinke, that is not in the skill and power of man to doe the like. Wilst we were recommending him and his grievous estate to the Lord, and intreating his Majesty in his behalfe, hee uttered these words: 'I must be gone.'

The next day being the Lords day, I came not to him untill about three a clocke in the afternoon, (finding company with him), at which time I used some speech, wherein I endevoured to prepare both him and his master's family, and also his parents . . . unto the holy exercise the day after to be performed. Towards evening, much people reported to the house. Then some words of exhortation were used by myselfe, for the sanctifying of so many of us, whose spirits God should stirre up [to] joyn in that solemne service and worship of God to be performed on the day following . . . This evening, and all the night long, [Satan] handled him more extreamly then before. At this time, among other things, the spirit retorted his tongue into his throat, and this he did often, whereupon many looked with a candle into his mouth, where they could see not tongue nor part of it, onely in his throat they beheld the root thereof. Hee uttered often these words, 'For corne, for corne', with a few more thereunto, noting the

unsatiable desire of gaine, or raising the price of corne in corne men
. . . This evening I requested the minister of that congregation, Mr
Aldridge, Mr Aldred, and Mr Halem, pastors of two severall townes
neere adjoyning unto Nottingham, to joyne with me on the morrow
in the minstration of the Word and Prayer, whereunto they
condescended . . .

In the morning, many of us were assembled together in the next
convenient and seemly roome to [the] place of his abode. The boy was
brought . . . by six or seaven strong men, who had all of them
enough adoe to bring him, and laid him on a couch in the midst of us
. . . All this day he was continually vexed and tormented by Satan,
having little rest at all, so as the same for vexation by the spirit, farre
exceeded any of the dayes before. His torments in his fits were most
grievous and fearfull to behold, wherein his body being swelled, was
tossed up and downe. In these fits his strength was very great, so as
being held downe with five strong men, hee did notwithstanding all
their strength, against their wills, rise and stand upright on his feet.
Hee was also continually torne in very fearfull manner, and disfigured
in his face, wherein sometimes his lips were drawne awry, now to one
side, now to the other. Sometimes his face and necke distorted to the
right and to the left hand, yea sometimes writhen to his backe.
Sometimes he thrust out his tongue very farre and bigge, and
sometimes turned backwards into his throat, gaping so wide that we
might afarre off perceive it. Now he gnashed with his teeth, now he
fomed like to the Horse or Boare, roaping downe to his breast,
notwithstanding there was one purposely standing by with a cloath
ever and anon to wipe it away. Not to say anything of his fearfull
staring with his eyes, and incredible gaping.

This day, notwithstanding he was so held, as is aforesaid, hee went
about to have choked and so destroyed himselfe. Speeches he used
none, save once in a great voyce, 'Corne!' And when I applied that
speech of our Saviour, 'All things are possible to him that beleeveth',
hee used these words, 'Thou liest'. Divers times he shrieked or cried
aloud in a strange and supernaturall manner. Sometimes he roared
fearfully like a beare, and cried like a swine.

Towards the evening, as I was treating of these words, 'Then the
spirit cryed and rent him sore, and came out, and he was as one
dead, insomuch that many said he is dead', the boy was rent sore
indeed, cryed, and that aloud. Then the people which were present
. . . cried out all at once, as it were with one voyce unto the Lord,
to have mercy upon him. And within a quarter of an houre (they
and he still crying alowd), he held down on a bed by five men, and
offering as though hee would have vomited, was on the sudden

violently cast, and his body there was turned, so as his face lay downwards to the ground, and at the beds feet, and his backe upward, with his feet on the beds head. And thus hee lay as if he had been dead for a season. Thus we have heard not only how it went with Sommers in the time of his possession, and at and little before his dispossession, but also how and by what meanes I came unto him, and being there, carried my selfe in the present action.

ABBREVIATIONS OF FREQUENTLY CITED SOURCES

Allen, *Satan*   Hannah Allen, *Satan His Methods and Malice Baffled* (1683)

Ashmole, Napier   Bodleian Library, Oxford, Ashmole MSS, casebooks of Richard Napier

Bateman, *Christall Glasse*   Stephen Bateman, *A Christall Glasse of Christian Reformation* (1569)

Brettergh   *A Brief Discourse of the Christian Life and Death of Mistris Katherin Brettergh* (1606 edition)

Bunyan, *Grace Abounding*   John Bunyan, *Grace Abounding to the Chief of Sinners*, ed. W.R. Owens (Penguin, London 1987)

Burton, *Anatomy*   Robert Burton, *The Anatomy of Melancholy* (1621), eds Thomas Faulkener, Nicholas Kiessling and Rhonda Blair (1989–94)

Clarke, *Generall Martyrologie*   Samuel Clarke, *A Generall Martyrologie* (1651)

Darrel, *Triall*   John Darrel, *The Triall of Maist. Dorrell* (1599)

Darrel, *True Relation*   John Darrel, *A True Relation of the Grievous Handling of William Sommers of Nottingham* (1641 edition)

Euing   *The Euing Collection of English Broadside Ballads* (Glasgow, 1971)

Ewen, *Witchcraft*   C. L'Estrange Ewen, ed., *Witchcraft and Demonianism* (Heath Cranton, London 1933)

Ewen, *Witch Hunting*   C. L'Estrange Ewen, ed., *Witch Hunting and Witch Trials* (Kegan Paul, London 1929)

Fairfax, *Demonologia*   Edward Fairfax, *Daemonologia: A Discourse on Witchcraft*, ed. William Grainge (Harrogate 1882)

Gifford, *Countrie Divinity*   George Gifford, *A Brief Discourse of Certaine Points of the Religion Which is Among the Common Sort of Christians, Which may be Termed the Countrie Divinity* (1584)

Haining, *Witchcraft Papers*   Peter Haining, ed., *The Witchcraft Papers* (1973)

Hoby, *Diary*	Margaret Hoby, *The Private Life of an Elizabethan Lady: The Diary of Lady Margaret Hoby*, 1599–1605, ed. Joanna Moody (Sutton, Stroud 1998)
Merry Drollery,	*Merry Drollery, or a Collection of Jovial poems, Merry Songs, Witty Drolleries* (1661)
Olde, *Short Description*	John Olde, *A Short Description of Antichrist Unto the Nobility of Englande* (1557)
Perkins, *Foundation*	William Perkins, *The Foundation of Christian Religion Gathered Into Sixe Principles* (1641 edition)
Powell, *Spirituall Experiences*	Vavasour Powell, ed., *Spirituall Experiences of Sundry Beleevers* (1652 edition)
Rogers, *Ohel*	John Rogers, *Ohel or Beth-Shemesh* (1653)
Rosen, *Witchcraft*	Barbara Rosen, ed., *Witchcraft in England, 1558–1618* (University of Massachusetts Press 1991)
Roxburghe	*The Roxburghe Ballads*, ed. W.M. Chappell (1871–1880)
Stubbes, *Christall Glasse*	Philip Stubbes, *A Christall Glasse for Christian Women* (1618 edition)
Thomas, *Religion*	Keith Thomas, *Religion and the Decline of Magic* (Weidenfeld & Nicolson, London 1971)
Walker, *Unclean Spirits*	D.P. Walker, *Unclean Spirits: Possession and Exorcism in France and England in the Late Sixteenth and Early Seventeenth Centuries* (Scolar 1981)

NOTES AND REFERENCES

For key to abbreviations of frequently cited works, see p. 187.

1. Introduction: The Social History of Satan

1. M.R. James, *Collected Ghost Stories* (Wordsworth, 1992), 241–2.
2. *Euing*, 277.
3. William Peter Blatty, *The Exorcist* (Corgi, 1972), 281, 293.
4. *Roxburghe*, I, 32; *Stand Up For Your Beliefe, or A Combat Betweene Satan Tempting and A Christian Triumphing* (1640).
5. Elaine Pagels, *The Origin of Satan* (Penguin, 1995).
6. An accessible introduction to the theology of evil is provided by Peter Vardy, *The Puzzle of Evil* (Fount, 1992).
7. For Augustine's discussion of the problem of evil, see *The Confessions of St Augustine*, trans. F.J. Sheed (Sheed and Ward, London 1944), 103–7. Augustine's theory of predestination is discussed in Gordon Leff, *Medieval Thought From Augustine to Ocham* (Merlin, London 1958), 37–9.
8. Jeffrey Burton Russell, *Mephistopheles: The Devil in the Modern World* (Cornell, 1986), 46.
9. Russell, *Mephistopheles*, 38.
10. Gilbert Dugdale, *A True Discourse of the Practises of Elizabeth Caldwell* (1604), B2r.
11. The historical debate about the doctrine of predestination in Elizabethan and early Stuart England is outside the range of this book. Nicholas Tyacke has argued that the doctrine was an essential component of the religious settlement until it was challenged by Charles I, whose innovations in the theology and practice of the established church eventually provoked a Calvinist 'counter revolution'. This interpretation has been contested by Peter White, who claims that Tyacke overestimates the extent of consensus on the doctrine prior to Charles' accession, and suggests that it was always treated with caution by the crown. The best recent collection of essays on this subject is Kenneth Fincham, ed., *The Early Stuart Church* (Macmillan, 1993).
12. Russell, *Mephistopheles*, 35, 37.
13. William Perkins, *A Discourse on the Damned Art of Witchcraft* (1608), reprinted in Haining, *Witchcraft Papers*, 126.
14. John Calvin, *Institutes of the Christian Religion*, reprinted in Alan Kors and Edward Peters, eds, *Witchcraft in Europe, 1100–1700: A Documentary History* (University of Pennsylvania Press, 1972), 204.
15. Rosen, *Witchcraft*, 172.
16. Martin Luther, *Commentary on St Paul's Epistle to the Galatians* (Philadelphia, 1875), 590–1.
17. Brian Levack, *The Witch Hunt in Early Modern Europe* (Longman, 1987), 110.
18. For a detailed account of this argument, see Christina Larner,

Witchcraft and Religion (1984),
Chapter Four.

19. John Foxe, preface to the 1570
edition of *Acts and Monuments*, in
L.J. Trinterud, ed., *Elizabethan
Puritanism* (Oxford University Press,
1971), 65.
20. The best account of Darrel's career is
in D.P. Walker, *Unclean Spirits*, 52–73.
21. Darrel, *True Relation*, A4rv.
22. Samuel Harsnet, *A Declaration*
(1603), 136–7.
23. Darrel, *Triall*, 22, 34–5.
24. *Ibid*, 66.

2. The Devil and the English Reformation

1. *A L Mery Talys* (1526), 1v–2v.
2. R.W. Scribner, *Popular Culture and
Popular Movements in Reformation
Germany* (Hambledon, London
1987), 88.
3. Halcyon Backhouse (ed.), *The Cloud
of Unknowing* (Hodder and
Stoughton, London 1985), 84.
4. Ronald C. Finucane, *Miracles and
Pilgrims: Popular Beliefs in Medieval
England* (2nd edition, Macmillan,
London 1995), 108–9.
5. *Mery Talys*, 6v.
6. For discussions of the dimensions of
hell see Piero Camporesi, *The Fear of
Hell: Images of Damnation and
Salvation in Early Modern Europe*
(Polity Press, Oxford 1990), 30–2.
A protestant critique of grossly
physical ideas of hell can be found
in Thomas Browne, *The Major
Works*, ed. C.A. Patrides (Penguin,
London 1977), 125.
7. This legend is described mockingly
by the protestant polemicist Stephen
Bateman in his *Golden Booke of the
Leaden Goddes* (1577), 29–30.
8. Eamon Duffy, *The Stripping of the
Altars: Traditional Belief in England,*

1400–1580 (Yale University Press,
1992), 216, 268–9, 279–81.
9. Finucane, *Miracles*, 204.
10. Augustus Jessopp, *Random Roaming
and Other Papers* (London 1894),
109–12.
11. The invocation of demons is
discussed in Richard Kieckhefer's
*European Witch Trials: Their
Foundations in Popular and Learned
Culture, 1300–1500* (Routledge &
Kegan Paul, London 1976) 34–5,
69–71. A detailed description of
invocation in sixteenth-century
England is contained in *The
Examination of John Walsh of
Dorsetshire* (1566).
12. *Tales and Quicke Answeres, Very Mery
and Pleasant to Rede* (*c.* 1530), C2r,
H1r, H3v; *Mery Talys*, 13r.
13. For the depiction of Satan in
medieval drama see *English Mystery
Plays*, ed. Peter Happe (Penguin,
London 1975), 393–4, 556–64.
14. Julian of Norwich, *Revelations of
Divine Love*, ed. Clifton Walters
(Penguin, London 1966), 84, 182,
199. For Margery Kempe see
Richard Kieckhefer, *Unquiet Souls:
Fourteenth-Century Saints and Their
Religious Milieu* (University of
Chicago Press, 1984), 183–4.
15. Richard Whytford, *A Werke for
Housholders, or for Them yt Have the
Gydiynge or Governaunce of any
Company* (1530), G1v.
16. Whytford, *Werke*, B3r.
17. Thomas Becon, *The Worckes of
Thomas Becon* (1564), I,
390v–391v, 423v–424r.
18. Martin Luther, *Commentary on St
Paul's Epistle to Galatians*
(Philadelphia 1875), 287–90. For
Luther's views on the devil see
Heiko Oberman, *Luther: Man
Between God and the Devil* (Yale
University Press, 1989), 102–6.

19. The most complete expression of Perkins' theology of the devil is probably *A Discourse of the Damned Art of Witchcraft* (1608).

20. William Chub, *The True Travaile of all Faithfull Christians* (1584), 137v.

21. Jeffrey Burton Russell, *Mephistopheles*, 30–3; see also David Nicholls, 'The Devil in Renaissance France', in *History Today*, November 1980, 25–30.

22. Whytford, *Werke*, E4v.

23. Perkins, *Foundation*, 3, 16.

24. Richard Sibbes, *The Saints Safetie in Evill Times* (1634), 6.

25. John Bradford, *A Godlye Medytacyon Composed by the Faithfull and Constant Servant of God J B* (1559), 27–8.

26. William Gouge, *The Whole Armour of God* (1627 edition), 28.

27. This advice is taken from point thirteen of 'a scoare of holesome preceptes' attributed to Richard Greenham in *Short Rules Sent by Maister Richard Greenham to a Gentlewoman Troubled in Minde* (1618).

28. Olde, *Short Description*, 29v.

29. Bateman, *Christall Glasse*, C1r.

30. John Reynolds, *The Triumphs of Gods Revenge Against the Crying and Execrable Sinne of . . . Murther* (1634), preface.

31. Olde, *Short Description*, 2v.

32. Gryffith Williams, *The True Church: Shewed to all Men, That Desire to be Members of the Same* (1629), 556.

33. *Euing*, 107.

34. William Perkins, *Lectures Upon the First Three Chapters of the Revelation* (1604), 57–8.

35. *Roxburghe*, III, 165.

36. Perkins, *Lectures*, 187; Perkins, *Foundation*, 3.

37. Gifford, *Countrie Divinity*, 26; Sibbes, *Saints Safetie*, 17–18.

38. Bradford, *Godlye Medytacyon*, 27.

39. Elizabeth Grymeston, *Miscelanea, Meditations, Memoratives* (1604), D2r.

40. Becon, *Worckes*, I, 314r.

41. S.S., *A Briefe Instruction for all Families* (1586), dedication.

42. Richard Carpenter, *Experience, Historie and Divinitie* (1641), 148.

43. See, for example, Bateman, *Christall Glasse*, D4r, J1r; Gouge, *Whole Armour*, title page.

44. Martin Seymour-Smith, ed., *The English Sermon, 1550–1650* (Carcanet Press, Cheadle 1976), 279.

45. On the royalist side see, for example, *The Devil Turn'd Roundhead: or Pluto Become a Brownist* (1642); for a parliamentarian version see Ellis Bradshaw, *A Dialogue Betweene the Devil & Prince Rupert* (1645).

46. Olde, *Short Description*, 30r–30v; Stephen Bateman, *The Golden Booke of the Leaden Goddes* (1577), 30.

47. Richard Kenneth Emmerson, *Antichrist in the Middle Ages: A Study of Medieval Apocalypticism, Art and Literature* (Manchester University Press, 1981), 207, 210.

48. Olde, *Short Description*, 7r–7v.

49. *The First Examinacyon of Anne Askewe, Latelye Martyred in Smythfelde . . . With the Elucidacyon of Johan Bale* (1546), 25r.

50. Perkins, *Lectures*, 354.

51. I.H., *The Divell of the Vault, or the Unmasking of Murther* (1606), 22.

52. Lucy Hutchinson, *Memoirs of the Life of Colonel Hutchinson*, ed. N.H. Keeble (Everyman, London 1995), 6, 58–9.

53. Bunyan, *Grace Abounding*, 55.

54. Clarke, *A Generall Martyrologie*, title page, 1.

55. Gouge, *Whole Armour*, 11.

56. Darrel, *Triall*, 34. See Chapters One and Six for Darrel's career.

57. *Strange Newes From Antwerpe* (1612), 6.

58. Perkins, *Foundation*, 3.
59. Gouge, *Whole Armour*, 11.
60. See, for example, *Gods Handy-worke in Wonders* (1615) and *A Wonderfull and Strange Miracle, or Gods Just Vengeance Against the Cavaliers* (1642).
61. Russell, *Mephistopheles*, 31–2.
62. *Cloud of Unknowing*, 59–60.
63. Greenham, *Short Rules*, no. 25.
64. Bateman, *Christall Glasse*, M4r.
65. See, for example, *Brettergh*, 25. The whole genre of deathbed literature is considered in Chapter Three.
66. Greenham, *Short Rules*, nos 21, 26.
67. Grymeston, *Miscelanea*, H1v.
68. Burton, *Anatomy*, III, 414–15.
69. Hoby, *Diary*, 51, 54.
70. The preface to Gough's translation is reproduced in Trinterud, ed. *Elizabethan Puritanism*.
71. B. Lowe, 'Religious Wars and the Common Peace: Anglican Anti-war Sentiment in Elizabethan England', *Albion* 28, 415–35.
72. Marten is quoted by Julian Lock in 'How Many Tercios has the Pope? The Spanish war and the Sublimation of Elizabethan Anti-Popery', *History* 81 (1996), 200.
73. Warwick County Record Office, 'MSS of the first Sir Richard Newdigate', 1626, MI/351/5/21; Welford-on-Avon churchwardens' receipt, 1635, DR911/7/1; Coventry City Record Office, corporation minute book, 1555–1640, A14a, 250v. For protestant opposition to a pro-Spanish foreign policy see the essays by Thomas Cogswell and Peter Lake in Richard Cust and Ann Hughes, eds, *Conflict in Early Stuart England* (Longman, London 1989).
74. Public Record Office, Kew (PRO), Bill of complaint from Stratford corporation to the star chamber, 1621, STAC 26/10.
75. Clarke, *Generall Martyrologie*, 391.
76. Vavasor Powell, *The Life and Death of Mr Vavasor Powell* (1671), 9–10; PRO, Star chamber proceedings against William Hall, 1622, STAC8/245/27.
77. William Perkins, *The Art of Prophesying* (Banner of Truth Trust, Edinburgh 1996), 93.
78. Ephraim Huitt, *The Anatomy of Conscience* (1626), 34–5.
79. Sibbes, *Saints Safetie*, 17.
80. Robert Harris, *The Works of Robert Harris* (1654), 254.
81. Samuel Clarke, *The Saints Nose-Gay, or a Posie of 741 Spirituall Flowers* (1642), 146.
82. *Merry Drollery*, II, 50.
83. See Christopher Haigh, *English Reformations: Religion, Politics and Society under the Tudors* (Clarendon, Oxford 1993), Chapter Sixteen and Conclusion, and Geoffrey Parker, 'Success and Failure During the First Century of the Reformation', *Past and Present* 136 (1992).
84. Gifford, *Countrie Divinity*, title page; Perkins, *Foundation*, epistle to the reader.
85. Hoby, *Diary*, 181.
86. John Fielding, 'Opposition to the Personal Rule of Charles I: The Diary of Robert Woodford, 1637–1641', *Historical Journal* 31 (1988), 769–88; Ann Hughes, 'Thomas Dugard and his Circle in the 1630's', *Historical Journal* 29 (1986), 771–93.
87. I.H., *The Divell*, 11.
88. Huitt, *Anatomy*, 34–5.
89. Harris, *Works*, 255.
90. Gifford, *Countrie Divinity*, 26.
91. Ephraim Huitt, *The Whole Prophecie of Daniel Explained* (1643), 226.
92. John Milton, *Prose Writings*, ed. K.M. Burton (Dent, London 1958), 6.
93. Elaine Pagels, *The Origin of Satan*, 180–1.

3. Living with the Enemy: Protestant Experiences of the Devil

1. Powell, *Spirituall Experiences*, 82–3.
2. R. Willis, *Mount Tabor, or Private Exercises of a Penitent Sinner* (1639), 108.
3. Rogers, *Ohel*, 427.
4. Burton, *Anatomy*, III, 422.
5. Allen, *Satan*, 22.
6. See, for example, the experience of Elizabeth Avery in Rogers, *Ohel*, 405.
7. Vavasor Powell, *The Life and Death of Mr Vavasor Powell* (1671), 8.
8. Bunyan, *Grace Abounding*, 29.
9. John Preston, *The Saints Daily Exercise. A Treatise Unfolding the Whole Duty of Prayer* (1629), 39.
10. Burton, *Anatomy*, 413, 415.
11. A survey and discussion of these phenomena was presented by Thomas Nashe in *The Terrors of the Night* (1590). Thomas Nashe, *The Unfortunate Traveller and Other Works* (Penguin, London 1990).
12. John Bradford, *A Godlye Medytacyon Composed by the Faithfull and Constant Servant of God J B* (1559), 44.
13. Rogers, *Ohel*, 419–20.
14. Powell, *Spirituall Experiences*, 272–3.
15. *The Journal of Richard Norwood*, eds W. F. Craven and Walter Hayward (New York 1945), 26.
16. Bunyan, *Grace Abounding*, 8.
17. Rogers, *Ohel*, 413.
18. Birmingham Central Reference Library, 'A Briefe Narrative of the Life and Death of Mr Thomas Hall', LF78.1 HAL/467148, 29.
19. Perkins, *Foundation*, 16.
20. Robert Bolton, *The Saints Selfe-Enriching Examination* (1634), 206–7.
21. A.W., *The Young Mans Second Warning-Peece* (1643), 4.
22. Bunyan, *Grace Abounding*, 29.
23. Allen, *Satan*, 3, 5.
24. Perkins, *Foundation*, 16.
25. Bolton, *Saints Selfe-Enriching Examination*, 206.
26. Powell, *Spirituall Experiences*, 173.
27. Allen, *Satan*, 15, 17.
28. Jane Turner, *Choice Experiences of the Kind Dealings of God* (1653), 25, 117–18.
29. Clarke, *Generall Martyrologie*, 458.
30. William Chub, *The True Travaile of All Faithfull Christians* (1585), 137r.
31. Warwick County Record Office (WCRO), notebook of Richard Newdigate, 1630, CR136/A14, 284.
32. Bunyan, *Grace Abounding*, 14.
33. Elizabeth Grymeston, *Miscelanea. Meditations. Memoratives* (1604), C4r.
34. Theodore de Welles, 'Sex and Sexual Attitudes in Seventeenth-Century England: The Evidence from Puritan Diaries', in *Renaissance and Reformation* 12 (1988), 50–1.
35. William Gouge, *Of Domesticall Duties* (2nd edn 1626), 47.
36. John Woolton, *The Christian Manuell, or Of the Life and Maners of True Christians* (1576), 189v.
37. William Perkins, *Lectures Upon the First Three Chapters of the Revelation* (1604), 186–7.
38. Richard Carpenter, *Experience, Historie and Divinitie* (1641), 102.
39. *Stand Up For Your Beliefe, or A Combat Betweene Satan Tempting and A Christian Triumphing* (1640).
40. Thomas Becon, *The Worckes of Thomas Becon* (1564), cccxiii r.
41. Willis, *Mount Tabor*, 208–9.
42. Allen, *Satan*, 16.
43. Powell, *Life*, 12; Richard Baxter, *The Life and Times of Richard Baxter*, ed. Orme, I, 243–4.
44. *The Miracle of Miracles* (1614), preface.

45. Turner, *Choice Experiences*, preface.
46. Gryffith Williams, *The True Church: Shewed to All Men That Desire to be Members of the Same* (1629), 556–7.
47. Rogers, *Ohel*, 429.
48. Powell, *Life*, 9, 12.
49. Powell, *Spirituall Experiences*, 34–5, 358.
50. Hoby, *Diary*, 10, 54, 105, 136, 143, 168, 180, 181, 182.
51. Hoby, *Diary*, 180–1.
52. WCRO, correspondence of Lady Anne Newdigate, CR136/B310, B314.
53. WCRO, 'MSS of the first Sir Richard Newdigate', MI/351/5/21.
54. William Gouge, *The Whole Armour of God* (1627 edition), 21.
55. Powell, *Life*, 9.
56. Samuel Clarke, *The Saints Nose-gay, or a Posie of 741 Spirituall Flowers* (1642), 146.
57. Perkins is quoted by Ralph Houlbrooke in 'The Puritan Deathbed, 1560–1660', in Christopher Durston and Jacqueline Eales, eds, *The Culture of English Puritanism, 1560–1700* (Macmillan, London 1996), 125.
58. John Gerard, *The Conquest of Temptations: or Mans Victory Over Satan*, translated from German by R. Bruch (1615), 111.
59. Clarke, *Generall Martyrologie*, 416, 472.
60. *Euing*, 198.
61. *Brettergh*, 12.
62. *Euing*, 198.
63. *Brettergh*, 13.
64. Stubbes, *Christall Glasse*, C3r.
65. *Brettergh*, 15.
66. Clarke, *Generall Martyrologie*, 416, 472.
67. Stubbes, *Christall Glasse*, C4r.
68. Stubbes, *Christall Glasse*, C3v–C4r.
69. *Brettergh*, 21–2, 37, 38.

4. The Devil in Popular Culture

1. John Aubrey, *Brief Lives*, ed. Oliver Lawson Dick (Penguin, London 1949), 114–15.
2. See J.J. Scarisbrick, *The Reformation and the English People* (Clarendon, Oxford 1988) and Christopher Haigh, *English Reformations*. The view that protestantism enjoyed strong popular support is set out in the revised edition of A.G. Dickens, *The English Reformation* (2nd edn, London 1990).
3. *The Historie of the Damnable Life and Deserved Death of Doctor John Faustus*, ed. H. Logeman (Amsterdam 1900), 38–9.
4. *Merry Drollery*, I, 103–4.
5. *The Examination and Confession of Certain Wytches at Chelmsford* (1566), in Haining, *Witchcraft Papers*, 33.
6. *The Disclosing of a Late Counterfeyted Possession by the Devyl in Two Maydens* (1574), 13–14.
7. Abraham Fleming, *A Straunge and Terrible Wunder Wrought Very Late in the Parish Church of Bungay* (1577), 2–3.
8. *The Miracle of Miracles* (1614), 3, 5.
9. Ashmole, Napier, MS 412, 115r, 141v.
10. Elizabeth Jocelin, *The Mothers Legacie to her Unborne Childe* (1624), 40.
11. *The Examination of John Walsh Before Maister Thomas Williams* (1566), in Rosen, *Witchcraft*, 69; Ewen, *Witch Hunting*, 304.
12. *Mother Shiptons Christmas Carrols* (1668), 2.
13. James Obelkivich, *Religion and Rural Society* (Clarendon, Oxford 1978), 276.
14. Keith Thomas, *Religion and the Decline of Magic* (Weidenfeld &

Nicolson, London 1971). For reinterpretations of Thomas' work see Eamon Duffy, *The Stripping of the Altars* and Jerome Friedman, *Miracles and the Pulp Press in Revolutionary England* (UCL, London 1994).

15. Rosen, *Witchcraft*, 69, 377.

16. Around 1635 Napier's nephew made a list of his uncle's patients who had been troubled by apparitions of various kinds. Ashmole, Napier, MS 1790, 108r.

17. Joseph Glanvill, *Saducismus Triumphatus* (1689), 325; for Aubrey, see D.R. Woolf, 'The Common Voice: History, Folklore and Oral Tradition in Early Modern England', *Past and Present* 120 (1980).

18. *Euing*, 108.

19. R. Willis, *Mount Tabor, or Private Exercises of a Penitent Sinner* (1639), 93.

20. Ewen, *Witchcraft*, 148.

21. *Roxburghe*, II, 370–1. This ballad is reproduced in Chapter Eight.

22. *Merry Drollery*, I, 103, II, 13.

23. *Euing*, 107; *Merry Drollery*, II, 27.

24. *Merry Drollery*, I, 7–11.

25. See, for example, *The Wonder: or the Devil Outwitted* (1736).

26. H.C. Porter, ed., *Puritanism in Tudor England* (1970), 279.

27. William Rowley and Thomas Dekker, *The Witch of Edmonton* (1658), 17. The play was possibly based on a witchcraft pamphlet published in 1621 and was first performed two years later.

28. *Strange Newes From Warwicke* (1642), 6.

29. *Sad and Dreadful News From Horsley Down* (1684); *The Devil and the Strumpet* (1701), title-page.

30. *Strange Newes From Warwicke*, 7–8. This tale is reproduced in Chapter Eight.

31. *Euing*, 108–9, 197, 227, 566.

32. Thomas Dekker, *Newes From Hell Brought by the Divells Carrier* (1606), preface, B2r.

33. *Roxburghe*, I, 331–6.

34. *Euing*, 569; *Merry Drollery*, II, 26–8.

35. *Merry Drollery*, II, 12–15.

36. *The Strange and Wonderful History of Mother Shipton* (1686), 8–9.

37. *Roxburghe*, II, 368.

38. Thomas Dekker and George Wilkins, *Jests to Make You Merie* (1607), 2; *Roxburghe*, II, 368.

39. Ewen, *Witchcraft*, 180.

40. *Roxburghe*, I, 224, 228, 396, 400; II, 496.

41. Dekker, *Newes*, B4v.

42. Samuel Clarke, *A Mirrour or Looking Glasse, Both for Saints and Sinners* (1654 edition), 23.

43. *Historie of the Damnable Life*, 4, 38.

44. *The Merry Devil of Edmonton* (1608), ed. William Amos Abrams (Durham, North Carolina 1942), 13–15, 107, 227–30. This edition includes the original source of the play and *The Life and Death of the Merry Devill of Edmonton* (1631).

45. R. Head, *The Life and Death of Mother Shipton* (1667), in *Mother Shipton: A Collection of the Earliest Editions of Her Prophecies* (Manchester 1882), 30–2.

46. *Mother Shiptons Christmas Carrols*, 2.

47. Head, *Mother Shipton*, 78.

48. *Mother Shiptons Christmas Carrols*, 3.

49. *Strange and Wonderful History*, 6–8.

50. Bateman, *Christall Glasse*, J1r.

51. R.W. Scribner, *For the Sake of Simple Folk: Popular Propaganda for the German Reformation* (Clarendon, Oxford 1981); *Popular Culture and Popular Movements in Reformation Germany* (Hambledon, London 1987), Chapters Three and Thirteen.

52. Tessa Watt, *Cheap Print and Popular Piety, 1550–1640* (Cambridge University Press, 1991).

53. Bateman, *Christall Glasse*, B1r, D2v, D4r, M4r.

54. William Gouge, *The Whole Armour of God* (1616), title page.

55. See, for example, *Newes From Hell, Rome, and the Innes of Court* (1642), title page.

56. *The Young Man's Conquest Over the Powers of Darkness* (1683).

57. Clarke, *Generall Martyrologie*, p. 388.

58. Thomas, *Religion*, 563.

59. *A Wonderfull and Strange Miracle, or Gods Just Vengeance Against the Cavaliers* (1642), 5.

60. *Strange Newes From Antwerpe* (1612), 2, 7, 9.

61. *God's Judgment Upon Hereticks, or The Infidel's Overthrow* (1729), 3, 7.

62. *A Most Horrible & Detestable Murder Committed by a Bloudie-Minded Man Upon his Owne Wife* (1595), preface, 1.

63. *The Examination, Confession and Condemnation of Henry Robson* (1598), 1, 6, 7.

64. Gilbert Dugdale, *A True Discourse of the Practises of Elizabeth Caldwell* (1604), dedication, B2r, C1v, C4r, D1r.

65. These texts are discussed by Peter Lake in 'Popular Form, Puritan Content? Two Puritan Appropriations of the Murder Pamphlet From Mid-Seventeenth-Century London', in Anthony Fletcher and Peter Roberts, eds *Religion, Culture and Society in Early Modern Britain* (Cambridge University Press, 1994).

66. John Reynolds, *Triumphs of Gods Revenge Against the Crying and Execrable Sinne of Willful and Premeditated Murder* (1635), preface, 371–80.

67. Lawrence Southerne, *Fearefull Newes From Coventry* (1642), title page, 5–6.

68. *Roxburghe*, II, 226–7; Head, *Mother Shipton*, 34.

69. Southerne, *Fearefull Newes*, 4, 6, 8.

70. *Roxburghe*, III, 29, 34, 137, 138.

71. *Roxburghe*, III, 156.

72. *Euing*, 108–9.

73. *Roxburghe*, I, 370.

74. *Euing*, 107.

75. *Roxburghe*, II, 224–8.

76. Ewen, *Witchcraft*, 192.

77. Ashmole, Napier, MS 404, 181v.

78. Samuel Clarke, *A Mirrour or Looking Glasse, Both for Saints and Sinners* (1646), 65.

79. Richard Kenneth Emmerson, *Antichrist in the Middle Ages*, 82–3.

80. Olde, *Short Description*, 4v, 30r.

81. John Gough, *A Godly Book* (1561), reprinted in Trinterud, ed., *Elizabethan Puritanism*, 32.

82. Emmerson, *Antichrist*, 228.

83. *The Divell of the Vault* (1606), 19, 22.

84. *Miracle Upon Miracle, or A True Relation of the Great Floods Which Happened in Coventry* (1607), 3.

85. *A Disputation Betwixt the Devill and the Pope* (1642), 2.

86. *Newes From Hell, Rome and the Inns of Court* (1642).

87. Ellis Bradshaw, *A Dialogue Between the Devil & Prince Rupert* (1645), 3.

88. John Booker, *The Bloody Almanack: To Which England is Directed to Fore-Know What Shall Come to Passe* (1643), 3, 4.

89. See, for example, *Six Strange Prophesies Predicting Wonderfull Events* (1642), and the later editions of Mother Shipton's prophecies.

90. *Historie of the Damnable Life*, 5, 9–10.

91. *Merry Drollery*, I, 104.

92. *Euing*, 107.

93. Rosen, *Witchcraft*, 64–7; Emmerson, *Antichrist*, 228.

94. This story was included in *The Tryal and Examination of Mrs Joan Peterson* (1652), 3–5.
95. *Grand Plutoes Remonstrance* (1642), 1–2.
96. *A Disputation*, 3.
97. *Ibid*, 4.
98. *Euing*, 107.
99. *Merry Drollery*, I, 103–4.
100. *Merry Devil of Edmonton*, 230–3.
101. *The Wonder: or The Devil Outwitted* (1736), 5, 8.
102. Head, *Mother Shipton*, 30–4, 60, 64, 78.
103. Haigh, *English Reformations*, 290.
104. Watt, *Cheap Print*, 126.

5. *Women and the Devil*

1. The best general account of women's religious experiences in the period is Patricia Crawford's *Women and Religion in England, 1500–1720* (Routledge, London 1993). Other valuable texts include Anne Laurence, *Women in England1500–1760* (Weidenfeld & Nicolson, London 1994) and Diane Willen, 'Godly Women in Early Modern England: Puritanism and Gender', in *Journal of Ecclesiastical History* 43 (1992).
2. For a discussion of these pamphlets see Jerome Friedman, *Miracles and the Pulp Press During the English Revolution*, 182–3, 195.
3. References to the Whore of Babylon were common in cheap print in early modern England. See, for instance, Bateman, *Christall Glasse*, D2v, *Six Strange Prohesies Predicting Wonderfull Events* (1642), 5, 7, and *Merry Drollery*, II, 51.
4. Nicholas Breton, *The Good and the Badde, or Descriptions of the Worthies and Unworthies of This Age* (1616), 27–8.
5. Friedman, *Miracles*, 179–80.
6. Richard Carpenter, *Experience, Historie and Divinitie* (1641), 66. The accession of Elizabeth spurred protestant thinkers to find theological justifications for female authority, which often involved reinterpretations of the story of Eden. See Amanda Shephard, *Gender and Authority in Early Modern England* (1993), Chapter Two.
7. William Gouge, *The Whole Armour of God* (1627 edition), 26; William Gouge, *Of Domesticall Duties* (1626 edition), 141, 329.
8. Hoby, *Diary*, 54, 75.
9. Jane Turner, *Choice Experiences of the Kind Dealings of God* (1653), 52–3.
10. East Sussex Record Office, Letter from Anna Temple to her daughter, Dunn MSS 51/54.
11. Crawford, *Women and Religion*, Chapter Eight.
12. Willen, *Godly Women*.
13. Bateman, *Christall Glasse*, H3r; Philip Stubbes, *The Anatomie of Abuses* (1583), F2r, Gv.
14. Bateman, *Christall Glasse*, H3r.
15. James VI of Scotland and I of England, *Daemonologie* (1597), 43–4. This view was shared by William Perkins, who claimed that 'the woman, being the weaker sexe, is sooner entangled by the devill's illusions with this damnable art than the man'. Alan Macfarlane, *Witchcraft in Tudor and Stuart England* (2nd edn, Routledge, London 1999), 161.
16. Turner, *Choice Experiences*, preface, 53.
17. *A Most Straunge and True Discourse of the Wonderfull Judgement of God* (1600), 2, 3, 10.
18. *God's Handy-Worke in Wonders* (1615), 5, 7.
19. *Euing*, 197.
20. Friedman, *Miracles*, 52, 180.

21. James Sharpe, 'Women, Witchcraft and the Legal Process', in Jenny Kermode and Garthine Walker, eds, *Women, Crime and the Courts in Early Modern England* (UCL, London 1994).
22. Clive Holmes, 'Women, Witnesses and Witches', in *Past and Present* 140 (1993).
23. *A Most Certain, Strange and True Discovery of a Witch* (1643).
24. Mother Shipton was first identified explicitly as a witch in Richard Head's *Life and Death of Mother Shipton* (1667), reprinted in *Mother Shipton: A Collection of the Earliest Editions of her Prophecies* (Manchester, 1882), 78.
25. Reginald Scot, *The Discovery of Witches* (1581), reprinted in Rosen, *Witchcraft*, 174.
26. Archives of the Yorkshire Archaeological Society, 'Presumptions against witches', DD146/12/2/10.
27. For a valuable survey of recent work touching on the links between English and continental witchcraft, see Bent Ankarloo and Gustav Henningsen, eds, *Early Modern European Witchcraft: Centres and Peripheries* (Clarendon, Oxford 1993), Introduction. See also Barry Reay, *Popular Cultures in England, 1550–1750* (Longman, London 1998), Chapter Four.
28. *The Examination and Confession of Certain Wyches at Chelmsford* (1565), reprinted in Haining, *Witchcraft Papers*, 28.
29. *A Rehearsall Both Straung and True of Hainous and Horrible Actes* (1579), reprinted in Rosen, 86; *The Apprehension and Confession of Three Notorious Witches* (1589), in Rosen, 184.
30. Haining, *Witchcraft Papers*, 73–4.
31. *Dr Lamb's Darling: or Strange and Terrible News From Salisbury* (1653), 5.
32. Joad Raymond, ed., *Making the News: An Anthology of the Newsbooks of Revolutionary England, 1641–1660* (Windrush Press, Gloucester 1993), 152, 153–4.
33. *Merry Drollery*, II, 12–15; *The Wonder: or The Devil Outwitted* (1736), 8.
34. *Roxburghe*, 335–6.
35. *The Wonder*, 8.
36. *Roxburghe*, II, 368–71.
37. *The Book of Margery Kempe*, ed. Barry Windeatt (Penguin, London 1985), 41–2.
38. Bunyan, *Grace Abounding*, 14.
39. Margaret Cavendish, *Poems and Fancies* (1653), preface.
40. Raymond, *Making the News*, 140–1.
41. Ellen Driver and Elizabeth Warne confessed in 1645 that 'pride was the cause' of their witchcraft. Ewen, *Witch Hunting*, 304, 305.
42. Ralph Houlbrooke, 'The Puritan Deathbed, 1560–1660', in Chris Durston and Jacqueline Eales, eds, *The Culture of English Puritanism, 156–1700* (Macmillan, London 1996), 136.
43. *Brettergh*, 12, 13, 15.
44. Elizabeth Jocelin, *The Mother's Legacie to her Unborne Childe* (1624), 33, 83.
45. Hoby, *Diary*, 54, 60.
46. *Book of Margery Kempe*, 46.
47. *The Young Man's Second Warning-Peece* (1643), 7.
48. Powell, *Spirituall Experiences*, 167, 168–9, 174–5.
49. Burrill's memoir is included in Rogers, *Ohel*, 413.
50. Gilbert Dugdale, *A True Discourse of the Practises of Elizabeth Caldwell* (1604), C1v.
51. Allen, *Satan*, 7–8.

52. Stevie Davies, *Unbridled Spirits: Women of the English Revolution, 1640–1660* (Women's Press, London 1998), 131.
53. Ashmole, Napier, MS 404, 289v.
54. Ashmole, Napier, MS 412, 150v.
55. Ottavia Niccoli, 'The End of Prophecy', in *Journal of Modern History* 61, (1989), 677, 680–2.
56. See, for instance, Moshe Sluhovsky, 'A Divine Apparition or Demonic Possession? Female Agency and Church Authority in Demonic Possession in Sixteenth-Century France', in *Sixteenth Century Journal*, XXVII/4 (1996), 1039–55.
57. For the tradition of visionary women in England, see Crawford, *Women and Religion*, Chapters Four and Five.
58. John Hacket, *Scrinia Reserata: A Memorial Offer'd to the Great Deservings of John Williams* (1692), 47–8.
59. Fairfax, *Daemonologia*, 62–4.
60. Crawford, *Women and Religion*, 107.
61. *A Strange and True Relation of a Young Woman Possest With the Devil* (1647), 1–2.
62. *The Most Strange and Admirable Discoverie of the Three Witches of Warboys* (1593), reprinted in Rosen, *Witchcraft*, 269.
63. Stubbes, *Christall Glasse*, C3v.
64. Davies, *Unbridled Spirits*, 128–33.

6. Possession and Exorcism

1. The main account of this case is *The Most Strange and Admirable Discoverie of the Three Witches of Warboys* (1593). This is reprinted in Rosen, *Witchcraft*, 280.
2. Ewen, *Witchcraft*, 452.
3. Ashmole, Napier, MS 412, 152r, 169r.
4. Gower's account is included in Clarke, *Generall Martyrologie*, 459.
5. Ewen, *Witchcraft*, 186.
6. *The Wonderfull Discoverie of the Witchcrafts of Margaret and Phillip Flower* (1619), in Rosen, *Witchcraft*, 377.
7. Ewen, *Witchcraft*, 180.
8. Ewen, *Witch Hunting*, 297.
9. Lyndal Roper, *Oedipus and the Devil: Witchcraft, Sexuality and Religion in Early Modern Europe* (Routledge, London 1994), 173–4, 177–80.
10. Alice Samuel's prosecution was supported by the godly chaplain of the Throckmorton family, Dr Dorrington, and the possessed man in Nottingham was exorcised by the zealous minister, Richard Rothwel. John Darrel presided at the dispossession of Thomas Darling and the victims of Edmund Hartley.
11. Darrel, *Triall*, 66.
12. James Sharpe, 'Disruption in the Well-Ordered Household: Age, Authority, and Possessed Young People', in Paul Griffiths, Adam Fox and Steve Hindle, eds, *The Experience of Authority in Early Modern England* (Macmillan, London 1996), 207–8.
13. John Hall, *Select Observations on English Bodies* (1679), 142–3.
14. Darrel, *Triall*, 17.
15. *A Strange and True Relation of a Young Woman Possest With the Devill* (1647), 2.
16. Darrel, *True Relation*, A2v.
17. Ewen, *Witchcraft*, 176, 186.
18. *Most Fearfull and Strange Newes From the Bishoppricke of Durham* (1641), 3.
19. See, for instance, Darrel, *Triall*, 17, *A Strange and True Relation*, 3, and Richard Baxter, *The Certainty of the World of Spirits* (1691), 47.
20. Fairfax, *Demonologia*, 54.
21. *Dr Lamb's Darling: or Strange and Terrible News from Salisbury* (1653), 6.

22. Thomas Wright, *Narratives of Sorcery and Magic*, II (London 1851), 139; *A Strange and True Relation*, 2.
23. Rosen, *Witchcraft*, 250.
24. Darrel, *True Relation*, A3r.
25. Wright, *Narratives*, 143.
26. *A Strange and True Relation*, 3.
27. Eamon Duffy, *The Stripping of the Altars*, 317.
28. Richard Carpenter, *Experience, Historie and Divinitie* (1641), 23.
29. Darrel, *Triall*, 50.
30. Wright, *Narratives*, 143.
31. Fairfax, *Demonologia*; Rosen, 256–8.
32. Ewen, *Witchcraft*, 176–81.
33. Darrel, *True Relation*, A2v.
34. *The Disclosing of a Late Counterfeyted Possession by the Devyl* (1574), 8, 11.
35. Haining, *Witchcraft Papers*, 131–2.
36. Clarke Garrett, *Spirit Possession and Popular Religion* (Johns Hopkins, Baltimore and London 1987), 5.
37. Baxter, *Certainty*, 47.
38. Roy Porter, *A Social History of Madness* (Weidenfeld & Nicolson, London 1987), 83–9.
39. *Disclosing*, 2–4.
40. Rosen, *Witchcraft*, 269–70, 285.
41. Sharpe, 'Disruption', 206.
42. Darrel, *True Relation*, A3r–v, A4r.
43. Clarke, *Generall Martyrologie*, 403.
44. *A Booke Declaringe the Fearfull Vexasion of One Alexander Nynde* (1573), 9.
45. Darrel, *True Relation*, A3; Ewen, *Witchcraft*, 191.
46. *Disclosing*, preface.
47. *Constitutions and Canons Ecclesiastical* (1605), LXXII.
48. Burton, *Anatomy*, III, 414–15, 422–3.
49. Allen, *Satan*, 3; Bunyan, *Grace Abounding*, 29.
50. Perkins, *Foundation*, 3, 16.
51. John Woolton, *The Christian Manuell* (1576), 179v.
52. This revision was first introduced in the 1552 prayer book and retained in the 1559 version.
53. John Milton, *Prose Writings*, ed. K.M. Burton (Dent, London 1958), 5–6.
54. Allen, *Satan*, 3, 8, 13–20.
55. *The Most Wonderfull and True Storie of a Certaine Witch Named Alse Gooderige* (1597), 16, 29–30.
56. Walker, *Unclean Spirits*, 54–6; Keith Thomas, *Religion and the Decline of Magic* (Weidenfeld & Nicolson, London 1971), 577.
57. Clarke, *Generall Martyrologie*, 402–3, 458–61. The account of the exorcism performed by Richard Rothwel was composed by Stanley Gower.
58. Clarke, *Generall Martyrologie*, 402.
59. *A Strange and True Relation*, 2.
60. *A Booke Declaringe the Fearfull Vexasion*, 5.
61. Jacqueline Eales, 'Thomas Pierson and the Transmission of the Moderate Puritan Tradition', *Midland History* 20 (1995), 81.
62. Anthony Fletcher, *Gender, Sex and Subordination in England* (Yale University Press, 1995); Lyndal Roper, *The Holy Household: Women and Morals in Reformation Augsburg* (Clarendon, Oxford 1990).
63. Extracts from Baxter's *Poor Mans Family Book* (1674) are reproduced in Mary Abbott, *Life Cycles in England 1560–1720* (Routledge, London 1996), 193–5.
64. Sharpe, 'Disruption', 205–9.
65. In 1591, for example, the verbal battle between Katherine Stubbes and the devil resembled a godly exorcism. When her adversary taunted her that her transgressions were so great that she was destined for hell, she responded by declaring that Christ's 'precious bloud [is] a

full satisfaction for my sinnes'
Stubbes, *Christall Glasse*, C3v.

66. *Brettergh*, 14, 17.
67. Rogers, *Ohel*, 423–4.
68. Walker, *Unclean Spirits*, 54–5.
69. Jane Turner, *Choice Experiences of the Kind Dealings of God* (1653), 2.
70. Richard Baxter, *The Certainty of the World of Spirits* (1691), 175.
71. Patricia Crawford, *Women and Religion in England, 1500–1720* (Routledge, London 1993); *The Declaration of John Robins* (1651), ed. Andrew Hopton (Aphoria, London 1992), 22.
72. Abiezer Coppe, *Selected Writings*, ed. Andrew Hopton (1987), 27, 80–1.
73. Samuel Clarke, *A Mirrour or Looking Glasse for Both Saints and Sinners* (1654 edition), 231–8.
74. Stephen Greenblatt, *Shakespearean Negotiations: The Circulation of Social Energy in Renaissance England* (1988), 97.
75. Darrel, *True Relation*, 6.
76. George Gifford, *A Dialogue Concerning Witches and Witchcraft*, reproduced in Haining, *Witchcraft Papers*, 94.
77. Clarke, *Generall Martyrologie*, 458–61.
78. *Booke Declaring the Fearfull Vexasion*, 5–6.
79. Darrel, *Triall*, 66.
80. Darrel, *True Relation*, 5.
81. Eales, 'Thomas Pierson', 81–2.
82. Clarke, *Generall Martyrologie*, p. 461.
83. Proceedings of the High Commission, Calendar of State Papers, Domestic Series (CSPD), 1634–5, 263.
84. For Harsnet's episcopal career, see E.J. Evans, *Seventeenth-Century Norwich* (Clarendon, Oxford 1979).
85. CSPD 1634–5, 263.

7. Witchcraft

1. James VI, *Daemonologie* (Edinburgh 1597), 35–6.
2. For a discussion of this phenomenon, see Stuart Clark, 'Inversion, Misrule and the Meaning of Witchcraft', in *Past and Present* 87 (1980), 98–127.
3. James Sharpe, *Instruments of Darkness* (Hamish Hamilton, London 1996), 131.
4. Sharpe, *Instruments*.
5. Ewen, *Witch Hunting*, 306, 312.
6. *Roxburghe*, II, 224–7.
7. Fairfax, *Demonologia*, 107–8.
8. *Euing*, 569.
9. Haining, *Witchcraft Papers*, 24.
10. Fairfax, *Demonologia*, 88–9. The superstitious connotations of witch scratching were noted in *The Witches of Northampton* (1612).
11. Rosen, *Witchcraft*, 69.
12. Barry Reay, *Popular Culture in England, 1550–1750* (Longman 1998), 113.
13. For a discussion of this practice, see James Sharpe, 'Women, Witchcraft and the Legal Process', in Garthine Walker and Jenny Kermode, eds, *Women, Crime and the Courts in Early Modern England* (UCL, 1994), 108–13.
14. Familiar spirits which took animal form and fed on blood were described in pre-Reformation cases of sorcery. In 1510, for example, John Steward of Knaresborough was accused of keeping bumble bees which he fed with 'a drop of blode of his fyngor'. G.L. Kitteredge, *Witchcraft in Old and New England* (Cambridge, Massachusetts 1929), 179.
15. Rosen, *Witchcraft*, 77–8, 86, 184, 138, 349, 358–9, 362.
16. Ewen, *Witch Hunting*, 309.
17. Rosen, *Witchcraft*, 350–1.

18. Lyndal Roper, *Oedipus and the Devil*, Chapters Nine and Ten. See also Malcolm Gaskill, 'Witchcraft and Power in Early Modern England: The Case of Margaret Moore', in Walker and Kermode, *Women*, 125–45.

19. Clarke, *Generall Martyrologie*, 458–61. This text is reproduced in Chapter Eight.

20. Richard Head, *The Life and Death of Mother Shipton* (1667), in *Mother Shipton: A Collection of the Earliest English Editions of Her Prophecies* (Manchester 1882), 32.

21. Ewen, *Witchcraft*, 188.

22. Rosen, *Witchcraft*, 254.

23. Ashmole, Napier, MS 412, 1634–5, 121r, 150v.

24. Ewen, *Witchcraft*, 189.

25. Ashmole, Napier, MS 412, 152r.

26. Ewen, *Witchcraft*, 177, 186.

27. Richard Baddily, *The Life of Dr Thomas Morton, Late Bishop of Duresme* (1669), 72–5.

28. Ewen, *Witchcraft*, 176–7, 180, 188–9.

29. Ewen, *Witch Hunting*, 252.

30. Ashmole, Napier, MS 412, 169r.

31. Rosen, *Witchcraft*, 272, 280.

32. Haining, *Witchcraft Papers*, 144, 167, 169.

33. Ewen, *Witchcraft*, 191.

34. This work has been undertaken by Brian Hoggard at University College Worcester. I am grateful to Brian for letting me use his material, and for other information included in this section.

35. M.R. Holmes, 'The So-Called Bellarmine Mask in Imported Rhenish Stoneware', *Antiquaries Journal XXXI* (1950), 173–9; John Allan, 'Some Post Mediaeval Documentary Evidence for the Trade in Ceramics', in *Ceramics and Trade: The Production and Distribution of Later Mediaeval Pottery in North-West Europe* (University of Sheffield Press, 1983), 37–45.

36. Denise Dixon-Smith, 'Concealed Shoes', *Archaeological Leather Group Newsletter*, 6 (1990).

37. To date, 53 bellarmines have had their location precisely recorded. Of these, 23 were beneath hearthstones or hidden in fireplaces, and another five were located beneath the doorstep or adjacent to it. After the hearth, the second most common location was under floors, where six bottles were found.

38. Ewen, *Witchcraft*, 188.

39. Joseph Glanvill, *Saducismus Triumphatus* (1689), 331.

40. Ralph Merrifield, *The Archaeology of Ritual and Magic* (BCA, 1987), 134.

41. Ewen, *Witchcraft*, 148.

42. William Perkins, *The Art of Prophesying* (Banner of Truth Trust, Edinburgh 1996), 111–12.

43. Olde, *Short Description*, 30v; S.S., *A Briefe Instruction for all Families* (1586), dedication.

44. John Reynolds, *The Triumphs of Gods Revenge* (1635), preface; R. Willis, *Mount Tabor, or Private Exercises of a Penitent Sinner* (1639), 91.

45. Warwick County Record Office (WCRO), Richard Newdigate's notebook, 1631, CR136/A7.

46. Rosen, *Witchcraft*, 161; Kittredge, *Witchcraft*, 180.

47. WCRO, Newdigate's notebook, 1626, MI /351/5/21, 581.

48. Alan Macfarlane, *Witchcraft in Tudor and Stuart England*, 189.

49. William Gouge, *The Whole Armour of God* (1627 edition), 11.

50. Stuart Clark, 'Protestant Demonology: Sin, Superstition and Society', in Gustav Henningsen and Bengt Akkarloo, eds, *Early Modern European Witchcraft* (Clarendon, 1993), 45–81.

51. Alison Rowlands has presented a nice test of Clark's thesis in a German context in 'Witchcraft and Popular Religion in Early Modern Rothenbury ob der Tauber', in Bob Scribner and Trevor Johnson, eds, *Popular Religion in Germany and Central Europe, 1400–1800* (Macmillan, 1996), 101–18.
52. Rosen, *Witchcraft*, 55–6.
53. Lichfield Joint Record Office (LJRO), episcopal visitation, 1636, B/V/1/58, 40r.
54. LJRO, episcopal visitations, 1614, B/V/1/29, 18; 1623, B/V/1/45, 18; 1629, B/V/1/52, 9; 1635, B/V/1/55, 18, 28; 1636, B/V/1/58, 40r, B/V/1/59, 119, B/V/1/61, 16; 1639, B/V/1/66, 17.
55. CSPD, 1634–5, 319–20.
56. Thomas Hall, *Fuebria Florae, The Downfall of May-Games* (1661), 11, 46.
57. Darrel, *Triall*, 76.
58. Macfarlane, *Witchcraft*, 183, 186–8.
59. Rosen, *Witchcraft*, 275.
60. Walker, *Unclean Spirits*, 64.
61. Rosen, *Witchcraft*, 288.
62. For the rejection of word magic by protestant demonologists, see Stuart Clark, 'The Rational Witchfinder', in Stephen Pumfrey, Paolo Rossi and Maurice Slawinski, eds, *Science, Culture and Popular Belief in Renaissance Europe* (Manchester University Press, 1991), 241–5.
63. Ewen, *Witchcraft*, 176, 178, 186.
64. Darrel, *A True Relation*, A2v, A4v.
65. Darrel, *Triall*, 34.
66. Clarke, *Generall Martyrologie*, 459.
67. Nowell was the half-uncle of Nicholas Starkie, whose daughters were dispossessed by Darrel in 1597. For Southerne's confession, see Rosen, *Witchcraft*, 358–60.
68. Fairfax, *Demonologia*, 38, 68, 87–9, 97.
69. Darrel, *Triall*, 25.
70. Rosen, *Witchcraft*, 290.
71. Matthew Hopkins, *The Discovery of Witches* (1647), 2.
72. Macfarlane, *Witchcraft*, 186.
73. William Lamont, *Puritanism and Historical Controversy* (UCL, 1996), 162.
74. Keith Thomas, *Religion and the Decline of Magic*, 597.
75. John Stearne, *A Confirmation and Discovery of Witchcraft* (1648), 3.
76. For Fairclough's career, see Samuel Clarke, *The Lives of Sundry Eminent Persons* (1683), 153–92.
77. Richard Baxter, *The Certainty of the World of Spirits* (1691), 52–5.
78. Ewen, *Witch Hunting*, 291, 292, 306.
79. Haining, *Witchcraft Papers*, 150, 154.
80. Matthew Hopkins, *The Discovery of Witches* (1647), 4–5.
81. Ewen, *Witch Hunting*, 303–4.
82. Kittredge, *Witchcraft*, 176.
83. Haining, *Witchcraft Papers*, 142, 157.
84. Rosen, *Witchcraft*, 367–8; Fairfax, *Daemonologia*, 107–8.
85. Sharpe, *Instruments*, 75–9.
86. For the case of Dr Lamb, see *A Briefe Description of the Notorious Life of John Lambe* (1628).
87. *Doctor Lamb's Darling: or Strange and Terrible News From Salisbury* (1653), 5–7.
88. Anthony Burges, *The Difficulty of, and the Encouragements to a Reformation* (1643), 18.

8. Conclusion

1. *The Devil Turn'd Round-head: or Pluto Become a Brownist* (1642), 4.
2. *A Short, Compendious and True Description of the Round-heads and the Long-heads* (1642), 6-7.

3. Robert Baillie, *Satan the Leader in Chief of all who Resist the Reparation of Sion* (1643), 33.
4. Ewen, *Witch Hunting*, 311.
5. *A Sad Caveat to all Quakers* (1657), 8–9, 11.
6. Turner, *Choice Experiences*, 110–26; Baxter, *Certainty* (1691), 175–6.
7. *The Just Devil of Woodstock* (1660), preface.
8. Baxter, *Certainty*, preface.
9. Thomas, *Religion*, 693–4.
10. Sharpe, *Instruments*, 243–4.
11. Greenham, *Short Rules* , no. 16.
12. See, for example, John Spurr, 'Latitutudinarianism and the Restoration Church', in *Historical Journal*, 31 (1988).
13. C.H. Sisson, ed., *The English Sermon, 1650–1750* (Carcanet, Cheadle 1976), 193–4, 196.
14. Woolf, 'The Common Voice', 50.
15. Margaret Spufford, *Small Books and Pleasant Histories* (Cambridge University Press 1981), 5.
16. Mary Williams, *Witches in Old North Yorkshire* (Hutton, Beverley 1987), 7.
17. Obelkivich, *Religion and Rural Society*, 277–8.
18. For Wesley's views on possession and witchcraft, see Henry Rack, *Reasonable Enthusiast: John Wesley and the Rise of Methodism* (Epworth, London), 195–7, 387–8.
19. Owen Davies, *Witchcraft, Magic and Culture, 1736–1951* (Manchester University Press 1999), 19-22.
20. Rack, *Reasonable Enthusiast*, 195.
21. R.W. Ambler, *Ranters, Revivalists and Reformers: Primitive Methodism and Rural Society in South Lincolnshire, 1817–1875* (Hull University Press 1989), 52, 73.
22. For an account of Southcott's struggles with Satan, see Marina Benjamin, *Living at the End of the World* (Picador, London 1998), 125–7.
23. Iain McCalman, *Radical Underworld: Prophets, Revolutionaries and Pornographers in London, 1795–1840* (Clarendon, Oxford 1993), 145, 191.
24. Robert Wedderburn, *The Horrors of Slavery and Other Writings*, ed. Iain MacCalman (Edinburgh University Press 1991), 153–4.

Appendix: Selected Sources

1. Jonathan Lumby, *The Lancashire Witch-Craze* (Carnegie, Preston 1995), 170; Rosen, *Witchcraft*, 368.
2. The complete text of this ballad is reproduced in *Roxburghe*, 368–71.
3. This account was appended to *Strange Newes From Warwicke* (1642), 7–8.
4. *God's Judgment Upon Hereticks* (1729), 3, 7.
5. Clarke, *Generall Martyrologie*, 458–61.
6. The woodcut illustrating the title page of Glanvill's book depicted the spirit as the devil beating a drum.
7. Joseph Glanvill, *Saducismus Triumphatus* (1689), 321–32.
8. Rosen, *Witchcraft*, 299–300.
9. This tract was originally published in 1599 as *A Brief Apologie, Proving the Possession of William Sommers*.

SELECT BIBLIOGRAPHY

CONTEMPORARY TEXTS

Allen, Hannah. *Satan His Methods and Malice Baffled* (1683)

Aubrey, John. *Brief Lives*, ed. Oliver Lawson Dick (Penguin, London 1949)

Baddily, Richard. *The Life of Dr Thomas Morton, Late Bishop of Duresme* (1669)

Baillie, Robert. *Satan the Leader in Chief of all who Resist the Reparation of Sion* (1643)

Bateman, Stephen. *A Christall Glasse of Christian Reformation* (1569)

——. *The Golden Booke of the Leaden Goddes* (1577)

Baxter, Richard. *The Certainty of the World of Spirits* (1691)

Becon, Thomas. *The Worckes of Thomas Becon* (1564)

Bolton, Robert. *The Saints Selfe-Enriching Examination* (1634)

Booker, John. *The Bloody Almanack: To Which England is Directed to Fore-Know What Shall Come to Passe* (1643)

Breton, Nicholas. *The Good and the Badde, or Descriptions of the Worthies and Unworthies of This Age* (1616)

A Brief Discourse of the Christian Life and Death of Mistris Katherin Brettergh (1606 edition)

Bradford, John. *A Godlye Medytacyon Composed by the Faithfull and Constant Servant of God J B* (1559)

Bradshaw, Ellis. *A Dialogue Betweene the Devil & Prince Rupert* (1645)

Browne, Thomas. *The Major Works*, ed. C.A. Patrides (Penguin, London 1977)

Bunyan, John. *Grace Abounding to the Chief of Sinners*, ed. W.R. Owens (Penguin, London 1987)

Burton, Robert. *The Anatomy of Melancholy*, eds. Thomas Faulkener, Nicholas Kiessling and Rhonda Blair (1989-94)

Carpenter, Richard. *Experience, Historie and Divinitie* (1641)

Cavendish, Margaret. *Poems and Fancies* (1653)

Chub, William. *The True Travaile of all Faithfull Christians* (1584)

Clarke, Samuel. *A Generall Martyrologie* (1651)

——. *The Lives of Sundry Eminent Persons* (1683)

——. *A Mirrour or Looking Glasse, Both for Saints and Sinners* (1646)

——. *The Saints Nose-Gay, or a Posie of 741 Spirituall Flowers* (1642)

The Cloud of Unknowing, ed. Halcyon Backhouse (Hodder and Stoughton, London 1985)

Coppe, Abiezer. *Selected Writings*, ed. Andrew Hopton (1987)

Darrel, John. *The Triall of Maist. Dorrell* (1599)

——. *A True Relation of the Grievous Handling of William Sommers of Nottingham* (1641 edition)

Dekker, Thomas. *Newes From Hell Brought by the Divells Carrier* (1606)

——, and Wilkins, George. *Jests to Make You Merie* (1607)

The Devil and the Strumpet (1701)

The Devil Turn'd Roundhead: or Pluto Become a Brownist (1642)

The Disclosing of a Late Counterfeyted Possession by the Devyl in Two Maydens (1574)

A Disputation Betwixt the Devill and the Pope (1642)

The Divell of the Vault, or the Unmasking of Murther (1606)

Doctor Lambs Darling: or Strange and Terrible News From Salisbury (1653)

Dugdale, Gilbert. *A True Discourse of the Practises of Elizabeth Caldwell* (1604)

The Examination, Confession and Condemnation of Henry Robson (1598)

Fairfax, Edward. *Daemonologia: A Discourse on Witchcraft*, ed. William Grainge (Harrogate 1882)

The First Examinacyon of Anne Askewe, Latelye Martyred in Smythfelde . . . With the Elucidacyon of Johan Bale (1546)

Fleming, Abraham. *A Straunge and Terrible Wunder Wrought Very Late in the Parish Church of Bungay* (1577)

Gerard, John. *The Conquest of Temptations: or Mans Victory Over Satan*, translated from German by R. Bruch (1615)

Gifford, George. *A Brief Discourse of Certaine Points of the Religion Which is Among the Common Sort of Christians, Which may be Termed the Country Divinity*

Joseph Glanvill, Saducismus Triumphatus (1689)

Gods Handy-worke in Wonders (1615)

God's Judgment Upon Hereticks, or The Infidel's Overthrow (1729)

Gouge, William. *Of Domesticall Duties* (2nd edn 1626)

——. *The Whole Armour of God* (1627 edn)

Grand Plutoes Remonstrance (1642)

Greenham, Richard. *Short Rules Sent by Maister Richard Greenham to a Gentlewoman Troubled in Minde* (1618)

Grymeston, Elizabeth. *Miscelanea, Meditations, Memoratives* (1604)

Hacket, John. *Scrinia Reserata: A Memorial Offer'd to the Great Deservings of John Williams* (1692)

Hall, John. *Select Observations on English Bodies* (1679)

Hall, Thomas. *Fuebria Florae, The Downfall of May-Games* (1661)

Harris, Robert. *The Works of Robert Harris* (1654)

Harsnet, Samuel. *A Declaration* (1603)

The Historie of the Damnable Life and Deserved Death of Doctor John Faustus, ed. H. Logeman (Amsterdam 1900)

Hoby, Margaret. *The Private Life of an Elizabethan Lady: The Diary of Lady Margaret Hoby, 1599–1605*, ed. Joanna Moody (Sutton, Stroud 1998)

Hopkins, Matthew. *The Discovery of Witches* (1647)

Huitt, Ephraim. *The Anatomy of Conscience* (1626)

——. *The Whole Prophecie of Daniel Explained* (1643)

Hutchinson, Lucy. *Memoirs of the Life of Colonel Hutchinson*, ed. N.H. Keeble (Everyman, London 1995)

The Just Devil of Woodstock (1660)

Jocelin, Elizabeth. *The Mothers Legacie to her Unborne Childe* (1624)

Julian of Norwich. *Revelations of Divine Love*, ed. Clifton Walters (Penguin, London 1966)

Kempe, Margery. *The Book of Margery Kempe*, ed. Barry Windeatt (Penguin, London 1985)

A L Mery Talys (1526)

The Merry Devil of Edmonton (1608), ed. William Amos Abrams (Durham, North Carolina 1942)

Merry Drollery, or a Collection of Jovial poems, Merry Songs, Witty Drolleries (1661)

Milton, John. *Prose Writings*, ed. K.M. Burton (Dent, London 1958)

The Miracle of Miracles (1614)

Most Fearfull and Strange Newes From the Bishoppricke of Durham (1641)

A Most Horrible & Detestable Murder Committed by a Bloudie-Minded Man Upon his Owne Wife (1595)

Mother Shiptons Christmas Carrols (1668)

Nashe, Thomas. *The Unfortunate Traveller and Other Works* (Penguin, London 1990)

Newes From Hell, Rome and the Inns of Court (1642)

Norwood, Richard. *The Journal of Richard Norwood*, eds W.F. Craven and Walter Hayward (New York 1945)

Olde, John. *A Short Description of Antichrist Unto the Nobility of Englande* (1557),

Perkins, William. *The Art of Prophesying* (Banner of Truth Trust, Edinburgh 1996)

——. *A Discourse of the Damned Art of Witchcraft* (1608)

——. *The Foundation of Christian Religion Gathered Into Six Principles* (1641 edn)

——. *Lectures Upon the First Three Chapters of the Revelation* (1604)

Powell, Vavasor. *The Life and Death of Mr Vavasor Powell* (1671)

Powell, Vavasour (ed.). *Spirituall Experiences of Sundry Beleevers* (1652 edn)

Preston, John. *The Saints Daily Exercise. A Treatise Unfolding the Whole Duty of Prayer* (1629)

Reynolds, John. *The Triumphs of Gods Revenge Against the Crying and Execrable Sinne of . . . Murther* (1634)

Robins, John. *The Declaration of John Robins*, ed. Andrew Hopton (Aphoria, London 1992)

Rogers, John. *Ohel or Beth-Shemesh* (1653)

Rowley, William, Dekker, Thomas, and Ford, John. *The Witch of Edmonton* (1658)

A Sad Caveat to all Quakers (1657)

Sad and Dreadful News From Horsley Down (1684)

A Short, Compendious and True Description of the Round-heads and the Long-heads (1642)

Sibbes, Richard. *The Saints Safetie in Evill Times* (1634)

Sixe Strange Prophesies Predicting Wonderfull Events (1642)

Southerne, Lawrence. *Fearefull Newes From Coventry* (1642)

Stand up for Your Beliefe, or A Combat Betweene Satan Tempting and A Christian Triumphing (1640)

Stearne, John. *A Confirmation and Discovery of Witchcraft* (1648)

Strange Newes From Antwerpe (1612)

Strange Newes From Warwicke (1642)

A Strange and True Relation of a Young Woman Possest With the Devil (1647)

The Strange and Wonderful History of Mother Shipton (1686)

Stubbes, Philip. *The Anatomie of Abuses* (1583)

——. *A Christall Glasse for Christian Women* (1618 edn)

Tales and Quicke Answeres, Very Mery and Pleasant to Rede (c. 1530)

The Tryal and Examination of Mrs Joan Peterson (1652)

Turner, Jane. *Choice Experiences of the Kind Dealings of God* (1653)

Whytford, Richard. *A Werke for Housholders, or for Them yt Have the Gydiynge or*

Governaunce of any Company (1530)

Williams, Gryffith. *The True Church: Shewed to all Men, That Desire to be Members of the Same* (1629)

Willis, R. *Mount Tabor, or Private Exercises of a Penitent Sinner* (1639)

The Wonder: or the Devil Outwitted (1736)

A Wonderfull and Strange Miracle, or Gods Just Vengeance Against the Cavaliers (1642)

Woolton, John. *The Christian Manuell, or Of the Life and Maners of True Christians* (1576)

The Young Man's Conquest Over the Powers of Darkness (1683)

The Young Mans Second Warning-Peece (1643)

EDITED COLLECTIONS OF CONTEMPORARY TEXTS

English Mystery Plays, ed. Peter Happe (Penguin, London 1975)

The Euing Collection of English Broadside Ballads (Glasgow 1971)

L'Estrange Ewen, C. (ed.). *Witchcraft and Demonianism* (Heath Cranton, London 1933)

——. *Witch Hunting and Witch Trials* (Kegan Paul, London 1929)

Haining, Peter (ed.). *The Witchcraft Papers* (1973)

Jessopp, Augustus. *Random Roaming and Other Papers* (London 1894)

Kors, Alan, and Peters, Edward (eds), *Witchcraft in Europe, 1100–1700: A Documentary History* (University of Pennsylvania Press 1972)

Porter, H.C. (ed.). *Puritanism in Tudor England* (1970)

Rosen, Barbara (ed.). *Witchcraft in England, 1558–1618* (University of Massachusetts Press 1991)

Raymond, Joad (ed.). *Making the News: An Anthology of the Newsbooks of Revolutionary England, 1641–1660* (Windrush Press, Gloucester 1993)

The Roxburghe Ballads, ed. W.M. Chappell (1871–1880)

Seymour-Smith, Martin (ed.). *The English Sermon, 1550–1650* (Carcanet Press, Cheadle 1976)

Mother Shipton: A Collection of the Earliest Editions of Her Prophecies (Manchester 1882)

Trinterud, L.J. (ed.). *Elizabethan Puritanism* (Oxford University Press 1971)

Wright, Thomas. *Narratives of Sorcery and Magic*, II (London 1851)

SECONDARY WORKS

Benjamin, Marina. *Living at the End of the World* (Picador, London 1998)

de Bruyn, Lucy. *Woman and the Devil in Sixteenth-Century Literature* (Compton Press, Wiltshire 1979)

Camporesi, Piero. *The Fear of Hell: Images of Damnation and Salvation in Early Modern Europe* (Polity Press, Oxford 1990)

Clark, Stuart. *Thinking with Demons, The Idea of the Witch in Early Modern Europe* (Clarendon, Oxford 1997)

Crawford, Patricia. *Women and Religion in England, 1500–1720* (Routledge, London 1993)

Cust, Richard, and Hughes, Ann (eds). *Conflict in Early Stuart England* (Longman, London 1989)

Davies, Stevie *Unbridled Spirits: Women of the English Revolution, 1640–1660* (Women's Press, London 1998)

Duffy, Eamon. *The Stripping of the Altars: Traditional Belief in England, 1400–1580* (Yale University Press 1992)

Durston, Christopher, and Eales, Jacqueline (eds). *The Culture of English Puritanism, 1560–1700* (Macmillan, London 1996)

Davies, Owen. *Witchcraft, Magic and Culture, 1736–1951* (Manchester University Press 1999)

Eales, Jacqueline. 'Thomas Pierson and the Transmission of the Moderate Puritan Tradition', *Midland History*, 20 (1995)

Emmerson, Richard Kenneth. *Antichrist in the Middle Ages: A Study of Medieval Apocalypticism, Art and Literature* (Manchester University Press 1981)

Fielding, John. 'Opposition to the Personal Rule of Charles I: The Diary of Robert Woodford, 1637–1641', *Historical Journal*, 31 (1988)

Finucane, Ronald C. *Miracles and Pilgrims: Popular Beliefs in Medieval England* (2nd edn, Macmillan, London 1995)

Fletcher, Anthony, and Roberts, Peter (eds). *Religion, Culture and Society in Early Modern Britain* (Cambridge University Press 1994)

Friedman, Jerome. *Miracles and the Pulp Press in Revolutionary England* (UCL, London 1994)

Garrett, Clarke. *Spirit Possession and Popular Religion* (1987)

Griffiths, Paul, Fox, Adam, and Hindle, Steve (eds). *The Experience of Authority in Early Modern England* (Macmillan, London 1996)

Greenblatt, Stephen. *Shakespearean Negotiations: The Circulation of Social Energy in Renaissance England* (1988)

Haigh, Christopher. *English Reformations* (Clarendon, Oxford 1993)

Henningsen, Gustav, and Akkarloo, Bengt (eds). *Early Modern European Witchcraft* (Clarendon, Oxford 1993)

Holmes, Clive. 'Women, Witnesses and Witches', in *Past and Present*, 140 (1993)

Hughes, Ann. 'Thomas Dugard and his Circle in the 1630s', *Historical Journal*, 29 (1986)

Kieckhefer, Richard. *European Witch Trials: Their Foundations in Popular and Learned Culture, 1300–1500* (Routledge and Kegan Paul, London 1976)

——. *Unquiet Souls: Fourteenth-Century Saints and Their Religious Milieu* (University of Chicago Press 1984)

Lamont, William. *Puritanism and Historical Controversy* (UCL, London 1996)

Levack, Brian. *The Witch Hunt in Early Modern Europe* (Longman 1987)

Lock, Julian. 'How Many Tercios has the Pope? The Spanish war and the Sublimation of Elizabethan Anti-Popery', *History*, 81 (1996)

Macfarlane, Alan. *Witchcraft in Tudor and Stuart England* (2nd edn, Routledge 1999)

Merrifield, Ralph. *The Archaeology of Ritual and Magic* (BCA 1987)

Niccoli, Ottavia. 'The End of Prophecy', *Journal of Modern History*, 61 (1989)

Nicholls, David. 'The Devil in Renaissance France', in *History Today*, November 1980

Obelkivich, James. *Religion and Rural Society* (Clarendon, Oxford 1978)

Oberman, Heiko. *Luther: Man Between God and the Devil* (Yale University Press 1989)

Pagels, Elaine. *The Origin of Satan* (Penguin 1995)

Parker, Geoffrey. 'Success and Failure During the First Century of the Reformation', *Past and Present*, 136 (1992)

Porter, Roy. *A Social History of Madness* (Weidenfeld & Nicolson, London 1987)

Pumfrey, Stephen, Rossi, Paolo, and Slawinski, Maurice (eds), *Science, Culture and Popular Belief in Renaissance Europe* (Manchester University Press 1991)

Reay, Barry. *Popular Culture in England, 1550–1750* (Longman 1998),

Roper, Lyndal. *Oedipus and the Devil: Witchcraft, Sexuality and Religion in Early Modern Europe* (Routledge 1994)

Russell, Jeffrey Burton. *Mephistopheles: The Devil in the Modern World* (Cornell 1986)

Scarisbrick, J. J. *The Reformation and the English People* (Clarendon, Oxford 1988)

Sharpe, James. *Instruments of Darkness: Witchcraft in England, 1550–1750* (Hamish Hamilton 1996)

Spufford, Margaret. *Small Books and Pleasant Histories* (Cambridge University Press 1981)

Stanford, Peter. *The Devil: A Biography* (Mandarin, London 1996)

Thomas, Keith. *Religion and the Decline of Magic* (Weidenfeld & Nicolson, London 1971)

Walker, D.P. *Unclean Spirits: Possession and Exorcism in France and England in the Late Sixteenth and Early Seventeenth Centuries* (Scolar 1981)

Walker, Garthine, and Kermode, Jenny (eds). *Women, Crime and the Courts in Early Modern England* (UCL, London 1994)

Watt, Tessa. *Cheap Print and Popular Piety, 1550–1640* (Cambridge University Press 1991)

Willen, Diane. 'Godly Women in Early Modern England: Puritanism and Gender', *Journal of Ecclesiastical History*, 43 (1992)

Woolf, D.R. 'The Common Voice: History, Folklore and Oral Tradition in Early Modern England', *Past and Present*, 120 (1980)

INDEX

Abbot, Francis 151
Acts and Monuments (Foxe) 10
Adam and Eve 5
Adams, Thomas 28
adulterers 68
Ady, Thomas 159
afterlife, medieval depictions 41
Alexander VI, Pope 85
Allen, Hannah 42, 49, 103, 123, 124
    and satanic thoughts 45–6
Allen, Thomas (mathematician) 58
alvas (witch-bottles) 147
Anatomie of Abuses (Stubbes) 93–4
and magic, witchcraft 158, 159
animal guises
    and the devil 13, 59–61, 76, 153
    and witches 138, 157–8
anti-popery 85–9
Antichrist 10, 28–9, 35, 38, 83–5
apparitions 41–3, 107, 165
Armada defeat 89
Ars Moriendi 117
Askewe, Anne 29
Aubrey, John 58, 62, 165
Augustine, St 5, 6
autobiographies 28, 41, 50, 53, 92–3, 100, 123–4

Bacon, Friar 68
Bacon, Roger 70–1
Baillie, Robert 161
Bale, John 29
ballads 37, 64, 65, 66, 97, 136

anti-popery 85, 87
    Civil War 37, 162
    comic 99, 169–71
    depicting hell 66–8
    godly 26–7, 31
    and popular beliefs 80–3
Balsom, Robert 125–6, 132
baptism 19, 123
Baptists 162
Bateman, Stephen 26, 33, 72, 73, 74, 75, 93, 94
Baxter, Richard 119, 126, 128, 156, 162, 163
beast, the: in Book of Revelation 28–9, 85–6
Becon, Thomas 23–4, 28, 35, 49
beliefs
    popular 80–9
    post-Reformation 164, 165–8
    pre-Reformation 3, 16–31
    suppression 35
bellarmines (witch-bottles) 145–6, 147
Bernard, Richard 153
bewitchment 117–18, 144, 153
Bilson, Thomas, bishop of Winchester 92
Blair Witch Project, The 1
blasphemy 76, 115, 120, 129
Blatty, William Peter 2
Bodenham, Anne 159
Bolton, Robert (pastor) 28, 45, 46, 122
Book of Common Prayer 123, 132, 155
    rites 11, 12
Book of Martyrs, The (Foxe) 10, 27, 29, 35

Bourne, Henry 165
Boyle, Robert 163
Bradford, John 25, 27, 44
Breton, Nicholas 91
Bretterg, Katherine 53, 55, 56, 101, 127, 131
Briggs, Agnes 121
Brinsley, John 153
Bunyan, John 28, 48, 100, 123, 160
    and apparitions 42, 43
    satanic thoughts and encounters 30, 45, 46
Burrill, Mary 44, 103
Burton, Robert (physician) 34, 41, 43, 122

Caldwell, Elizabeth 5, 77–8, 103, 104
Calling of the Ministry, The (Perkins) 147–8
Calumy, Edmund 156
Calvin, John 5, 6, 7–8, 24–5
Calvinism 6, 8, 164
Carlisle cathedral 19
Carpenter, Richard 28, 49, 92
Casting the Runes 1
catechisms 25, 27, 28, 37, 48
catholicism 74–5, 105, 131
    as the Antichrist 10, 28–9, 38, 83–5
    association with witchcraft 148
    demonisation by protestants 26, 28, 76, 83
Cavendish, Margaret, duchess of Newcastle 101
Cennick, John 166

211

swellings (bodily) in
  possessions 14, 115,
  142–3, 152, 160, 180,
  182

tales 66, 163, 165, 173–7
  of the devil 18, 21, 82,
  161–2
  judgement 95–9, 171–3
  merry 30, 68–9
  of murder 76–80
  of witchcraft 136–7
Temple, Anna 93
temptation 25–7, 45–57
  and the devil 81–3, 173–4
  and possession 122–7
  sexual 48–50
Tewkesbury abbey 19
Thomas, Keith 61, 135, 137
thoughts: impious and
  satanic 45–57, 123
Throckmorton family
  108–10, 114, 116,
  117, 120, 123, 126,
  142, 143, 144
Tillotson, John, archbishop of
  Canterbury 164
Tovey, Joyce 126
tracts 34, 72–80, 91, 96, 97
  see also pamphlets
*Tragical History of Dr Faustus,
  The* (Marlowe) 87
Trapnel, Anna 108
*True Relation of the Grievous
  Handling of William
  Sommers of Nottingham,
  Being Possessed with the
  Devill, The* (Darrel)
  181–6
Turner, Jane 47, 50, 92–3,
  95, 128, 162

'unclean spirits' 14, 17, 112,
  133, 178

vanity 93–5, 101

visionaries 105, 106–8
visions 40–5
Voltaire, F.-M.A. de 4

Walker, John 13
Walsh, John 137
Walsingham shrine 28, 148
war with Spain 10, 35
warfare
  religious 35–6
  spiritual 49
watch (pocket), and the devil
  58
Watt, Tessa 73, 89
Wedderburn, Robert
  (preacher) 168
Werke for Housholders, The
  (Whytford) 23
Wesley, John 166
Whitgift, John, archbishop of
  Canterbury 12, 13
Whole Armour of God, The
  (Gouge) 74, 149
Whytford, Richard 23
will and power of God: and
  evil 5–7
Williams, Gryffith 26
Williams, John, bishop of
  Lincoln 106
Wilson, Thomas 36
Witch of Edmonton, The
  (Rowley, Dekker and
  Ford) 64, 97, 141
witch-bottles 138, 145–7
witch-hunts 134, 135–6,
  154–60
  emergence 9–10
witchcraft 94, 97, 150, 167
  continental influences
  135, 138
  and the devil 134–47
  and 'familiars' 62, 63, 98,
  149, 154, 177–8
  as a female vice 97–8
  and folklore 136–7, 151,
  155

and magic 158, 159
and obsession/possession
  13, 141–5, 180–6
in popular beliefs/culture
  136–47
and religion 8–9, 147–60
trials 97, 98–9, 111, 149,
  150, 151
witches
  animal guises 157–8
  East Anglian 134, 135–6,
  139–40, 154–60
  as females 97–8
  and folklore 136–7, 151,
  153, 155, 156, 157
  of Pendle 139, 153
  sabbats 134
  and satanic connection
  9–10
women
  and domestic strife 102–4
  female authority 108–10
  perceptions of Satan 90–1
  portrayal in popular
  literature 95–9
  and protestantism 49–50,
  92, 93
  religious/spiritual
  experiences 91,
  99–104, 105–10
  and sexual equality 92,
  93, 95
  social roles 92–9
  and witchcraft 97–8
  writings 90–1
woodcuts: and popular
  imagery 28, 33–4, 68,
  73–5
Woodes, Nathanial 84
Woodford, Robert 37
Woolton, John 49, 123
Worcester cathedral 18
Wright, Catherine 115
Wright, Elizabeth 142
Wright, Sara (prophetess)
  104, 108, 109, 128